Searching for Freedom

Ten Christians forsake the technological life to start over.

"Build houses and dwell in them and plant gardens and eat the fruit of them" Jeremiah 29:5

A Novel by Arnold Kropp

A century and a half ago, Abraham Lincoln said:

"We have been the recipients of the choicest bounties of heaven. We have been preserved these many years in peace and prosperity. We have grown in numbers, wealth and power as no other nation has ever grown.

But we have forgotten God. We have forgotten the gracious Hand which preserved us in peace, and multiplied and enriched and strengthened us; and we have vainly imagined, in the deceitfulness of our hearts, that all these blessings were produced by some superior wisdom and virtue of our own.

Intoxicated with unbroken success, we have become too self-sufficient to feel the necessity of redeeming and preserving grace, too proud to pray to the God that made us."

"Without morals, a republic cannot subsist any length of time; they, therefore, who are decrying the Christian religion, whose morality is so sublime and pure...are undermining the solid foundation of morals, the best security for the duration of free governments." - Charles Carroll to James McHenry, November 4, 1800.

Searching for Freedom

All rights reserved by the author.

This is a work of fiction and any reference to any living persons is strictly incidential. There are references to historical persons and their quotes are gleaned from historical records. Local cities and towns mentioned may be real or imagined by the author, and any other references to local landmarks may be real or imagined.
 Scriptures used are from the Holy Bible. This is an edition, an update of the novel published in 2012 titled 'Montesquieu, New World Island,' which is no longer available.

The views expressed are of the author himself,

Copyrighted 2024 by Arnold Kropp

ISBN: 979-8-218-36666-7

Yes, Let's start.

Chapter 1

Mark and Susan are pre-bedtime relaxing in their side-by-side leather recliners, tuned into the ten-pm Omaha news, but not paying close attention. Mark's left arm extended up with his hand cupped behind his head, his right forefinger on the mute button when the commercials increase the volume. Suddenly, the nightly news broadcast switches gears, announcing that an earthquake had just rattled the northern Pacific. Huge waves of tsunami proportions are predicted to hit Alaska's Aleutian islands, eleven hundred miles north, the Western coastal States, and the Hawaiian Islands, directly south, about 1500 miles from the epicenter and eastern Russia.

The earthquake occurred in an area known as the Mendocino Fracture Zone and Pioneer Fracture Zone. Both of those two areas have experienced quakes. The weather professionals warn people living in the surrounding areas to take cover and move inland away from the beaches and low-lying areas near the Pacific. It's 8:20 at night on the west coast. The earthquake is about twelve hundred miles west of San Francisco. The weather channel predicts the tsunami will hit the San Francisco area at about two a.m. while most people will be sleeping, so they have notified and authorized the local officials to sound the alarm to send out text messages to every cell phone owner who could be affected by the rush of the sea waters, interrupting every radio and TV broadcast with the warnings of the approaching tsunamis.

According to federal laws, if the people do not reply to the original Homeland Security text messages, then the message is sent over and over again until the cell phone registrant hits the reply button. If there is still no response after a specified time, depending on the type of disaster, the local police are given the order to knock on the non-responders doors until they are made aware of the situation. The police are also explicitly authorized to wake up every homeowner located near the beaches and beach-level areas of the Pacific and direct them to gather their belongings and valuables and get to higher ground. Millions of people will be affected by this tsunami, the weather channel warns. The federal government is notified, and thousands of agents enter a national emergency.

"There they go again," Mark says to Susan, waking her up as she had dosed off.

Irritably. Susan says, "What?"

"Susan, the weather channel has just interrupted the news about an earthquake in the Pacific."

"So what?" Susan responds. "Good night, I'm going to bed." Susan gets up and brushes Mark's arm as she passes by his chair to the bedroom. "Are you coming?"

"Not yet," Mark replies as he watches the forecasts.

The broadcasters shift gears, showing pictures of the 2004 tsunami that caused massive damage to the islands of Indonesia. Mark changes the channel and hears one of the announcers tell of the earthquake of April 2012 that was initially expected to send tsunamis to Indonesia again. The waves never developed over three feet high.

Changing channels again, Mark hears that the federal emergency response team is already being alerted to the possible flooding that this earthquake could cause. Switching back to the original news broadcast they were watching, he hears the announcement that the earthquake in the Pacific was recorded at a magnitude of 7.9, a bit below the 9.1 – 9.3 recorded in 2004 that devastated the Indonesian islands. He hears one of the weather geologists say that this area of the Pacific is usually quiet, that an earthquake in this area is very rare, and because of that, they do not predict much of an upheaval nor much damage and that it is far enough out in the pacific that any waves created by the disturbance will diminish significantly in size before it hits land. But, the geologist said the government is right in sending out the warnings anyway, as it is better to be safe than sorry.

Mark turns off the TV and heads to bed.

In the wee hours of the morning, another earthquake happens in the same area, then another, and another soon after that. In seven hours, five earthquakes occurred in the same location. They resend the tsunami warnings as a matter of concern for those previously notified. They put the Eastern coast of Russia on alert.

The geologists warn that the quakes create a reverberating effect, increasing the intensity of the waves. Those waves are going to hit the shores as none ever has. The damage is going to be huge. Forecasters predict people are going to be devastated. Last night, right before retiring, Mark thought the forecasters were overreacting as usual. Calling out the agents from DHS and having the local police knock on doors to get those closest to shore evacuated immediately was overly cautious. It appears to be a once in a hundred years catastrophe. Millions will be affected.

All across the country, people are glued to their TV and internet news just as Americans were glued to the news when the Twin Towers went down in 2001 and when New Orleans suffered from the surges of water from Katrina and the Indonesian earthquake-driven tsunami of 2004. The Navy and the UN have hundreds of planes watching and following the waves, sending live videos to the news broadcasters, the federal governments, and the UN. Every TV program is being interrupted by the news. Ships in the North Pacific have almost been turned upside down by the surging waves, which quieted down, then another surge, a period of quietness, and then another surge; five of those surges.

Millions of people in the target areas have packed up and left the coastal areas as quickly as traffic will flow.

The forecasts are that the tsunami will first hit the sparsely populated Aleutian Islands, along with the numerous small islands off the Gulf of Alaska and the coast of British Columbia, rippling down the western coast and hitting the coast of Washington and Oregon. Farther down the coast, the experts predict the tsunami will decrease in velocity toward the southern shore of California and should eventually run out of steam along the Mexican coastal areas. The Islands of Hawaii are expected to be hit as never before. The coastal people are panicking. The government of Hawaii is trying to calm the people, informing them that coolness and preparedness in the face of a storm are the best defenses. The Hawaiian news is broadcasting their advice to hit the hills and reach higher ground.

Mark awoke at his usual time, made his coffee, poured a glass of orange juice, connected to the internet, and immediately saw the latest developments. *'This is massive.'* He reflects, thinking, *'Five earthquakes in the same area.?'*

Then he opened the scriptures for his morning reading in Habakkuk's book: *"How long, Lord, must I call for help, but you do not listen? Or cry out to you, Violence! But you do not save? Why do you make me look at injustice? Why do you tolerate wrongdoing? Destruction and violence are before me; there is strife, and conflict abounds."*

He continues reading all of Habakkuk's complaints and the Lord's answer. A specific answer captures his thoughts; *"See, the enemy is puffed up; his desires are not upright-but the righteous person will live by his faithfulness __ indeed wine betrays him; he is arrogant and never at rest. Because he is greedy as the grave and like death is never satisfied, he gathers to himself all the nations and takes captive all the people."*

Mark is glued to the internet news when Susan awakes an hour later. "Susan, this is massive, like an end-of-days event that could wipe out millions of people."

Not quite fully awake, Susan asks, "What?"

Mark says, "While we were sleeping, five earthquakes shook the Pacific like never before, and the weather people are watching the tsunami waves form as they head for the west coast."

"Hmm, Thank God we live here in fly-over country where we just get tornadoes," Susan remarks as she pours her coffee and butters a toasted English muffin. Sitting down and biting into the muffin, she mumbles, "Yeah, if only we had several hours notice every time a tornado was heading our way."

"Mark, don't forget we've got company coming tomorrow. Bruce and Wendy, along with Janet, driving in sometime tomorrow for the Halloween festival. We've got things to do." Susan announces while Mark seems involved in reading the news on his notebook. "Oh, and good morning, Mark. Did you hear me?"

"Yes, Susan, I'll get going on that stuff soon. Could you make a list for me?"

"Good morning, Mark," Susan says again, this time with a bit more emphasis.

"Yes, Good morning, honey." Mark finally replies.

"Mark, what is so interesting in the news you're looking at?" Susan asks, questioning his concentration.

"It's the earthquakes out in the Pacific. There's never been an earthquake in that area before. These are different. The UN expert seismologists and geologists are flying over the area of the earthquakes for a visual inspection. They say that a land mass appears to be rising above sea level. Nobody's ever seen anything like it before. One said it's like seeing lands develop like it must have happened millions of years ago."

"Well," Susan says, "the trash needs to be taken to the road before the truck comes by, and you do remember that Bruce, Wendy, and Janet will be here sometime today. Could be before noon."

"OK? I thought they were coming in tomorrow." Mark questions.

Susan adds, "Just checking if you were paying attention."

"OK, I got it. I'll get the trash out first while you prepare that list for me." Mark responds as he shuts down the notebook, and walks to the back door.

Susan reaches for another English muffin to put in the toaster, turning on the notebook to see what's so interesting about earthquakes in the Pacific. One of the headlines reads: "Earthquakes shake the earth." Another: "Huge earthquakes send walls of water to shorelines." And another: "Is this Armageddon?" Another says: "Hawaii may not be." "Tsunami turns ships upside down."

"We've got things to do." Susan thinks as she turns off the notebook and starts writing the to-do list for Mark. Her cell phone rings, and she sees it as being from her son George.

"Hello George, how are you?"

"Everything is just fine, Mom. I was just calling to see if you guys had heard about the earthquakes. There's something different about these quakes."

"Yeah, we saw a glimpse of it last night, and your Dad was completely bitten by the news this morning. I had to force him to put it aside and get busy. You know your dad when he gets involved in something." Susan answers.

"Yeah, for sure. We'll that's all mom. Oh, I told you we're coming in for that Halloween festival too, didn't I?"

"Yes, you did. We'll be looking forward to seeing you again. When will you guys be here?" Susan asks.

"We'll be there late Thursday and will stay until the 2nd. Is that Ok?"

"Of course it is, Dear. Your dad is excited too, and you know that our friends Bruce, Wendy, and Janet will also be here. They should be here Wednesday."

"Yep, see you then, Mom. Bye."

"Bye, sweetie pie."

The phone rings again; this time, it's her daughter, Melody. "Good morning, Mel. How are you doing today, and did you hear about the earthquakes?"

"Well, yes, of course." Melody answers. "How did you know I was going to ask if you'd heard about them?"

"I just got off the phone with George, and that's why he called."

"I should have known. Has Thomas called yet?"

"No, he hasn't," Susan answers.

"Gee whiz, I beat one of them to the punch this time. What's wrong with Thomas, as he usually beats George," Melody remarks.

"Yes, he does. Perhaps he's become like your dad and can't escape the news. Too busy to call. Anyway, how are things there in Denver?"

"Everything's fine, Mom, but I'm sorry I will miss the big Halloween festival this year. Work is going strong, and I've got a long report the agency wants on the 30th, so I'll be tied up with that. Say Hello to Dad for me and have fun. Next time, I'll beat George. Bye, Mom, I love you."

"Love you too, Mel, and take care," Susan says as she hangs up.

Soon, Mark walks in looking for the list of chores as Susan returns to touching up the kitchen.

"The trash is out; what's next?"

"George and Melody called. They each wanted to be the first to ask if you'd seen the news about the earthquakes." Susan informs Mark. "Oh, and George and Ruth are coming Thursday. Melody is busy at work, so she can't make it."

"I didn't think George could get away," Mark answers.

"Something must have changed then, as he just told me they'd be here Thursday,"

"Well, good. Now, do you have that list for me?" Mark asks while looking down at the counter, picking up the note with numbers followed by handwriting, and reading the list softly. "This is it?"

"Yes, that's it. That's all I can think of right now." She replies.

"Fine, then I'll have more time to work on that Haunted House display."

Just then, the phone rings, and Susan is the first to grab it, suspecting it's Thomas. "That's got to be Thomas," Susan says as she picks up the phone before Mark reaches out to get it. "Hello Thomas, yes, we heard about the earthquakes, honey. So what's up with you guys?"

"Good morning, mom. Well, ah, goodbye then." Thomas says and clicks the phone once.

"Thomas, are you there? Did you hang up on me?" Susan says quickly.

"No, mom, I'm still here. Well, I guess George and Melody beat me to it, right? They did it again."

"Yes, Thomas, they did, and yes, we did hear about the quakes. Anything new there with you guys?"

Thomas then informs her that the latest is that a volcano has just erupted in the same location as the earthquakes. "We can't make it there for the Halloween festivities this year as we couldn't get the time off. Sorry, Mom," Thomas says. "Is Dad there?"

"Yes, he's standing right here. Take care, Thomas, and I love you. We'll see you then at Thanksgiving." Susan says as she hands the phone to Mark.

"Hey, son, how are things up there?"

"Good dad, just like it was last week. Will you have that Haunted House display as you did last year?"

"You bet." Mark answers. "The adults enjoyed that one. Remember, it was a room labeled 'Irritable Revenue Sharing' as in IRS. I'm thinking of a new angle this year. I'm putting together a series of rooms; one has two people sitting at their desks looking over stacks of paper. As each new group of folks enters the display, the stack of paper explodes; the room goes dark, and then flashes of light fill the room as the two behind the desk change into Roman Knights in armor spitting out rule violations, calling for an investigation of a citizen, citing certain misbehaviors.

Another room is labeled as DHS: Demented Home Safety. Another is ATF: Attaboy Tough Feds. We've got a video showing four Roman Knights with swords getting out of a government van and approaching a house. So, I wish you were coming to help with some of the electrical work."

"Sorry, Dad, I'd love to, but can't do it this year. Let them have it. Eh, I've got to go. I'll call you later, and keep an eye on the developments in the Pacific. The tsunamis could be terrible. Bye."

"Talk to you later, Thomas," Mark signs off and replaces the cell phone on the table in front of Susan.

Mark reaches over to get the notebook, opens it, and sees the headline: "Volcano blows the Earthquake."

"Susan, look at this. In the same area as those earthquakes, a volcano is slowly rising above the earthquakes, which caused the sea bottom to rise above sea level. Those UN geologists claim that we're witnessing how millions of years ago the earth's lands developed."

Looking at the video, Susan says, "Amazing, this planet is under repair. Mark. Is God warning us, and we could be looking at the explosive end times beginning right in front of us, in our time."

Mark replies, "I'm surprised these geologists don't use trillions of years in their guesswork, as spending trillions is as normal as wasting billions. Maybe this earth created land masses just thousands of years ago. Their guesses are as reliable as their forecast about the tsunamis wiping out Hawaii."

"Mark, put that thing down and get to work. We've got company coming." Susan emphasizes.

Later in the afternoon, Mark is busy putting together some pieces to his invention outside the old barn. He's tried many different ways to capture the rays of the sun, storing the power. He cone-shaped it, wanting it to act like a funnel, but each battery failed to keep the generator running for more than an hour. *There's got to be a better battery system than this. The magnifying glass is working, doing its job; it's just not big enough.* He gets his tools and dismantles the battery, carefully placing the parts in order of assembly. He reaches for a different chemical to add to the forty cells within the casing, trying out one he had not tried before.

Putting it all back together, he hooks up the wiring to the magnifying glasse, the rotator, the batteries, and the generator and places the unit directly under the sun. He immediately notices that the rotator motor is ever so slowly following the sun's path. *"Well, that's working so far."* He thinks to himself. *The meter is reading high.* *"I'll just let this sit, come back, and monitor it later."*

"Mark, are you out here again?" Susan asks disappointingly.

"Yes. Why? What's up? I've completed your list, did some work on the Haunted House, and thought I'd work on this. But I'm finished for now. What can I do?"

Susan then tells Mark that a man called about your plan to lease some acreage and asked if he could come over and chat about it. "You didn't have your cell phone with you, so I told him sure, any time tomorrow morning, say about ten a.m. Mark, please remember to take your phone."

"Yeah. OK. I'm sorry."

Chapter 2

Mark and Susan, waking up to the break of daylight, found a considerable rainstorm enveloping the area on the day their friends were to arrive. "Oh well, that's nature not getting the message." Susan irritably voices her disappointment.

"Mark, what did you intend to get done outside today before our friends show up?"

"Really, there's not much at all, and it can wait. Bruce can help when it clears up tomorrow," Mark informs her as he turns on the notebook to check the latest news.

"Another Volcano Erupts" is the first headline Mark notices. Reading further into the article, near the bottom is a statement from the UN volcanologist saying there is something different about how this island is being formed compared to how they've seen other islands develop in recent history.

Another headline reads: "UN observing all activities." "Volcanic ash will spill over the west coast this afternoon. All residents alerted." And another Report reads: "President declares a national emergency." "Homeland Security is springing into action." "VP and congressional members fly over the area." "Congress ready to pass spending authorization." "Media sending camera personnel." "Hawaiians packing up, moving to higher ground."

Mark continues reading the latest news while Susan is busy baking an apple and banana cream pie for the company later on.

Mark hears a knock on the front door, but Susan passes the door on her way to the bedroom and opens it to a gentleman. He introduces himself as Jason Walker from the Department of Agriculture, showing her an identification badge.

"Mark," she calls out. "It's a gentleman from the Department of Agriculture," she says, and invited the youngish man out of the rain.

"Now what?" Mark mumbles to himself as he approaches the vestibule.

"Greetings, Mr. Tebonson. I'm the Department of Agriculture agent Jason Walker, and I want to talk with you about your intent to lease out your acreage."

"Good morning, Mr. Walker. Come on in and have a seat. It's a nasty, wet morning roaming around here in rural Nebraska. But come, have a seat."

"Thank You, Mr. Tebonson. Yes, it is, and your place out here is not that easy to find."

"So, Mr. Walker. Did you say your first name is Jason?"

"Yes, sir," Jason replies.

"Has anyone ever called you jay walker?"

"Oh, yes, sir. Kids had a big time with that in school. I then showed them how to walk like a J. I would kick my right foot forward and bring it back in front of my left foot, and then the same with the left foot. I've been kidded about it at the office, too."

"Well, anyway, what's on your mind?" Mark Asks. "Did I hear you say something about my intentions to lease out my acreage?"

"Yes, you did. We in the department are concerned that your leases will not violate our agreements concerning selling your crops to the ethanol industry." Mr. Walker tells Mark.

"Well, ahh . . . how old are you son?" Mark asks the young man.

"I'm twenty-six, sir," He replies.

"Well, son, I know this started many years ago, way before your time in the crib, but why should the taxpayers subsidize me for growing corn or any other crop? Concerning what I do or not do is my business. Don't you think you should read up on the rights of private property owners first before spending all that money and time coming way out here wanting to know what kind of lease I'll be negotiating with another private citizen? I agreed with the department to sell my crops to the ethanol industry because they paid more per bushel, and you people offered me more tax write-offs for that guarantee. It's what you call economic incentives. I got much more than I would have from Del Monte. Do you blame me for that? That agreement was between us for seven years, and that time is ending."

"Well, yes, that's right. We did. But the department still has the right to continue those guarantees to another party, and we'd like your assurance that those provisions will be part of your lease. All you have to do is sign here." Mr. Walker informs Mark.

"Well, sorry about that, but when and if I lease out any or all of my land, that will be an agreement between the two of us only, two private citizens entering into a mutually agreeable contract. It's none of your business. I will not insert any provision of that nature in our contract. You'll have to contact the party I'm leasing the rights to and deal with him. And what he or she does with the property after we sign will be none of my business.

"This conversation is over Mr. Walker, and you can relay that information to your head honcho in Washington. So, goodbye, young man, and if I were you, I'd find another vocation." Mark finishes as he shows the young man the front door.

On the way out, the young man, appearing rattled, says, "Mr. Tebonson, We could condemn this land of yours, and I'm sure you'll be hearing some more from the department."

"Is that a threat? Get out of here, now." Mark exclaims with a raised voice.

After the man left and the door was closed, Susan says, "Mark, you're going to get us in trouble yet."

Mark replies to Susan, "Well, it is none of their business, and we'd all be better off if those high and mighty watchdogs in

Washington kept their nose out of our business. It wears me thin when something like this happens, and it's happening more often than not nowadays. I get the feeling to leave. Every year. there are additional restrictions on top of last year's intrusions. Gad zooks, a girl can't even put up a lemonade stand outside her home anymore because some zealous watchdog says her drinks are not FDA inspected. And, the preparation area does not conform to current health safety standards."

"Calm down, Mark, eh? Bruce and Wendy are coming in this afternoon, and Janet too. So, please try not to get off on one of those rants of yours while they're here."

Mark tries to calm down by turning on his notebook and selecting to play a game of solitaire. Finishing one game, he closes that and selects internet, going to his home page for a glimpse of the news, if any, of the volcanoes in the Pacific.

"Hey, Susan, three more volcanoes are erupting in the Pacific."

"So?" Susan replies as she prepares another treat for the guests.

"Well, it's a historic event happening right here in front of us. All the major news covers the event full-time; the experts say it's not over yet. Seven major earthquakes and six volcanoes so far".

"Listen to this. As the volcanoes have risen out of the ocean, there has been an unusual formation of sub-surface land rising above the ocean level first, and then the volcanoes erupted. The previous ocean floor is now actually above the sea. A new island is being made, one about the size of mainland Hawaii. The UN scientists and geologists are beside themselves, calling this a million-year phenomenon, a view into prehistoric history when the earth went bang."

"Hey, Susan, do you want to move to an Island in the Pacific?" Mark asks. "We've had the idea in the back of our minds the last few years of finding a permanent beach home somewhere."

"Mark, turn that off and help me get ready?" Susan begs.

"Sorry, what can I do?"

"Here, peel the potatoes for me. Then slice these tomatoes into 1/8" thick slices. Then slice the onions and the green peppers." Susan informs Mark. "I'm going to make meatloaf for dinner, with our corn on the cob, green beans, and a salad. And then finish it off with a slice of apple or banana cream pie. Check on the wine for me. Thanks, Mark, you're a big help when I can get you away from your toys."

"Well, they're really not toys as in Tonka trucks," Mark responds. "You've got your toys too, my dear."

"Yeah, I know. Susan replies. "We all like to play with our toys, don't we? When do we grow up and put away our childish things? After we reach sixty-five?"

"No, not then either," Mark adds. "Then we do go back and start play-acting again. I've seen many retired men restoring an old car they wanted since high school. Some old-timers suddenly get the urge to retrieve the baseball card collection from the fifty's, which they haven't looked at for fifty years. Somehow, they seem to find the old high school baseball glove and then start rubbing neats-foot oil on it while watching the Cubs play on TV. Some take up a new hobby like woodworking, modernizing an old kitchen, or gardening."

"Mark, I've still got a couple of dolls from when I was, about five or six. And somewhere in the attic are the dresses I used to dress up with at that age. Mom made those dresses for me. They were so big I'd step on them if I moved too fast. Yeah, I'd sneak into Mom's bedroom and try on her one pair of high heels, ones she'd only wear to special events with Dad. Kids growing up stuff. Mark, when do you think Ruth or Annabelle will provide us with a grandchild? I hope they don't wait too long so we can spoil them and watch them grow up."

Mark answers, "Thomas told me they're trying, and George hasn't said anything to me about it."

Susan responds, "Yeah, that's what I heard too. Honey, slice the tomatoes a bit thinner than that and then cut the slices into smaller pieces for the salad."

"OK, how's that?" Mark asks.

Looking at the chopping block, Susan says, "That's perfect. Now, I'm not sure Melody will ever want a child, even if she does find a good man. Poor girl. I think she's still holding back, resisting any thought of a relationship with a man, as she may not be totally over that rape. It may still be haunting her."

"Has she said anything about it recently?" Mark asks.

"No, she hasn't. And I don't want to bring up the subject." Susan responds.

"But," Mark adds. "It'd be best if she did look that devil right in the eye and say the haunting must stop and go on with life, neglecting those tormenting images and feelings every time they make a re-appearance. We can allow the past to control us, or we can move forward regardless of our history."

"Yeah," Susan responds. "But that's Melody's choice, Mark. One that she'll make when she's ready. I hope she finds a way soon, as sometimes it's hard not to suggest that she hasn't faced it yet."

Marks adds, "Maybe she has, but hasn't found the right guy yet."

Susan says, "Mark, one more thing. Thanks a bunch. Now do your thing, whatever that may be. And, take your cell phone, please."

The rain has been slowing down a bit as Mark exits the kitchen into the rear-covered deck, just wandering without a purpose of why he came out, looking without noticing the lights shining through the windows of the old barn, hearing without sensing the thundering in the background. He's looking at the rain gauge, which shows the rainwater inside the tube at the 1½ inch mark. *'That's good.'* Mark thinks to himself while looking out over the rear yard and into the gently rising farmland in the background, the row of oaks and elms rising 40 feet into the rain to his right. *'Now, it'd be nice if the rain stopped.'* Just then, a lightning bolt streaked across his path of vision from right to left, looking like it had the old barn as its target. The loud explosion shook Mark from his stupor and jolted him backward into the roof support.

"Wow. My God, that was close." Mark explains to the air.

"Mark, are you alright?" Susan asks as she bursts out onto the deck. "Did that one hit anything around here? It sounded like it was right there. Mark, say something. Are you alright?"

"Yeah, yeah, sure, I'm fine." Mark manages to squeak out. "Looking around now, I don't see any downed trees; the barn is not burning. It's got lightning rods. It could have hit the tower. Do you see anything, Susan?" Mark announces, "I'll get in the jeep and look around."

"Mark, you shouldn't go out in this. It's storming, and the lightning is still all around us." Susan exclaims. "Be careful. I'm going in. Do you have your cell phone?"

"Yes, I got it, and yes, I'll just look around a bit. I need to check on the solar system." Mark enters the garage from the covered deck and turns around, remembering he doesn't have the jeep keys. "I guess I need the keys." He tells Susan as he re-enters the kitchen, retrieving the keys off the rack.

"Be careful," Susan warns.

"Hey, how many times have we been caught in a storm like this while driving on an interstate somewhere?" Mark reminds Susan that there should not be a problem while he's in the jeep to satisfy his curiosity about where that bolt struck.

With the garage door open, he notices that the trees in the front yard still stand tall as he pulls the jeep out of the garage, turns it around, and heads toward the barn area. He can barely see the row of oaks and elms through the heavy rain as he heads in a parallel direction toward the barn.

The old barn is the first barn his grandfather built fifty-some years ago, which Mark now uses as his workshop and a place where he tinkers with his many ideas. It's one of the classic style buildings farmers erected in the early 1900s. The red paint slightly worn through, but the barn still stands strong.

Mark had his solar power generator outside the rear of that barn in the direct path of the sun so that it would receive all of the sun's rays throughout the day. Turning the corner around the rear of the barn, he sees that the magnifying glass panel had been knocked on its side, resting on the ground, leaning against the generator. He stopped the Jeep to get out for a closer look and thought, *"It was this that got a direct hit from that lightning bolt."* He then remembered not considering putting any lightning protection around the panel. Upon further inspection, he saw that the battery was burned. The power of the strike burned the generator wires together. Opening the door to the barn, Mark starts the front-end pallet loader to bring the unit inside. He stoops for closer inspection inside the barn and out of the rain, and all his previous notions are correct. *"The unit definitely was hit by that bolt."*

The magnifying panel is Ok, just dislodged, the battery is burned up, and as he takes a closer look at the pieces to the battery, he sees the meter, still intact, had recorded the highest ever numerical reading, indicating that the unit had been generating power, quite a bit of power.

"It was working." He shouts in excitement. "It was working. Working before the storm came."

Mark then remembers when he first came out of the kitchen onto the deck before the lightning bolt hit; looking around from under cover of the deck's roof, he briefly noticed that the lights to the old barn were on. At the time, it did not seem strange; it was just lights inside the barn left on.

"Could it be?" He thinks again as he looks down at the generator, looking to see if he had changed the chemical of the batteries the other day, if he had hooked up the power cord from the generator to the barn's lights. "Yes, I did."

"We're going to have solar power! It was working!"

He removes his rain gear and starts to disassemble the battery parts. He's been at it for over an hour when the phone rings.

"Hello, Susan." Mark answers.

Susan excitedly asks: "Where are you? Where have you been? I was getting concerned."

"Guess what, Susan," Mark replies.

"We're going to have solar power. My unit was hit by lightning because I had not thought of installing any lightning protection around it. It was working. The generator had two one-hundred-watt bulbs in the barn burning all night." Mark tells her. "I've been working on taking it apart to start over with new parts and put it back together again. Do you know what this means if my assessment is correct?"

"Oh, that's great, Mark," Susan affirms.

"Is anything else damaged?"

"No, not that I could see. Everything else seems fine," Marks informs her. "Hey, I'll be out here r making notes and taking this thing apart. Ok?"

"But keep me informed if you leave to get parts or anything," Susan asks. "It's 11:15, Mark, and we should be seeing Bruce and Wendy fairly soon. I don't expect Janet until later on. I'll call when I see them driving up. Meanwhile, the news reports that there have been three more Volcanoes and another earthquake this morning, all in that same area of the Pacific. The tidal waves are not as bad as they had predicted. There's something different about this one, they said. That's about it. Oh, and the weather radar shows our storm is passing over and should continue to move northeast out of our area in about an hour. The local weather says we've received one and three-quarters inches. That's it, Mark."

"Thanks, sweetie," Mark responds, putting the cell phone on the desktop.

Chapter 3

A couple of hours have passed, the storm has blown over, and the sky is clearing. Mark finished repairing his invention and took another tour of the farm, inspecting for any damage from the fierce lightning. The new barn, which stores all his farm machinery, suffered no damage. He was concerned about it as this is where the Haunted House display will be. His jet is fine. The aircraft hanger is fine, and even all the trees survived the storm. The only damage was that big strike on his solar panel.

Relieved, he returned to the house and turned on the notebook at his desk to view the latest about the volcanoes. Just then, he hears a car approaching.

"It's Bruce and Wendy." He calls out to Susan in the kitchen. "They're here."

Rushing to the front door, Susan beats Mark, opens the door, and skips out to the car as Wendy opens the passenger door. "Oh, it's so good to see you again, Wendy," says Susan as she hugs Wendy.

Mark was right behind her, approaching the driver's side to greet Bruce. Shaking his hand, Mark greets his high school friend. "Glad you could make it, buddy. Did you bring your clubs?"

"Sure did, Mark, and we're thrilled we could get away to enjoy the relaxing time with you two and to witness this festival you're having. We'll get out for a round some time, I hope. Have they done anything to change the course?"

"A few minor changes, but that's it."

Mark turns around to greet Wendy, giving her a hug; "We're thrilled you guys could make it. You're looking better than ever, Wendy, so Bruce must be treating you good."

Susan takes her turn, hugging Bruce, "You're looking as youthful as ever. Come on in you two and have something. It's a long drive from Omaha out here. How was it? You've got the top-up, so you must have run into that storm that passed over?"

"We'll get that luggage later, Bruce. Come in and relax awhile first," Mark tells Bruce as he was about to open the luggage compartment in his BMW convertible.

As they're comfortably seated in the living room when Susan says, "Bruce, we've seen you in a few more golf equipment commercials. You're doing well."

"Yes, doing those commercials has been a blast, and the last one, well, I couldn't get my lines straight, so it took most of the day to film it. I couldn't even get three sentences together. We all laughed so hard at my blunders that it was hard to keep a straight face. The camera crew was having the time of their lives while I was sweating. I'm not sure the advertiser will call me again. Over all, doing those are fun and quite rewarding."

"Well, it turned out great," Susan replies. "Wendy, how's the nursing going? You're into surgical nursing now, right?"

Wendy answers, "Yes, several months ago, the hospital experienced a shortage of nurses, so I applied and got the opportunity to see the insides of the body every day as the surgeons cut them open, exposing parts that I've only seen pictures of before. At first, I was scared that I'd get sick and throw up all over someone's heart and lungs. But it wasn't that bad. I've been through over forty major surgeries already, and now the sight of inside our skin is an everyday affair. I've come to love it.   Except that, the endless paperwork is most demanding."

Wendy then inquires about what's the latest around this neck of Nebraska.

Susan answers, telling them that Janet is on her way up from Texas A&M. "That's about a fifteen-hour drive."

"How's she doing down there?" Wendy asks. "Has she found a guy yet?"

Susan replies to Wendy, "I guess she's enjoying her classes, and as far as a man in her life yet, we'll have to wait to ask her. We expect her sometime later today or early tomorrow."

Bruce asks, "OK, Mark, brief us on this Halloween festival you've got coming up. And how can we help?"

Marks starts by telling them that the festival began two years ago as just a place where kids could come out to a farm and ride around sitting on hay bales by a horse-drawn wagon with pumpkins all over the place, enjoying the outdoors and seeing some decorations Susan had placed hanging in nearby trees.

"They had a great time," Marks explains. "And when evening came, we had a big campfire roasting marshmallows as certain town folks told spooky stories trying to scare the kids. You know, the typical Halloween stuff. In the first year, we had about thirty kids and their parents. Last year, there were over eighty children, plus the parents and grandparents. Can you picture a campfire big enough for over a hundred people? I had to hook up an audio system so everyone could hear the stories. We were overwhelmed. So, this year, we knew we needed help, and here you are. We'll get busy tomorrow."

"But there's always someone who gets upset at something." Mark continues. "One of the fathers commented on my Haunted House displays, asking, "What do these political displays have to do with Halloween?" He said, pointing to the <u>Irritable Revenue Sharing</u> sign and the Roman soldiers. He assured me that Halloween was always about the kids, not a time to scare adults about the federal government."

"I responded to the guy, don't you think it's time people got concerned about the intrusions the federal officials are mandating? I'm scared, aren't you? I would rather have them concentrate on protecting our freedoms rather than spending trillions of our grandkids' money regulating us and our freedoms. The man was irritated and declared he would not bring his kids out here this year."

Bruce then adds, "Another one of those left-wingers. Even out here in a predominately conservative area of the country, some just don't get it, don't want to . . . the proverbial ostrich."

Wendy asks, "Will any of the parents from town come out and help?"

Susan answers, "Yes, twenty-five parents and grandparents have indicated a desire to pitch in this year. It's been an amazing experience for us and this town of twenty-five-thousand."

"Hopefully, we won't get snow in the next few days." Mark chips in. "Today's thunderstorm was unusual for this time of year, as historically, late October will bring a few snowfalls and no rain showers. We've had five inches of snow on Halloween before. The past couple of years must result from that global warming thingy," he adds.

"Anyway, from what I hear, the townspeople are excited whatever the weather brings; they'll wear their coats if necessary or wear shorts and tee shirts if called for." Susan pipes in.

"Sounds like a good deal for the town, and I hope they appreciate the work you put into this," Wendy exclaims.

Susan announces that she should call Janet to see where she is and her approximate arrival time. While she calls, Mark and Bruce unload the luggage and place the bags in the spare bedroom. Wendy meets them in the room to unpack a few things, bringing Susan a beautifully wrapped gift.

Susan announced that Janet told her she was about three to four hours away. She crossed over into Nebraska a short while ago.

"What's this?" Susan asks as Wendy hands her a gift package. "Now, I thought we had that gift-sharing thing settled."

"Oh, go ahead and open it. You guys are special to us, and we just wanted to show a little appreciation."

"Well, thank you," Susan says. Then Wendy announces, "You may not want to thank us after you open it."

"Hmm," Susan carefully removes the paper, laying each piece of wrapping aside as Mark and Bruce look on.

"It's labeled a thingamajig, but looks like an ordinary flashlight?" Susan announces. "I don't get it."

Looking at the bewildered expression on Mark's face, Bruce explains, "Well, just in case the solar invention blows out all your lights and power."

"Yeah, thanks, buddy. I got a story about that thingamajig of mine that happened this morning. I won't need that stupid flashlight." Mark says, sounding a bit irritated.

Looking at Mark, Susan understands what Mark is doing and then glances back to Wendy and says, "Thank you, how thoughtful." And then to Bruce,, "You did well to put this thingamajig together. Are there any directions for it?"

Bruce and Wendy, looking at each other, are stunned that their friends are irritated by the playtime gift. They've done things like this in the past, and they never seemed offended. Wendy tries to apologize to Mark, asking his forgiveness. Mark and Susan, winking at each other, burst into soft chuckles.

"Gotchya," Mark says, pointing his index finger at Bruce's belly, while Susan says the same to Wendy.

"You guys!" Wendy exclaims. "We've never been able to pull one on you two. You're so quick at turning things around to bite us. I should have known."

Bruce, pointing his fist at Mark, says, "I'll get you. Just wait till we tee off."

"Hey, we got time. Let's run into town and get a bite to eat, Okay?" Mark suggests. "It's on you, Bruce. A fairly new family-owned restaurant serves the best chicken fried chicken I've ever tasted. What say you?"

Looking at Bruce first, Wendy tells Susan and Mark, "We've changed and have turned ourselves into vegetarians. I read this book about meat products, especially chicken or pork. It's so bad for the heart, and the digestive system gets torn up with all that fat. We've been at it for two months, and I'm sold. Bruce has trimmed down and lost some of that belly roll, and we both feel so much better. I almost want to get pregnant and start a family. I feel so good."

Susan replies, "I'm glad for you guys. Mark, I've already got dinner about ready. Oh shoot, it's meatloaf, and now you guys have quit eating meat. Well, it'll keep. This place does have some fantastic salads.   And the decorations are amazing. Very historical. You'll love it. So let's go, all right. I'll save the meatloaf for Janet."

Susan locks up the house while Mark backs the SUV out of the garage, and they head for town, a ten-minute drive through the rural gravel roads to US 83, across the Platte River, passing by the Railroad Museum and into town. Mark pulls into a good-sized parking lot where the restaurant, Jeffers Depot, is located.

"Well, here we are," Mark announces, finding a parking spot on the street. "You're going to enjoy this place; the owner is a descendant of the Union Pacific president during the heydays of the forty's."

Outside the entrance are two old-time railroad crossing gate guards on opposite sides of the front door. Entering the vestibule, several customers patiently wait for an open table.   Mark recognizes a couple as he extends his hand out to greet Bill and Sandy Wright, friends and members of the church, standing in line with the others.

"How are things going for you guys?" Mark quizzes.

"Good, as usual," Bill responds. "It looks like we'll have decent weather for the festival."

Mark answers, "Yes, the forecast is looking good."

Susan bends in and hugs Sandy, saying, "nice to see you again. We'll see you at the festival again, right?"

"We'll be there Sue. Wouldn't miss it, and I'll be out early to help some."

Susan asks, "Where's Matthew?"

"Oh, he's recovering from a cold. His grandmother has him tonight feeding him chicken soup and having him inhale eucalyptus steam so he'll be better for the festival." Sandy informs Susan.

Mark turns and introduces Bruce and Wendy to Bill and Sandy. After the initial greetings and handshakes, Bill tells Bruce and Wendy, "You're gonna love this place. Rural people in these small towns can do amazing things when left alone."

Mark turns to their eight-year-old son Joshua, extending his arm, elbow slightly bent with his palm face up. "Give me five, Josh," as Josh concentrates on his arm swing, aiming for Mark's open palm. Mark quickly moves his hand away from the slap, causing Josh to miss. Mark's hand is available for another try, and Josh swings his arm toward the palm, missing again. Mark is quick enough to move his palm away from Josh's hand, either to the left or right, confusing Josh. Finally, Mark keeps his hand in position, and Josh strikes it hard with a very satisfying look.

"Oooh, That hurt!" Mark slowly says. "Are you going to be Superman again this year?" Josh looks at his mother, knowing that his costume is still undecided. "Aah, you want to surprise me. OK."

Bill tells Mark, "You guys called in a reservation, as I see Joe is ready for you."

"Good evening, Mr. and Mrs. Tebonson. Good to see you again," Joe, the greeter says as he opens the second set of doors, entering the restaurant and leaving the rest waiting for their turns. "Your table for four is ready for you, sir?"

"Good evening, Joe. Meet a couple of our good friends from Omaha: Bruce and Wendy Wilcox." Mark replies to the greeter.

Reaching out to shake Bruce's hand, Joe greets Bruce, who seems to be overtaken, looking around at the interior decorations. "Wendy. We're thrilled to have you."

"Right this way, please. How long are you guys going to be in town?" Joe asks Wendy. "And, if you don't mind my saying so, you're beautiful. Those eyes of yours are stunning."

Quite surprised at a stranger complimenting her, Wendy says, "Well, thank you. We'll be here for the rest of the week, and you've done a fantastic job decorating this place. It's amazing."

"Not my work, Wendy. Peter and Marge Jeffers, the owners, did all this. Here's a nice booth for you guys. Enjoy your meal."

Sitting down, Bruce is captivated by the model railroad track around the restaurant's perimeter, running right there next to the booth as a model train passed by carrying food on the flatbed cars. Bruce remarks: "I thought that model railroading was a bygone hobby."

"Not here, Bruce. This town was born of the railroad industry, and the hobby shops here still sell many model railroading equipment. We passed the Museum on the way in. We might get a chance to tour the old but still-used railroad depot. Peter and Marge started this place several years ago."

Bruce and Wendy look around the room at the decorations; everything is railroad, signs, pictures, ornaments, old lanterns, caps and uniforms, photos of the town in the twenties and thirties, and an actual caboose has been built into the rear wall.

A model train with Union Pacific markings pulls up and stops alongside their booth, bringing the menus, glasses of ice water, and napkin-wrapped silverware on a flat car behind the engine. A voice announces: "Greetings, and how you folks doing this evening?" startling Wendy, sitting next to the wall and the train track, turning her head in the direction of the voice, seeing the train engine as a two-inch tall man pivoting out of the engine booth of the tiny train says, "My name is Ralph, and I'll be serving you, hopefully without spilling anything. The conductor likes to go fast. Can I take your drink orders?"

Turning her head and eyes toward Susan and Mark, Wendy exclaims, "This is something else. What ingenuity."

Susan says, "I'll have a cup of hot tea, please."

"Hot tea for the lady in red." The conductor says. "And for you, sir."

"Coffee for me," Mark informs.

"Coffee for Mr. Tebonson," is the reply from the conductor. "And now for the lady on my left. What can I get you?"

Wendy tells the tiny man with a big voice: "I'll have a hot tea also. Would you have Constant Comment?"

The man says: "A Constant Comment hot tea for you, Madam." And now, for the gentleman who lost part of his belly roll sitting next to this beautiful lady, what would you have, sir?"

Bruce says, "Huh?' toward the train, and then, "Make mine a Bud light."

"Sure thing, Mr. Wilcox. Coming right up. Do you mind if I take your picture? The tiny man asks.

"You better," Susan replies.

"Ok, good, now smile, and you, the gentlemen on the end, please lean in a bit." A tiny light flashes, and then: "Thank you all, and look for engine number 9845."

A set of crossing gates descend, the whistle blows, and the toy train moves down the tracks away from the table.

Bruce says, "This place ought to get national coverage. Unbelievable!"

"It has received lots of coverage." Mark answers. "Popular talk show hosts have been here, along with many from the entertainment industry, movie stars getting their pictures taken, and media people documenting the scenery. You must have missed all that coverage. Journalists from Europe have also visited, and that Prince of England and his wife stopped by one day on their latest trip."

"This is amazing, Mark," Bruce says, " They must have spent a fortune on it. Now, where is the guy communicating with us through that toy engine? He can see us, knows what color clothes, and our names. Where is this guy doing all this from? Looking around, I don't see any central booth."

"Modern technology," answers Mark. "On the back of the menu is a short explanation and the history of how it developed. Look over there to the back corner. Notice the track rising and going through that tunnel. It's heading to the control room; the two other tracks exit straight back into the kitchen. Inside the engine is a video camera transmitting the images and sound to the computer in the control room, where the announcer can see us and communicate back and forth. When the food comes out, there will be two engines side by side pulling four flatbed cars holding the plates of food. We'll get the picture he took along with the bill and a nice thank you note."

"Parents love to bring their kids here," Susan says. "Peter and Marge love to play around with kids and have lots of fun talking to the kids through that conductor. Kids love it."

"They've intentionally kept the prices on the children's menu as low as feasible. The caboose along the back wall is for small parties, and did you notice the actual rail car along the side wall? That was a real Union Pacific dining car from the forties that can be reserved for larger parties. The waiters dress up just as they did back then: white shirts, ties with white napkins hanging over their forearms. They'll see moving landscapes along the outside windows as if the car was passing through the mountains. And get this, Peter wanted the customers to experience the motion of railroads, so he built in pistons and shock absorbers moving the car as if it was going down a track at seventy miles per hour, just so his customers could feel like they are traveling."

"Wow. Amazing. What ingenuity." Bruce exclaims.

Susan says, "Peter and Marge will be coming to the farm for the Halloween festival, so you'll get to meet them. They're terrific people. They've got a gold mine here Oh, speaking of Marge, I see her coming out now."

Standing up as she approached the booth, Mark said, "Marge, meet some good friends of ours from Omaha, Bruce and Wendy Wilcox."

Reaching in to shake Wendy's hand first, "Great to meet you guys." Marge says, also shaking the hand of Bruce, who has stood to his feet. "Did you come in for the Halloween bash?"

"Yes, we did. Bruce answers and then compliments her on the restaurant, adding, "I'll be telling all of my friends back home about this place, Marge. You've done an unbelievable job here."

"Well, thank you. It was good of Mark and Susan to bring you here, and I suppose we'll see each other on Friday then. Enjoy your meal, and let us know if there's anything else we can do. I've got to get back to the kitchen and control room. Thanks for coming, and enjoy your meal."

"Nice to meet you too, Marge," Wendy and Bruce say together.

Wendy asks Susan, "This place is packed. How did you get us in so easily? Twenty people were waiting, and the waiter seated us right away."

"All it took was a phone call and a few pieces of information like Bruce losing his belly roll," Susan answers back.

Then Wendy says, "You guys are something else. I'm so glad we came. We almost canceled, as the hospital wanted me to work, especially because of Halloween and the accidents that always disrupt the festivities, but they relented, and here we are. I'm thrilled. And coming to see this place is an added benefit."

Mark asks Bruce, "How's the golf game? You're not playing in any tournaments anymore, are you?"

"No, Mark, my game has gone sour the last few years on the senior tour, so for my mental health and the pocketbook, I gave up the traveling and now concentrating on a teaching jig at the country club: teaching kids and the high rollers, and once in a while I'll do a commercial spot for equipment manufacturers. I also write a few magazine stories and some YouTube instruction clips. It keeps me busy enough."

"Oh, Mark," Bruce then asks, "have you been keeping up with those volcanoes and earthquakes in the Pacific? The latest we heard over the car radio was that the UN is preparing a group of scientists to inspect the new island. What have you heard?"

"Ah, nothing much more than that, Bruce. It's amazing to see something like that being created right before us. Imagine an entirely new island forming in what looks like the perfect location, not too hot or cold, halfway between the US and Russia. Perhaps the world is seeing how the land masses were formed thousands of years ago, like Hawaii and all those in the South Pacific."

A whistle blows, the crossing gates descend, and the double side-by-side toy train engines stop with the drinks loaded on a flatbed car. The voice from the train says, "Your drinks are here. Please carefully remove them. The first one is hot tea going to the lady on my right. Next is Constant Comment hot tea going to the lady on my left. The Bud Light goes to the gentleman on the left, and the old guy gets the coffee. Be careful now; don't spill it. Thank you. Are you ready to order, or do you need some more time?" Bruce snickers at hearing the train calling Mark the old guy.

"Yes, I think we're ready," Susan announces to the toy man and gives him her order. And around the table as each makes their food requests.

The whistle blew again, and off the toy train went.

"Old guy? Huh."

Mark says to Wendy, "I thought you said you've turned vegetarian."

"Ah, we were pulling your leg. Do they treat all customers so personally?" Wendy asks. "The way the world is now, I would be very hesitant about making remarks like that: the guy and his belly roll, and that old man remark. People are so easily offended these days."

Mark says: "I've not heard any complaints from anyone, and Peter hasn't said anything about it. You're here in flyover country now, away from the big cities where all these things supposedly happen and get the big publicity. These are ordinary people out here, decent people who know how to take it and instinctively know where to draw the line."

Wendy adds to the conversation, "the rules and procedures we've got to follow in the hospital would have been brave new worldish twenty years ago, perhaps even ten years ago. It's unbelievable what's happened to our society since those twin towers went down. Oh, there I went. I started on a rant of mine when I told Bruce that I wouldn't get off on that subject while we're here."

"That's OK, Wendy," Mark responds. "I think we're all on the same page, and we all feel the same rage seeing America run by ideological tyrants bending over to a bunch of spoiled brats who won't get off their fat butts, demanding their right to a decent job, to a house, to the latest hybrid car, two cell phones, and all of it paid for by someone else. It tees me off, too, and I've made several remarks to Susan lately about just selling it all and getting out of Dodge and finding a nice condo on a beach somewhere in the Bahamas. President Reagan said: *'Freedom is never more than one generation away from extinction.'* This younger generation may be it."

"The sad thing," Bruce adds, "is that whoever is elected President or as a congressman can't change a thing because the rules and regulations get deeply entwined in every aspect of our lives. Every agency has ties to follow the lead of the next agency, yet supposedly each working independently, yet tied together with invisible strings so that no one understands the entire scope of any law that has been passed, enabling bureaucrats to add legalese of their own. How could anyone understand a bill that's over two thousand pages long filled with 'the Secretary shall' . . . ?"

"Outrageous, isn't it," Mark adds. "They said we'd find out what's in it after the president signs the bill."

Bruce adds to the talk. "Everyone has their hands tied, not knowing where to start dismantling agencies, and no one wants to start pulling those strings, which would unravel the entire system. Too many people would be affected. It doesn't matter which party is in charge anymore; the corruption stays, and the lobbyists spread it to different offices when new reps are installed. Politicians get re-elected term after term by sending pork projects home and getting pictures taken with the receivers of the pork. Ah, there I go. I'm sick of it, too."

"Mark, when you find that condo, let us know, and we'll be right there with you. Hey, think of that for a moment: we could play golf on some of the most beautiful courses, go fishing, eat fresh crabs, play cards watching the sunset sink below the ocean, go snorkeling among tropical fish, and read mystery novels sitting in an easy recliner. I might even start smoking a pipe. I don't think I'd own a TV set, and the internet could do without me. I wouldn't miss a thing. We'd get up in the morning, not caring whether it was Monday or Friday; it was just another beautiful day without a care in the world. We could just hang out enjoying these later years."

The whistle blows again, and engine 9845 stops. The announcer says, "Here you are, folks; you're fantastic, tasty, and deliciously prepared meals using the finest ingredients expertly cooked to perfection by the best chefs anywhere. Please be careful lifting your plates off the delicate Union Pacific railroad.

"Enjoy your meal, folks. Thanks a bunch." Sitting next to the tracks, Susan and Wendy handle the plates of food. The whistle blows as the train gathers speed, leaving the booth.

Getting ready to eat, Bruce asks, "They have not been monitoring our conversation, have they?"

"No," Mark answers. "The microphone and all are inside the train engine, so they can't hear us when it leaves the table. I've been in the control room where the operation was explained to me as I watched the gentleman operating the trains and the video cameras and talking to the patrons at their tables. Peter put a lot of thought into this."

The food was fantastic, the conversations were energetic, each catching up on the daily lives of the other, their accomplishments, and future desires. Knowing Mark and Susan, several local people came by the table to greet them and inform them of their intent to attend the Halloween festivities. One of them, a doctor, said he would be there and be available in case anyone was injured. The mayor would also come by for a few moments. One of Susan's friends offered to help.

Bruce and Wendy were continually amazed by the restaurant's atmosphere, the decorations, the model train service, and the friendliness of everyone. Bruce commented that you knew you were in an exceptional place from the moment you entered.   Bruce took pictures with his cell phone of the decorations hanging around the walls and the train operations, the caboose, and the dining car.

Capping off the evening, the train stopped with the bill, to be paid at the front service desk on the way out, along with the picture of the four of them, which Wendy quickly put in her purse.

"Well, gang, let's head for the house, shall we?" Mark said, getting up from the table. "I got this one, Bruce. You're our guests, remember.

Chapter 4

The time is now eight-fifteen as they head back north on Highway 83, then turn west onto the gravel roads leading to Mark's farm. Looking around at the darkened landscape as the sun has settled down for the night, Bruce asks, "Is this part of your farm Mark?"

"No. Not yet. Most of my land is north of the house."

Turning into the driveway as the garage door opens, Susan announces: 'Well, here we are. Are you guys awake back there? Anyone for a piece of pie?"

Wendy answers, "Not for me; remember, I'm on a strict vegetarian diet now."

"Yeah, sure you are," Susan says.

Wendy headed for the bathroom as soon as she entered the house. Upon entering the kitchen and passing by the notebook, Mark notices messages on the computer screen reading "Another volcano in the Pacific." And another message reads: "A new Island is taking shape." And another below that: "UN scientists delay their inspection because of recent activities." The last headline says: "US declaring the new land as their territory."

While Mark was scanning those tweets, Bruce looked over his shoulder and said, This may change the political cohesiveness the major countries agreed to a few years ago under the UN leadership. There's going to be a big fight over who has the rights to this new island while the UN will probably declare the land as theirs."

"Interesting," Mark replies.

"Well, let's sit and relax while waiting for Janet to arrive," Susan says, trying to get the guys away from the computer. "How about that piece of pie, Bruce? Apple or Banana cream?"

"Sounds good, I'll take Apple. You made these? I think Wendy would prefer the banana cream."

"What'd you like to drink with it?"

"Coffee will be fine," Bruce answers.

"Mark, I know you want apple and coffee too," Susan said as she pushed the button on the coffee machine, then reached into the refrigerator, retrieving the banana cream pie.

Wendy enters the kitchen, noticing Susan preparing to slice that beautifully topped dessert. "Yeah, I'll have a piece of that. You make the best banana cream pie. A cup of tea will do me. Where do I find it?"

"In that cabinet behind you, on the second shelf. There are several different kinds, so pick your favorite." Susan tells her. All four have their drinks and pie and head into the living room to continue catching up.

"Bruce, tell us more about your activities at the club," Mark asks.

Replying, Bruce says, "Well, basically, I spend most of my time teaching the game, much of it to kids, teenagers, some of them on the high school golf team, and even some eight-year-olds just starting to play. Sometimes, a foursome of members would hire me to play nine holes with them, instructing them as we played. I enjoy that, as I get to play, and the camaraderie with those guys is a lot of fun. We try hard to keep politics out of it, but some members are involved in local and national politics, so just a remark will tip one of them off, and then it starts.

Hearing what these lawyers, doctors, and businessmen say is fascinating. They are very much concerned about the future. The tips can be great if my instructions result in an improved game. One guy gave me a thousand bucks because he broke through an old habit and had reduced his score by seven strokes for nine holes, from a 48 to a 41. That part is icing on the cake. They seem to like what I do. And I'm getting much more involved with the kids. The high school coach has sought my advice several times, and I've been able to attend several of their tournaments, walking along with the kids and their parents. It's paying the bills."

"Sounds like the ideal job for you, Bruce." Marks adds.

"It is, I'm having a ball."

"Wendy." Susan asks, "Tell us some more about your hospital duties."

"Well, where do I start?" Wendy ponders.

Mark asks, "How has technology changed the surgery room procedures?"

"Mark, I've only been in the surgery room a few months, so I can't tell you what changes were made before my entrance. But it is awesome equipment we use. Much of our time is spent tending to the equipment. I had several days of instructions before I was authorized to participate in actual procedures, and it's a daily briefing we go through to keep abreast of the latest developments: the equipment and the regulations, too."

Mark then asks, "What comments have you heard from the doctors about the government's involvement in the medical field?"

"Oh, Mark, don't get me going on that subject. I'd be moaning and groaning all night long." Wendy answers.

"Just as I figured."

Wendy then says, "You may have read about this, Mark. It went viral, was all over the Internet news. A seventy-two-year-old gentleman was involved in an accident, having his hip and legs broken in the wreck, along with a broken rib barely puncturing one lung. He was rushed to us. Normally, I don't get involved in emergency room operations, but this time, it was quiet in the planned surgical room, so the administrator asked me to help during the lull. Putting bones back together is not a big deal; even pinning a broken hip is a relatively simple procedure. The punctured lung got this man in trouble, and we too. Upon opening his chest, the doctors saw that his lungs were heavily colored from his long-term tobacco use, even though, at his age, he did not have asthma, or any signs of cancer, or any other lung problems.

But, according to recent changes in Medicare coverage, the bill would not be paid through Medicare because he was a smoker. It took time to collect the data, waiting for the insurance company's approval to handle the Medicare coverage while the man was lying on the emergency room table, doctors waiting, while we kept monitoring the patient.

"The hospital administrators had to wait to see who was going to pay the bills. It would have been easier and cheaper if the doctors had immediately treated the man, sending him home for rest and allowing his bones and all to heal. In three months, he would have been back to normal. But, the insurance company said no, as they could not collect from Medicare recouping their payments to the hospital. The charges would fall completely on him and his family.

"If I remember right, the charges would have been around $65,000. The man was not wealthy, but healthy at his age. He had been retired and on Medicare for almost eight years. Financially, he was surviving well enough, living on his social security benefits and not being a burden to anyone; his house, being paid for, was worth about $45,000. His one sibling, a single daughter, did not have the resources to pay the bills, as she had been unemployed for six months and was on unemployment insurance."

Wendy pauses and continues, "Under the directions of the Patient Care Act, the hospital was informed to flip the switch, reasoning that at eighty-two and being a smoker, it would be best under the circumstances to save the resources of the hospital, letting the patient suffer no more and die under anesthesia. Later, the hospital found that someone had mistakenly put his age at eighty-two on the report instead of seventy-two, as listed on the hospital records."

"Yes, I remember reading about that," Mark says. "We're seeing things like that more and more. In the UK, it's even worse. It seems they withhold food and water to the elderly patients deemed incurable by simple tests, letting them die from malnutrition. The UN is beginning to get involved too, declaring that major resources ought to be focused on the young rather than throwing good money on the elderly, who are going to die soon anyway."

"Eugenics is what it is, but they see it as saving resources for those contributing to society," Bruce interjects.

Susan says, "Can't we discuss something more positive or edifying? All I've heard recently is how bad the system is and how our society is being torn apart. You hear it everywhere. It's getting rather depressing. Don't you think these are isolated cases and not the norm? Now that we've got instant news that was not available twenty years ago, we know what's happening anywhere in the world at any moment by just pressing a button or two. Modern technology has changed the world tremendously. Do you think things like that could have happened thirty years ago, and we did not hear about it?"

Wendy breaks in and says, "Yes, I think that's part of it. Before the advancement of technology, news was broadcast at certain times of the day, and that was it. They either tuned in at six pm or missed it and would have to wait until ten. They read the daily newspaper, and most of that was local news or a major story, a story of a real calamity somewhere, not a story of a Walmart robbery in New Jersey, a bank hold-up in California, or a forest fire in Colorado. Those things were considered local news. Look how much more information is broadcast about the daily weather.

"Twenty years ago, if a tornado was heading our way, the only warning we got was the sound of the sirens going off. We'd look out the window or go outside and look at the sky. Now, the weather forecasters break into any program telling us to run for cover, a tornado might be heading your way, and show us graphics with arrows pointing in the direction it's heading, the wind velocity, and how much rain is falling. We should seek cover immediately, showing us videos of the tornado tearing up the roof of a house twenty miles away. "Seek cover immediately," the announcer in a town fifty miles away would tell us, because the tornado just might, it could, it's possible, it could change course and head our way. You can't be too careful, you know. We became afraid to take a minute to look out the window before we grab the flashlight, pillows, blankets, and some valuables and run to a small central closet, or if we had one, an underground shelter praying all the way, causing our heart to beat faster. Modern technology has spoiled us, making us dependents."

Mark says, "Wendy, I think you hit the nail. We have become dependent upon it. But what can be done to reverse the dependency? Nobody wants to give up the technology. We've all come to love it, thinking it gives us freedom. It does provide us with more time for other things, but then we get addicted to keeping up with what's happening . . . in ah, Cambodia."

Again, Susan is dismayed at all the negative and asks again to change the conversation. "Let's talk about our plans for the Halloween festival, shall we? It's coming up shortly, and we only have a couple days to get ready," Susan says, letting the phone ring a few more times to finish her sentence.

"Hi Janet, where are you?" Susan asks.

"I'm lost. I can't find you guys. I'm somewhere north on 83, coming up to Stapleton. I must have missed your road."

"Hang on, Janet. I'll give the phone over to Mark. Mark, Janet missed the side road and is up near Stapleton."

"Hello, Janet." Mark says, "when you get to 92, the crossroad leading into Stapleton, turn left off 83, stop at the convenience store about a half mile on the right, and wait for us. It's only about a ten-minute drive up there from here. What kind of car are you driving?

"OK. We'll be there shortly."

Arriving at the convenience store, Mark pulls in next to the pale green Honda CR-V, seeing Janet standing next to the driver's door. Susan and Wendy open their doors and embrace their friend as Mark and Bruce briskly walk around the minivan, ready to greet Janet.

"Oh, it's so good to see you gals," Janet says.

"How are you doing?" Susan questions. Mark and Bruce take their turns greeting the long-time friend.

"Janet then says, "Mark, I don't know how I missed the road, as you gave me specific directions. I must have missed the sign you said you'd place alongside the road, as dark as it is out here in nowhere."

"Oops. Ah, Sorry Janet, I forgot all about that sign." Mark replies. "My fault. I've been so busy."

Susan adds, "Janet, I was supposed to remind him and forgot too. Forgive us. But you're here, we're here, and we're glad you could make it. Let's get home and let you relax. Wendy and I can ride with you."

Janet handed Susan the car keys and said, "Here, you drive. I'm worn out."

Wendy gets in the back seat, where there is enough room next to the hanging clothes rack.

"Are you sure you want me to drive Janet?" Susan asks.

Janet tells her, "I sure am. Get me to a bed, Susan. I'm tired." Comfortably seated after familiarizing with the controls, Susan pulls onto the main road behind Mark.

Janet says, "It's a long way up here, 935 miles. I stopped in Wichita, Kansas, for the night after that ten-hour drive, and then today, it was almost four hundred, so I'm beat. Not used to these long trips. But now that I'm here, I already feel rested . . .ah . . . well . . . relieved."

Wendy says from the back seat. "We've got a few days to catch up. No rush. Just sit back and leave the driving to us, although I have a thousand questions."

"That's OK, Wendy. We'll have time unless Susan and Mark have the next few days planned out like a menu. Susan, Tell me about this Halloween festival you guys are putting on for the town."

"Oh, Janet, we'll get into that later, but the short version is that this is the third year we've done it. Last year, about eighty children and their parents came out and had a great time. We said we'd do it again. Mark has finished much of the heavy work. We need to fill in the details over the next few days."

Wendy adds, "You've heard the phrase 'the devil is in the details,' so guess what we'll be."

"Yeah, I can't wait," Janet answers.

"Hang on, Janet, these gravel roads are not the smoothest, and the dust is irritating."

After a short twelve-minute drive back to the house, they gather around Janet again, saying they were looking forward to her arrival. "So, let's go inside. You can rest while filling us in on all your exciting news." Mark tells her.

Bruce hands Mark a bundle of hanging clothes as he retrieves her luggage from the trunk. Inside, Susan directs Janet into the living room and a nice comfortable chair while Mark and Bruce take Janet's items back to the spare bedroom she'll use.

Susan asks: "What can I get you to drink? Anything? Coffee, Tea, Beer, Wine?"

Janet says: "A good cup of Starbucks espresso dark roast, two creams with a squirt of chocolate, Susan." And quickly adds, "You asked."

Susan returns, "I have some bold-flavored coffee, cream, and I'm sure I've got some chocolate in the cabinet. Will that do it?"

"Sure, you bet."

Looking at Wendy, Susan asks, "Wendy, how about you? Can I get you something?"

"A glass of water will be fine for me. Thanks."

As Mark and Bruce enter the room, Mark notices that Susan is not there, so he turns back, leaving to help his wife in the kitchen.

Looking at the chairs and recliners available, Bruce picks one close to Janet, asking: "Anything new at the University?"

"Oh, Bruce, we'll have a chance to get into all that later. Right now, I'm enjoying getting here and seeing all of you guys again. You don't know how much I've missed you. I have thought of you often when I hear the professors asking me if I'd like to play a round of golf. Bruce, I've only played once this year. Can you believe that? You must have seen that I brought the clubs along, hoping we could get out and hit that white ball around."

Bruce answers, "Yeah, I saw the clubs. I brought my bag, and Mark and I have already mentioned it."

Susan and Mark enter the room with the drinks, bringing Bruce his favorite before-bedtime drink: Shiner Bock.

"Thanks, Susan, that coffee looks and smells better than Starbucks. I hope it's not too hot because I'm pooped." Janet says.

The five of them chat for fifteen minutes, and then they turn in. "You guys know the drill: make yourself at home getting up whenever," Susan says.

Chapter 5

After breakfast, Mark and Bruce head out to the new barn to work on the Haunted House displays and the solar panels. The ladies spend the day preparing the costumes, the hanging spider webs, the pumpkin carvings, and checking with the boys in the barn every so often. They spruced up the fifth-wheel camper for George and Ruth, who expect to arrive later that evening. After lunch, a few of the parents from town came out to help for a few hours. One of the parents had brought dozens of pumpkins she had carved. Another had skeletons. Another had special treats.

Around five in the afternoon, the ladies start dinner. Mark had planned on having steaks smoked on the grill tonight. Janet asks Susan about the restaurant in town featuring the toy trains and whether she would have a chance to see it, telling Susan that a professor at the University was raving about the place.

Susan answers, "We did plan to take you there after George and Ruth come in. Tomorrow evening, we'll all go. We took Bruce and Wendy there last night before you arrived. I'll call the boys so they can clean up and prepare the smoker, so we can eat about seven."

Janet asks Susan if it'd be alright for her to lay down for an hour; those long drives are not as easy as they used to be; thought she got a good night's rest, but evidently not as preferred, still tired.

While Mark and Bruce were assembling the batteries for the solar magnifier, Mark told him about the lightning strike the other evening and that he saw two one-hundred-watt lights burning inside the barn right before the direct hit tore up the unit.

"I'm onto something here Bruce. It just might work. And all I'm doing is adding pieces of magnifying glass in front of and behind the silicon arrays, magnifying the sun's power, while the rotor moves the unit as the sun moves. I've shaped it like a funnel, magnifying and funneling the rays, magnifying and funneling, funneling and magnifying. It looks like a TV satellite disk and acts like a funnel. Pour a bunch of water into a funnel, and the water backs up if the mouth is too small, so I made the mouth of the funnel moveable, opening and closing depending on the strength of the sun's rays, allowing more or less rays through to be captured in the batteries. Do you realize what this will mean if this thingamajig works in any meaningful way?   It may be enough to provide our own electrical needs?"

"Mark, your inquisitive mind is always coming up with a better way of doing something. Why can't you use that ability in your golf game?   When are we going to get out?"   Bruce questions.

"Bruce, I planned on taking you guys to the club tomorrow morning. George and Ruth will arrive later today. We'll see how late it is when they get here. Either way, I've covered us with tee time for eight am tomorrow and at ten-thirty on Saturday. All seven of us could play then." The phone rings. Answering it, Mark says it was Susan asking them to start the smoker and clean up for dinner.

Sitting around the table on the covered back deck eating the smoked pork chop dinners while enjoying the beautiful late October weather, the conversations got around to Janet and her duties at the university. Mark asks, "So Janet, how many students do you have in each class? Give us a rundown of your daily activities."

Replying, Janet says, "Where do I start? I have just three classes a week, from fifteen students in one, to seventy-five and ninety-two in the others. The subjects are principles of agronomy, basic soil science, and then a class on 'Issues in Sustainable Agriculture,' which the department wanted me to hold. That last one is a doozy, exploring what the experts around the world, under the direction of the UN Agriculture Council, expect the issue of climate change will change the agriculture industry. But, I've made it a 'think about it' course with students doing most of the research. From their findings, they ask questions, and then I ask questions back, and they think about it some more, forming their own opinions. It's a futuristic course. It's been a lot of fun debating how climate change will affect food availability for the next generations. When they find out I don't completely accept the global warming hysteria, some of them are offended. I've been reported to the administrators."

Changing the subject, Susan asks Janet if there's a man in her life yet.

"No, there is not, and I'm not sure I'm ready, or will ever be ready for a serious relationship again. Most of the professors are married or are gay. While I'm on that subject, the administration has allowed one new teacher, who claims he's bisexual, to dress as a male one day, and the next day teach his students dressed up as a woman. Oh, sorry, I shouldn't have opened that subject. But it's irritating to most of us, the kind of impressions they are giving to these kids that anything is OK, as long as no one is denied their right to . . . ah . . . happiness. Yes, happiness."

Changing that subject, Wendy asks: "How did you get the time off right here in the middle of the year? Don't you have classes every week?"

Janet answers, "This is what the university declared fall break week. It was approved a few years ago so students could go home for Halloween."

"Go home for Halloween?"

"Yeah, for Halloween, to celebrate spooks and goblins, just like what we'll be doing here Friday night," Janet replies.

Mark then asks, "How about Thanksgiving? Do they get time off then?"

Janet responds, "No, we have classes on the day after Thanksgiving this year. When they approved Halloween as a holiday time, they took away the long Thanksgiving weekend, claiming the holiday was too patriotic to one country in this time and age of globalism, and they deemed it as also religious in nature. Someone also determined that it was too dangerous, as millions of people were driving somewhere for the weekend. Tell me that that makes sense. They also did not want to be seen as providing favoritism to one religion, as all are equal.

"Unbelievable." Mark asserts. "These idiots are removing everything America was built upon. What's next? Christmas and Easter?"

Janet starts by replying to Mark's questions, "Yes, there have been discussions about that too. The gays have their holidays, the atheists have taken over Halloween, African Americans have a special day, Hispanics have Cinco de Mayo, the Muslims have Ramadan, the greenies have World Wetlands Day, Water Day, Forestry Day, and then there is Earth Hour, where on our campus, the administrators fully cooperated turning the lights off for an hour. Thousands of students were encouraged even to turn off their headlights if driving. I heard some UN big shot wanted to honor Al Gore with a worldwide holiday celebrating Climate Change Science."

Bruce adds that he heard that unions are suggesting that Mondays be a permanent holiday because, historically, it has been a hard day for working people to get back into the swing of the work week. Having Monday off would help them adjust."

"Eh gads, whatever happened to our understanding of common sense?" Mark says.

Susan then declares, "Why is it that our conversations always seem to get so political? I'm tired of it."

"Well," Mark replies, "we could spend our time talking about football, and you ladies could spend your efforts discussing the latest purse designs. Susan, if by informing ourselves of these events tearing this country apart, perhaps average people would organize other like-minded people into a resistance movement and stop the degradation of our moral standards. George Washington said: *'Of all the dispositions and habits which lead to political prosperity, religion and morality are indispensable supports.'*

America cannot survive when political special interest groups tear away the agreements of basic morality. Our morality was built upon Biblical tenets, 'do unto others as you would have them do unto you,' along with the Ten Commandments."

"Another drink for anybody?" Susan asks, as she gets up and heads into the kitchen. Wendy offers to help as Janet, Mark, and Bruce give their orders to Susan. In the kitchen, Wendy asks Susan if she's OK. "Susan, I don't remember that you've interrupted Mark like I've seen you do several times."

"Yes, I'm fine, but I don't know what's gotten into Mark lately. He seems to be different ever since we heard about the earthquakes and Volcanoes forming that new island out there in the Pacific. He's changed. It's like he wants to move out there and escape. He even made that comment one day. He said he was joking because we were talking about moving to the Bahamas to get away, to sit back, relax, and enjoy our hard work. We deserve it. And now, whenever I hear about what's happening to this country, I know that this increases his desire to leave, and that would be the reason he desired to move, not because we loved each other and desired to be together more than we've been able to when we were working so hard raising the kids and all. Yes, I'm troubled over it, but please don't say anything to Bruce about this, Ok?"

"No, of course not," Wendy says. "Mark is an inquisitive, intense, focused, and determined man, as you know, and I'm sure he wouldn't do anything as drastic as forsake all these comforts to start anew on some volcanic island way out in the Pacific. That would be insane. Try not to let this affect you, Susan. It can tear you up."

"Yeah, this island has got his focus already."

"I can't see that happening," Wendy says.

"I know, you're right, moving out there would be insane when we've got everything right here. Now, let's get these drinks out there. And maybe we can talk about the beautiful moon or something." Susan tells her good friend, not noticing through the kitchen window the headlights of a car coming down the drive. "Thanks for listening."

Back on the deck, Wendy asks everyone, "Isn't that a beautiful moon?"

"Yes, gorgeous," Janet answers, just as George and Ruth walk around the corner of the house, surprising them all. After the hugs and initial greetings, Susan offers the desserts she made, asking Ruth if she'd mind helping.

"No problem, I'd be delighted," Ruth answers, sensing that Susan desired to chat. After Susan explains Mark's change, Ruth confirms that she'd try to keep the conversation away from politics.

"Thought we'd bring it all out, and you can get whatever you want," Susan announces as she and Ruth place the pies, plates, forks, and napkins on the table. "Help yourself."

Looking at Mark, Janet asks, "Isn't this an unusual weather pattern for this time of the year here in western Nebraska?"

"Yes, it is Janet, as some years we could already have seen a foot of snow, so we're enjoying the warmer evenings like this, with mid-afternoon highs in the low seventies. The forecast for Friday evening is in the mid to high fifties, perfect for our Halloween fest."

George asks about the plans and how he can help get things ready, while Ruth asks about how many they expect and what she could do to help. Mark briefs them all on the plans, what they've done already, and what needs more work.

Finishing off his apple pie, Bruce brings up the subject of playing golf in the morning. "George, you did bring your clubs, right? Your Dad has tee times in the morning at eight."

Then Susan says, "Yeah, the three of you go out and play in the morning, and we girls will do our thing here getting ready for the evening's festivities?"

"Sounds good to me," Janet confirms. "My game is horrible, and I'd ruin it for you guys."

"Me too." Ruth agrees.

Wendy adds, "Good, that's settled. You guys go enjoy yourselves."

Susan then adds, "Yeah, go play. We girls will get the details taken care of, as we expect quite a few mothers from town to pitch in also. If any of the fathers come out, we'll put them to use on the heavy stuff, like hanging the spooks and spiders in the trees and placing the pumpkins."

With that, Janet says she's ready to hit the sack.

George asks, "I assume the camper is ready for us."

"You got it, son," Mark tells him. "So go ahead and turn in, but be ready to leave at seven." Bruce then announces that he will also turn in while Wendy grabs a few items from the table, helping Susan put things away.

While Susan is cleaning up the kitchen and the guests have retired, Mark turns on the notebook computer to catch up on the latest news, seeing the headline: "UN officially declares a new island has formed." The story indicates that the current size of the new island is now about the size of Hawaii, and their scientists hope to be able to physically inspect it before the year is up, giving the lava flows, which seem to have stopped, time to cool. Mark looks at his weather page and checks for further information about how solar companies make out financially.

"Let's go to bed, Mark." Susan declares. "I told the girls they could sleep in as long as they wanted, as that's what I intend to do, or if they get up before me, to make their coffee and help themselves to whatever. So, Mark, don't wake me in the morning, go play golf, but take your cell phone, and please, before you come home, call to see if there's anything I need while you're there."

"Sure."

"Good night, dear," Mark tells Susan as he leans over, kissing her, wrapping his arms around her, and snuggling up.

Chapter 6

The round of golf went well, although Mark was beaten by his son George, who shot a 78. Bruce was his usual self, finishing with a one-over par. During the round, Bruce gave Mark and George tips to improve their swings or concentration, reminding them that practice makes perfect, along with his smart remarks. At one point during the game, Mark had a small pond between him and the green and was debating which club to use when Bruce told him he can hit one more club or two more balls.

"You're still away," Bruce told Mark when his putt ran past the hole, stopping farther away.

"Nice swing," as Mark's tee shot landed in the woods.

On the way home, Bruce remarks, "They've made some improvements in the course since the last time; some bunkers were enlarged, some smaller, and a few fairways have been enlarged. It looks good. The ground-keepers are doing a good job, Mark."

George says, "Dad, you asked me to remind you to call Mom to see if there was anything we needed to get while here in town?"

"Oops, thanks for reminding me," Mark says, reaching toward the dash-installed hands-free cell phone, and soon enough, Susan answers. "Hey Susan, we've just finished. You got a shopping list?"

Susan answers, "Yeah, we're OK here, Mark. The town folks have helped a bunch and also brought some interesting decorations. Most of them are still here. And, Mark, I put a couple of the men preparing the campfire area. They put a small barrier around the fire pit, protecting anyone from getting burned, and moved the firewood nearby. It was their idea for the barrier, as they remember last year when a kid nearly burned his hand in the fire. They've also finished off the wagons, putting bales of hay around for the people to sit on. All you'll have to do is hook up the horses."

"Sounds good, babe. We'll be there in a few minutes."

The men get home, grab a sandwich, and then get busy greeting volunteers from town and finishing the Haunted House.

"Well, it's as it is, and that's that."

Finding Susan, Mark asks her if anyone has commented to her about the Haunted House displays.

"Nothing negative, Mark. I noticed that others who saw it got a kick and laugh. No one complained about it to me. Someone suggested you put a sign on the door saying, 'Enter at your own risk. Contents may be offensive to some.'"

Mark says, "Ok, we'll do that. Warning signs are everywhere, even on baby cribs. And now, I've got to warn people that this is a free speech zone."

Susan tells Mark of Sandy's idea regarding giving out candies at the various stations along the hay bale ride. She suggested that the children would get off the wagon at the stations and hunt for the candies like kids hunting for Easter eggs. She stated that our generation had spoiled kids at Halloween as all they had to do was knock on doors, and they'd get candy. And she related it to welfare; the children grow up thinking all they have to do is knock on a few welfare office doors, and they get money from the federal government. She wanted her kids to know that one had to work to get the things of life."

Mark says, "That's brilliant. We'll work on that, and I'd like to thank her personally."

Bruce and George discuss implementing the changes as Susan takes Mark off to find Sandy.

"I approached her, and she was helping some others place the carved pumpkins along the driveway into the farm."

"Sandy," Susan says. "Tell Mark your idea about the candy treats."

"Hi, Mark." Sandy starts by telling him how much she has enjoyed the Halloween festival here the last two years, how her kids raved about it on the way home, and how much she and her friends appreciate the work the two of you were doing for the town.

"Anyway," Sandy continues, "I got to thinking about how we've just shoved candy and goodies into the children's baskets at Halloween time, and I compared that to Easter when we make the kids hunt, run, and find the hidden eggs. Some kids got more than others, some less. That seemed more of reality, more like what life was about. But then along comes Halloween, and we throw them the candies, as all they have to do is go from door to door. I talked it over with Bill, and he agreed that we should change Halloween so the kids can understand the principles early in life."

"You know you are right," Mark replies. "I never thought about it in those terms before. Halloween is not a Christian holiday like Easter. The Easter egg hunt represents a Biblical principle, whereas the free Halloween candy represents a devilish one. That's a brilliant thought you had, Sandy. How can we implement this idea into our little festivities out here?"

Sandy says, "Well, I've thought a little about that too. Mark, if I recall correctly, you took the kids for a ride on the horse-drawn hay wagons last year. I remember that a spook would pop out from behind a tree or shrub and throw candy at the kids at various points. At one point, a devilish, costumed man got on the wagon and gave each kid some candy. At another point, the candy came down from a tree, and another had a Spiderman jump in the wagon and give the kids candy. My husband and I discussed that it could be changed so that the kids would have to show a little effort to get the candies, perhaps get off the wagon and search.

That's as far as we got. I don't presume to desire to take over your show here, Mark. It's your show, and we'd still appreciate what you're doing."

Mark tells Sandy, "Listen, Sandy, this has become a team effort starting last year when so many of you volunteered to help. In the first year, we got some help from a few friends from church, but it was basically our idea, and now it's growing with more and more help from people like you, and more ideas are added to the festival. So we appreciate your ideas, and again, I think you hit upon something we should change. What are your ideas on changing it? Come on, I'm sure you have a few thoughts."

Sandy then adds, "One thing I've thought about is that we should eliminate all of the spooky stuff that's been traditional Halloween standards, replacing that with just fall-oriented decorations."

As they were talking, a car drove into the farm entrance, and two men dressed in suits and a well-dressed lady got out and inquired of one of the volunteers where they could find the farm owner.

Mark notices the three of them walking over in their direction and tells Sandy, "I'm sorry, but I guess I need to see what these people want. Sandy, get with Susan and go ahead and start working on those ideas of yours. I'm all for it."

"Good afternoon, gentlemen. I'm Mark Tebonson, the owner of this farm. How can I help you?"

"Good afternoon, Mr. Tebonson. I'm Jack Billingsly of the Food and Drug Administration. This is Tom Whitehead of Homeland Security and Nakita Samson from Health and Human Services. We got word that you may violate several of the federal guidelines concerning the safety of children during this festival of yours. We want your permission to inspect and advise. Our sources tell us that your actions could be offensive and that you may not be taking the need to protect children seriously."

"Oh my God," Mark exclaims. "Where did you get that information? Don't you people have anything better to do than to bother us? This is private property. Instead of bothering citizens. Well, anyway." Mark quells some thoughts, and says, "Here, it is two o'clock, and we've got hundreds of town people coming out here in a few hours, and you guys show up to inspect at this last minute. Unbelievable! And it takes three of you!"

"Watch what you say, Mr. Tebonson. "Would you cooperate and show us around, or must we call for help?"

"I don't believe it," Mark exclaims. "I suppose the help would be the State Police and swat teams. If I asked to see your search warrant, you'd tell me you don't need one, as this is just an inspect and advise mission, but if I resisted, the help would arrive at six pm when the festivities begin."

"Mr. Tebonson, are you going to cooperate or not?"

Mark softly answers. "Where do you want to start?"

"The three of us can fan out." Mr. Billingsly says. "Mr. Whitehead can look around the barn areas. Ms. Samson can check in on the candies and your food supplies, and I'll review the equipment. Mr. Tebonson, you can go on with whatever you're doing, and we'll get back to you shortly. Okay?"

Mr. Billingsly and Ms. Samson walk away.

"I see you've got a couple of wagons loaded with hay over there. Were you planning to use them? How would they be transported? Will children be riding in the wagons? What age groups? And where did you plan to take them on the wagons?"

At that moment, Mark remembers the man who got offended and left in a hustle last year. Mark fresponds, "We planned to have the children in the wagons, which two horses will pull. We will drive them around the area, around the wooded area, next to the trees, in and among them. Same as last year," Mark informs, pointing towards the row of trees bordering the farm. "During the ride, we planned on having adults dressed in costumes jumping out from behind the trees and shrubs, throwing candies into the wagon for the kids to pick up. One of the adults was going to be in a tree, and as the wagon came under the tree, he would be dropping candies on the wagon. Parents would be on the wagon holding small kids. Totally safe as it was last year, no one got hurt, and they all had a good time."

"Hmm, I see." Mr. Billingsly says. "Our sources tell us you plan to have a big campfire, too. Where would that be?

"Over there in the open area," Mark says. "And we've put a barrier around the actual fire so that no children could accidentally fall into the fire."

"Very thoughtful of you," the gentleman from the FDA says. "Mark, go ahead and continue what you were doing, and I'll just wander around on my own, OK? We'll get back to you shortly."

Mark leaves the feds to look for Susan and Bruce. Finding Bruce first, Mark tells him about what's happening. "Bruce, see if you can detour that gentleman from entering the old barn and place a tarp over my solar equipment. I don't want them to see that, for sure."

"Gotcha, Mark, I'll see what I can do," Bruce responds.

Finding Susan, Mark informs her of who the visitors are and what they want.

"Well, Mark, What are we going to do?" Susan asks.

Mark responds: "I agreed to let them inspect and advise. That is what they said this was—just an inspection. I was so mad I was ready to throw them off the farm as they didn't have a search warrant and no legal right to search our private property. The alternative was to let them look around; we may still have our festival.

"One even warned me about what I said, as it could be used against me. So Susan, we only got a few more hours to prepare this thing, so let's continue doing as we were. Tell the ladies to ignore the strangers. I'm more concerned about the Haunted House displays and those signs than anything else. How could they possibly be against the traditional Halloween activities, even though we go overboard a bit? The campfire may be a problem to them, but the hayride or the candy giveaways? But, we'll see in a little bit when they advise."

"Mark, you did the right thing," Susan tells Mark as she walks toward the new barn, where one group of volunteers sorts out the candies. Another group designs the systems of effort the children must partake in to receive candies. Another group is preparing more pumpkins, placing candles inside them, while George and Ruth decorate the horses, the carriage, and the wheels of the wagons.

" Oh, Mark, I almost forgot. The mayor called and said he'd be out about three-thirty or four."

Mark tells Susan that he will take the golf cart back to the old barn to see what's happening there and to look at the campfire site, among other things. Circling toward the rear of the old barn, Mark noticed a tarp had been placed over his solar equipment, hiding it from easy view. Looking through the window, Mark saw Bruce inside but decided against going in and instead headed out along the tree line inspecting the route they hoped to take with the wagons, looking up in the tree at the platform an adult would be to drop candies into the wagon. *That looks OK to me,*"

Continuing along the planned path, he stops at each area, looking at the rigs hooked up that would activate mannequins dressed in costumes to jump out, drop-down, or fly over the wagon as it passed by. *Ok, these are ready to go.* He turns the golf cart around, heading back toward the campfire area. Upon arriving, he notices one of the feds talking with a volunteer, placing the firewood at various points along the barrier. A mound of dirt was constructed behind the fire pits for the speakers to stand on as they delivered their stories. Not wanting to get involved with the bureaucrats, he headed back toward the new barn area, where Susan was busy with the other volunteers.

An hour passed, and those three from Washington were still looking around. *'I wished the mayor would drive up soon before these guys gathered together comparing notes and presenting me with their advice,'* Mark was hoping just as Susan came over to talk.

"Well, Mark, two of them came in here looking around carefully at all the candy items, the pumpkins, and the tricks we intend to pull on the kids and talking with some of the ladies. Sandy said she got mad at the man and told him to beat it, to get out of this area and leave us alone. She told them she was a Christian and wasn't doing anything wrong, that her kids would be out there that evening, and she and her husband could watch over their safety themselves. She did not need anyone's help from Washington."

"Good for her," Mark responds. "But it might also just piss these people off." He adds, then says, "I've stayed out of their way, as I know the intrusions got me mad too, and then who knows what they would do if I resisted. They know they have the upper hand and can make us do whatever, or shut us down using the power of the State or federal police to do it. I could sue, but then we'd be out millions, and they would move millions of tax monies to their defense. We'd be tied up in court for years. They know that, too.

At times like this, I want to resist with all I got. Get the guns and run them out of here. But then we'd have another Janet Reno shoot out."

"Thanks for resisting those urges, Mark."

"After this is over, I will write to our congressmen, even though that will be useless too," Mark says. "Did any of them ask to get in the house?"

"No, Mark, not to me," Susan responds. "Can I get you something to drink?"

"No, not me, but maybe it might be a good idea to offer those three goons a cool drink," Mark suggests.

Turning around to see if he could see where they were, he noticed the three bureaucrats slowly walking toward them from the area of the old barn. "Never mind, here they come. Stay here with me. You'll be my moral support and elbow me if I start to get off on a rant of mine. Ok?"

Mr. Billingsly, Tom Whitehead, and Nakita Samson approach, and Mr. Billingsly begins, "Mr. Tebonson, The volunteers we talked with were very helpful, except for one who appeared upset. We thank you for your cooperation. We've made our notes and taken a few pictures for our records. Before coming here, we talked with the mayor, who supported your plans, saying that all of the codes are followed to his knowledge. We were also wondering what efforts you made to welcome minorities. Our sources mentioned that there were no minorities present last year. That's disappointing, don't you think so?"

"Well," Mark says, "Your eyes may have been closed to the fact that two or three minorities are helping us prepare for the start of the festivities. Invitations went out to the entire community and all churches in the area. Is it my fault that no minorities showed up last year?"

"Yes, but what about the Hispanics?"

"Gads, I don't go around asking everyone what ethnic group they belong to, and I, we don't keep records for statistical purposes. Asian folks? Some Vikings may show up. Do they count? And what group should I put the half-whites in?" Mark answers, feeling the elbow in his side.

"No, but you should reach out more aggressively to make them feel welcome."

"How do I do that? I will not send cars out looking for a few token minorities to make the statistics favorable to your expectations. Did you notice that I'm not white like a piece of paper, just a different shade of tan, like you? Now, is that all? I've got work to do." Mark replies, being upset with their insinuations that he's racist.

Mr. Billingsly responds. "There's another thing that could be a problem for some people: those signs you have in the Haunted House. They're disgusting. But don't you think you've gone a bit too far with that ATF thing, suggesting that soldiers would come out arresting people? That could frighten some folks. That's overboard, Mr. Tebonson. The signs are OK, but the film of soldiers dressed in Roman costumes with swords is unacceptable. We suggest you do not show the film. Another suggestion is to place a comment at the door noting that what's inside is your opinion only."

"Oh, another thing unrelated to Halloween is your private jet and whether you file flight plans with the FAA before every take-off. We'll be checking on that. That's it, Mr. Tebonson. Our inspections are complete, and you can proceed as planned. We'll send you a written report soon. And it would be best if you made a stronger effort to attract minorities. We expect that you will. I appreciate your cooperation."

Stunned, Mark says: "Thank You."

As they left, the mayor stopped and parked in front of Mark and Susan. Opening the door, the mayor, James Olsen, says, "It looks like I arrived just in time to miss the feds."

Mark responds, "Yeah, perfect timing, James. But it went better than I first expected, and we can proceed with their blessings. Thank you for your comments to them before they came out here. They said they had a visit with you."

"Oh, you're so welcome, Mark. Susan, you're looking good as usual. How are the displays going? Are we ready to give the children a good time?"

"We are," Mark announces. Susan then asks the mayor if he'd like to come in for a drink before the guests start arriving.

"Sure, thanks, and you can fill me in on what you want me to do." He responds.

The guests arrived a bit before six as George and another young man from town directed the parking, and pointing to where they would begin the festivities. By seven pm, over three hundred people from the area had arrived, and the celebrations were in full swing. It went well, with just about everyone having a great time. The weather was perfect, cooling down to 45° later for the campfire stories and marshmallow roasts. Mayor Olsen opened with a few remarks. Then, the Boy Scout leader told some stories, and Pastor Allan related how Halloween got started.

At eleven-twenty, everyone had left, leaving those seven enjoying a nightcap on the deck. Mark summarized the event by saying, "Boy, am I glad that's over. Dealing with those yackos from the feds just about had me unglued, but thanks to Susan, who helped me keep my cool, and to the rest of you for your tremendous help. We could not have done it without you. Tomorrow morning, we will relax and tidy up the grounds. Tee-off time was changed to one-thirty, and we'll hit a ball that does not go where we want it to go.

Then we'll all go to Jeffers Depot for dinner. Good night."

Chapter 7

It's late March when Mark and a long-time friend, Jim Nordingham, are having dinner at the Doubletree Hotel in Bethesda, Maryland, catching up on what's been happening in each other's lives while Mark is in town securing his patent on the solar magnifier and electrical generator.

"Is this the first time you've been in Washington this time of year?" Jim asks Mark.

"Did you forget about our year together with the Justice Department living in that dump of an apartment just west of the Arlington cemetery?" Mark reminds him.

Jim replies, "Oops, I did there for a moment. That year was one I'd like to forget. The work was horribly boring, sitting at a desk all day researching old law journals and looking for legal briefs substantiating the department's actions. I still don't know why I wanted to be a lawyer."

"Yeah," Mark says. "I couldn't stand it either. The department head called me one day to tell me I was on the list for a promotion. He then brought up some of the comments I'd made regarding the duality of a department stance during those sexual revolution years of the early eighties. So, after our discussion, I knew I did not want to make a career in the department, and I was thinking that a promotion might change my mind after some time, so I decided to submit my resignation and leave."

Jim says he remembers Marks's joy and excitement when he returned to the apartment that night. "I left shortly after that, remember?" Jim reminds Mark. "That year was a turning point for both of us. I went to work managing an electronics store, and you moved back to Omaha and went to work for your grandfather, right?"

"The best thing I did was get out of here," Mark says. "And here we are, Jim, 33 years later, having done quite well for ourselves.

Jim asks, "Tell me about that solar invention you got the patent for."

"Well," Mark goes on to explain his newest invention. "I got the idea while looking for a different alternative power source for the farm. I looked at wind, which I ruled out. While looking at solar panels, I was not too fond of anything on the market, and I started thinking of an improvement. All I did was add pieces of magnifying glass on both sides of the current solar panels on the market today, shape it conclave like a funnel, concentrating the sun's power even more, and then made it small enough to fit on the roof of a house, making it look like a TV satellite receiver, with a rotor that would move it following the suns' path throughout the day. A battery about the size of current air conditioning units is formulated to hold the power for two to three days, then connected to a generator. Connecting a second battery would almost double the storage capability. It was a lot of fun, but it took most of two years to perfect it. And now, I've got the patent."

"Congratulations, Mark. Let's have a toast to your new riches." Jim suggests.

"Jim, have you been keeping up with the earthquakes and volcanoes in the Pacific?"

"No, not that much," Jim responds. "There's a new island, and that's all I know about it."

Mark confides, "Jim, there is just something about this phenomenon that has captured my attention. I catch myself reading every bit of news that comes out now. You remember Janet Studebaker, don't you?"

Jim replies, "Sure do. She's down in Texas somewhere teaching agronomy, right?"

Mark says, "Yeah, she's at Texas A&M. She just returned from a tour of the Island with a few university scientists and some UN geologists collecting rock samples and such for research. They walked around several areas, inspecting the rock formations and collecting samples for research. She felt the soil level was unusually high, considering the circumstances. It was more salty than ashy. She was aware of my interest, called us at home, and asked if I had any plans to fly over the place to look at it. She said I'd be surprised at what I saw. Would you like to fly out there and look at it?"

Jim answers, "Yeah, but when? I'll be tied up here for another month before I can get away."

Mark replies, "Well, about the same for me as farming duties are calling me to work the one hundred acres I kept for myself. This time of the year is hectic for farmers, and I promised I'd help one of the guys who just leased six hundred acres. Perhaps we could both go at the end of April? Would you be game?"

Jim answers back: "You're on. I'd love to see what's cooking out there."

Mark answers, "Alright, I'll plan on it. You can fly to Denver, and I'll pick you up there."

Jim then asks, "What's on the menu for tomorrow? This time of year is beautiful here in Washington. Tomorrow, as you take care of business, you must drive around to see the Cherry Blossom Trees all over the area. At the convention center, there will be a ceremony honoring the gift of the trees by the mayor of Tokyo way back in 1912."

"Yeah, the trees are beautiful, Jim. But I can't stand this city anymore, and I wouldn't come here unless I had to, which I did. I'll be going home in the morning. Dealing with all the codes, the endless dots and tees that must be crossed in a certain way, drives this country boy mad. I want to scream. Whatever happened to those days when a good handshake closed the deal?"

Jim responds to that, "I know what you mean, but this is the twenty-first century, and everyone wants a part of your deal at no cost to them, no obligation to them or responsibility by them, so all of those liability statements must be all-encompassing without a chance of an ant sneaking through. Back in North Platte, you may be confident in another's handshake, but those days are ending there, too."

"Jim, do you want me to send you a ticket, a boarding pass, and a liability statement for our trip to see the Island and pat you down before you can get on my airplane? You'll be as a passenger in my private jet, and you never know what could happen. You could be hiding something in your butt, or I could have intentions of flying into a schoolhouse."

Responding to that sarcasm, Jim says, "You will never inspect my butt. I'll have my attorney call your attorney."

"Eh, with that. Now I've got to turn in right after I call Susan." Mark answers.

Jim tells him that he's got a meeting in the morning to resolve some problems with the accountants. "I'll keep in touch and let you know my plans."

They shake hands and turn to leave in their respective directions, Mark heading for the elevator and Jim walking toward the desk, asking that his car be brought around.

In his room, he pushes #1 on his iPad to get Susan while turning on the TV to get the latest news. "Hello Susan, How are things there?"

Susan answers. "Great, Mark. I miss you. When will I see the jet coming in?"

Mark responds, "I'll be taking off here at ten, so I should be there around eleven- ten your time. I'll call as I circle the landing strip."

Susan informs him, "Be careful. There's a storm brewing from Omaha to Indianapolis."

Mark says, "Thanks. I haven't had a chance to look up the weather situation yet."

Susan responds, "Oh . . . Mark, you got a FedEx letter from the Energy Department. They want to discuss your solar device and something about the needs of the national community. You'll need your lawyer to decipher the actions they suggest."

"What?" Mark asks.

"Sorry, I shouldn't have mentioned it." She responds.

Mark then questions whether he should stay another day in Washington, taking care of it eye ball to eye ball. Susan assures him he would be better off coming home directly, reading the letter himself, and calmly getting his thoughts together. The energy department thought a letter would be sufficient, so a delayed response should be adequate, too."

"Just be careful on the flight, and please keep me informed as you progress. The storm is a big one encompassing your direct path."

"OK, Susan, I'll let you know. I love you."

"Love you too," Susan says. "Bye"

Glancing at the TV news, he notices a great-looking young blonde talking about the new Island in the Pacific.

Turning up the volume, he hears her saying: ". . . the UN inspectors have been examining the rocks and soil from the new Pacific Island. They declare the area a modern-day example of how our current land masses formed millions of years ago, enabling life to evolve and be sustained. We are privileged to see the beginning of this planet's land masses. The UN is asking each country to make this new island formation a central part of the educational development of the world's children. The educational arm of the UN is preparing those materials. The UN has declared that life on the island will take millions of years to develop, so humans must leave this new island alone. They would like to see the island develop life on its own, just as Mother Earth did millions of years ago."

Mark shouts at the TV: "Gobbledygook. Hogwash!" changing to the weather channel, thinking that the only thing that girl knows is how to read a script. She's got people fussing over her makeup and her hair, and she has a selection of clothes chosen for her by Neiman Marcus. And she gets paid thousands to look good on the air, attracting viewers, and the faster she can talk, the more time she has for commercials. On the weather channel, he noticed the storm was expected to hit the Philadelphia area by mid-morning. He decides to leave earlier, taking the southern route over Atlanta, then west to Birmingham and up from the south, avoiding the storm. Calling Susan back, he informs her of his change of plans and that he'll touch down much earlier.

"Good." Susan says, "I'll have breakfast ready for you. Still, keep me informed in the morning. I Love you."

Mark calls down to the desk for a wake-up call at five.

In the morning, he gets the clearance to take off at seven-ten. He heads out over the Atlantic, then south along the coast, turning west at Charlotte toward Atlanta, over Birmingham, turning northwest toward Memphis, across Arkansas, descending as he passes over Joplin, Missouri to get a closer look at the tornado rubble, and then over Wichita and home calling the control tower commanded by Susan getting the signal to land.

Putting the jet away in the hanger, Mark climbs aboard the golf cart for the short ride to the house, noticing that the solar magnifier is churning away, and seeing Susan standing on the deck waving a greeting.

"Good morning, my love." Mark greets her. "Every time I'm away for a few days, you look more beautiful than ever."

"Hmm, what do you want now?" Susan suggestively responds.

"Breakfast," Mark tells her.

"Is that all?" she questions.

"We'll see about that later." Mark answers.

"Your favorite will be ready in a few minutes. Here's that letter I told you about." Susan tells Mark as he sits down to the breakfast nook. Reading the letter, Mark begins tapping his foot, sighing, ripping it up, and throwing it in the trash. "The nerve of those people," Mark exclaims to Susan while she places the plate of scrambled eggs topped with cheddar cheese, three sausage links, and a toasted English muffin before him.

"I hope you're hungry." Susan declares as Mark bows his head toward the plate, fork in hand.

"Wow! That's beautiful, Thank You."

"Mark, you should not have thrown that letter away. It asked for a response by a certain date." Susan tells him as he lifts a fork of eggs off the plate.

Mark tells her, "What the energy department wants is certain rights for my invention, implying that with their expertise, their wide range of resources, and close contacts, they could greatly help in the manufacturing and distribution of the solar magnifier, taking all of those worries and hardships off my back. The sob story they present is that the poor need this, the world full of hungry people need this, the children of the world need this, and I should think about their needs first rather than selfishly benefitting myself. In other words, I should be one of their puppets and let them and their experts handle all the details. They would be generous by paying me a fee for each item sold as my compensation or some other arrangement. Did you notice the threat at the bottom of the letter? If I disagree, then other means are at their disposal."

"Sorry, but bring it on. They can go fly a kite. Who do they think they are?"

Susan asks, "How did they find out about it so quickly? The letter was here before you finished the paperwork on the patent."

Mark says, "That's easy. Red flags go up when certain hot issue items are mentioned. I'm beginning to feel like my solar magnifier is that mysterious motor of Atlas Shrugged. The generator is supplying most of our electrical needs now, and I'd like the kids to have it, but the government will never get it. Never. Never! They don't have enough money. They can't print enough. The UN could not confiscate enough. I'll do with it what I want, and that's it."

"Susan dear, calm me down by telling me some good news." As he shifts his weight on the oak chair, Mark suggests, "Susan,

I'm getting very irritated by all this. Perhaps we ought to look into that Caribbean beach house?"

Excitedly, Susan replies, "I thought you'd never bring it up. I've got some brochures I sent off for. Let me get them for you."

"You've got brochures?" Mark questions.

Susan answers, "Yes, I do. I sent off for them. Let me get them for you. Oh, Mark, we would be so happy watching the sun setting over the ocean horizon, sipping pina coladas, playing bridge with some new friends, knocking that golf ball around the palm trees with no worries, no tractors to fix, no corn to harvest. Mark, you deserve it. We deserve it."

Mark then says, "Yeah, the house is paid for, the farm is free and clear, there's money in the bank and the market, and there's enough coming in monthly from the leases on the farm, and the payments for the Business Solutions Software Company I sold, to keep us quite comfortable. I suppose I could even bring the solar magnifier down there and set one up on the roof of the beach house. I might even get into reading mystery novels sitting on the veranda while you keep cool drinks at my elbow."

Susan asks if he'd like another cup of coffee, a cinnamon roll, or anything. "Mark, let's take a trip down there to see for ourselves. We could leave this afternoon and be in the Bahamas by dusk."

Mark replies. "No, I can't go yet. I promised our neighbor Larry that I'd help him with his tractor problems after I got back. I will take a good look at those brochures this evening. But the next month is always quite hectic to get the seeds planted on time. Hopefully, the equipment does not break down. You know how it is. And I'm meeting with Jim in Denver at the end of April."

Susan replies, "I could go myself and have a look around. Perhaps George or Thomas could get away for a week-end. Surely, I could get a friend from church to go with me. Or, Melody? Yeah, Melody. She'd love to get away, and it'd be good for both of us. You know, that mother-daughter thing. What do you say?"

Mark answers, "Well, call Melody and see if she can get away and when. And I'll take a good look at those brochures this evening."

"You already said that," Susan replies.

Mark answers that, "Honey, I will. Did we get any other letters while I was gone? Did anything else happen around here that was of interest to me?"

Susan replies, "That cat jumped over our fence again."

"Very funny. Thanks for breakfast. It's good to be home, and now I should be heading over to Larry's to see what I can do."

"You've only been here for an hour. Sit and relax a bit. Let's talk some more. I've missed you."

"There's a bunch of information about the Bahamas we could get over the net," Mark informs. "Have you tried any of that?"

Susan responds, telling him how much time she has explored the areas they might be interested in, such as Bermuda, Cayman Islands, Barbados, and St. Thomas.

"Right now," Susan says, "all of them seem very attractive. But, I know we'll need to explore this more. Mark, it would be best to explore from your angle. You're so much better at handling these computer programs than I am, and I'm sure you'll find much more than I could. That's why I sent for the brochures."

Mark says, "If Melody can get away and a date is set, I'll have some connections set up for you when you arrive and show you around, pointing in the best direction. Possibly even a realtor to show you some sample homes for sale. Yes, I can handle all of that."

"Mark, I still sense from you that you're not really ready to make this kind of a move. You're not, are you?" Susan asks him.

"Well, ah, no. I guess that I'm not ready right now. In three months, six months, a year? I don't know. I've still got irons in the fire to finish first, and I can't honestly say when that'll be. It's dependent on too many other people. But an exploratory trip would still be a good thing to do, and I'm all for that. It's just that right now, I don't feel free to leave for a week or more. Looking for a future home in an area we're not familiar with will take more than a week, possibly a month.   Gathering information is preparatory work, and that's where we're at right now."

Susan answers, "I understand that you're not ready to start packing yet, even after all the government bullets you've had to dodge, something is still holding you back. What is it?"

Mark says, "Well, there is something, and I'm not sure what that is yet. We've got a good life here. It's not easy to leave when our fortune is at stake."

"You mean this is not like picking out a pair of shoes at the mall?"

"In a sense, it is. Buying a home works similarly; only the cost and contractual arrangements differ."

Chapter 8

It's the end of April, and Mark has picked up Jim at the Denver Centennial airport. They are on the way to San Francisco to fuel up and then off to view the new Island in the Pacific. Jim is telling Mark that since their meeting in March, he has been trying to keep up with the news about the island: what the experts are saying, the stance of the various nations interested in claiming the land as their own, and what the UN desires to do when the Island is declared hospitable for humans.

"Mark," Jim questions his good friend. "You've probably answered this question before, but why do you have such an overwhelming interest in this Island."

Mark replies, "You know, I'm not exactly sure myself what it is that's driving me to such an extent that I'm willing to spend the time flying out for a personal viewing that antagonizes Susan. She was very upset that I'd take the time and spend the money flying out to a no man's land rather than a trip to look at Bermuda. We're investigating the possibility of retiring to a beach home in the Caribbean. We're just beginning to explore those possibilities. And now, here I am going to look at an uninhabited volcanic island in the Pacific while she's at home exploring Google Earth, thinking of sipping Pina Coladas and watching the sunset through the palm trees."

Jim tells Mark, "I know you pretty dag gone good. You're the definition of a right-wing extremist. You decided long ago that you would earn your way through your ingenuity and hard work.

Over the years, you've developed distrust and dislike for any government body or official that interferes in any way. And now you know that moving anywhere in the civilized world will result in you subjecting yourself to demands from outsiders. This island may be your pilgrimage where you would establish something of your own, without any outside interference whatsoever."

"Wow," Mark responds. "Yes, I think you just hit the nail on the head. I guess this is a pilgrimage for me. Perhaps this may be the new land where I can live free without interference. I'd captain the first boat taking off for the Americas. The pilgrims wanted freedom of religion as the King established and mandated church attendance in the state-sanctioned Anglican Church. Every other religious observance were banned under the threat of imprisonment. Although religion is still somewhat free in America, there are too many who wish to see our faith regulated, and that process has already started. They always use a few idiots to illustrate why we should be regulated. The IRS can cancel a church's tax-exempt status just because the pastor has endorsed a particular candidate. Our freedoms of expression are watched for offensiveness. Church bells have been silenced. Crosses placed alongside highways commemorating the loss of a loved one are banned. The Ten Commandments were removed from schools.

"Where's it going to end?

"Our rights to bear arms are being attacked every time a madman shoots up a theater. History is repeating itself. America's Constitutional Republic has lasted beyond its time, as two hundred years is as long as democracy has ever lasted. America has become a democracy, pushing the republic part off the cliff. Jim, are there thousands of like-minded people here in America right now who desire to live free of established out-of-control government busybodies, people who wish to start over under a new form of government on a brand new Island? Am I the only one that is considering such a possibility? I doubt it."

Jim responds by saying: "It's very likely."

"Well, here we are over San Francisco. We'll land, fuel up, and I've got to file a flight plan with the FAA," Mark announces as he throttles back, entering landing mode.

Mark is told Inside the FAA office that the UN has declared the Island off-limits to any private persons, even for a flyover, and that his destination could not be approved. He must cancel those plans. "How about LA or San Diego?" He asks. "Nope, and not Spokane either. Nowhere in the contiguous 48 could he get approval," the agent insisted.

Mark then changed his destination to Anchorage, Alaska, where he believed the local FAA administrators would be friendlier and less restrictive.

"Well, Jim, we've got to go to Anchorage, a five-hour trip. We'll have to stay overnight there. It seems that the FAA has submitted to and reinforced the request of the UN declaring the Island off-limits to private parties. I told the guy we would not land, just circle over the island and return. I told him I had read the actual restrictions the UN had placed, and it specifically restricted the actual touching of the land setting foot on the island. It did not restrict flying over the Island, which hundreds do regularly. He informed me that the official US stance was the same as the UN. No private planes were to go within viewing distance of the Island.

"While trying to reason with the idiot, the administrator called dispatch in the control tower, putting a hold, a no-take-off permit for my plane. We were locked down. While you were getting a bite to eat, I was directed to another office, which turned out to be Homeland Security, investigating me as a possible terrorist, someone who was not cooperating, a troublemaker just because I had argued with the FAA official. And now they're heading out to the plane to inspect it for explosives. If they find it free of any dangerous material, we'll be free to go on to Anchorage."

An hour later, the FAA coordinator called Mark into the office, informing him he is cleared to take off.

"Let's get out of here. Quick."

At the Anchorage airport, Mark filed a flight plan for the morning, heading toward coordinates 40°14'22.30N by 149°42'57W directly on the path toward Hawaii, and he was assured there would be no problem. It was approved immediately. His expected return time would be seven hours after take-off, giving Mark about a half hour to look around and take pictures. He was told by the attendant that there had recently been numerous requests by private individuals who also wished to view the island for themselves. The attendant indicated that some California airports had turned down those sightseers; Seattle was denying flights over the island. The attendant stated they had no information from headquarters to deny exploratory flights near the new Island.

"Jim, let's get a bite to eat and then turn in. I want to be in the air by seven, as we are approved for a seven-hour trip out and back, and we'll want to fly over the entire Island at least once, giving us time to look around. We'll also reserve the room for tomorrow night and head home Thursday morning."

"Sounds good to me." Jim signifies. How does Alaskan Salmon sound to you?"

Approaching the newly formed land mass, they are amazed at its size, the volcanoes' height, and the expanse of the relatively flat lands between the circular peaks. Circling the island, Jim clicked the camera mounted under the wings, taking hundreds of pictures of the volcanoes, the lakes, the beaches and harbors, the plateaus, and peaks. They did not see any volcanic activity or hot lava streaming down the sides. In one harbor, they noticed a stationary ship with UN identifiers and a group of people (10) walking along a high plateau overlooking a narrow beach area.

"Have you seen enough?" Jim asks.

"Yes, I think so. Quite amazing," turning the plane back toward Anchorage. They discuss what they saw, concentrating on different areas, and then get into what Mark intends to do with the information.

"I'm not sure, Jim," Mark says. "Last week, I was reading in Jeremiah, and a few verses captured my attention. *"Build ye houses, dwell in them; plant gardens, and eat their fruit. And seek the peace of the city whither I have caused you to be carried away captives, and pray unto the Lord for it: for in the peace thereof shall ye have peace."* I'm not sure if that specifically applies to me or what, but it has stayed with me, and over and over again I think specifically about the phrase: *"in the peace thereof shall ye have peace."*

"About this island, all I can surmise right now is that the earth has supplied us with a new land mass that sometime in the future will be either a new country or part of an existing country, most likely under the control of the UN. It's bigger than I envisioned. I did not see any signs of vegetation, did you? Perhaps some moss, but that would be about it."

Jim says, "No, it's way too early for that process to start, but seeing that UN ship down there indicates they are gathering as much information as possible. According to news sources I've come across in the past month, the UN is observing the Island. They have collected rock and soil samples from various locations while still declaring that all other governments should remain away, letting them and their host of scientists make a safe and scientifically intelligent assessment. Their stance now is that this is a teachable modern-day moment of how various segments of the earth were formed, of how the land masses and oceans separated millions of years ago. I read one article quoting a UN geologist saying there is something different about how this island came to be compared to how they envisioned other volcanic island creations. They even speculated it could have something to do with global warming. They have indicated that their esteemed group of scientists will reach a consensus and release the data to the various interested governments, the press, and the schools for instructing society in due time."

Having called Susan the day before informing her of the detour they were forced to take, she knew of their approximate return to the States.

"Hello, Susan," Mark says into his cell phone. "We're on the way back to Anchorage, where we'll stay for the night, and then early in the morning, I'll head toward Denver to drop Jim off and then back home again. Possibly, see you around seven or eight tomorrow evening. How's everything there?"

"Good," Susan responds. "We had another lightning storm the other night when the power went off for a moment, but everything is working just fine. What did that new island look like?"

"You'll see the pictures when I get home. It's amazing."

"Thomas and Annabelle are coming down for the weekend sometime Friday evening."

"Great, it'll be good to see them again," Mark responds. Thinking about that, he tells her he'll be in Denver Thursday evening to drop Jim off, and they could ride home in the jet with him.

Susan says, "I'll call Thomas. Ah, no, Mark, why don't you call Thomas, as the two of you will have to make those arrangements anyway."

"Sure, I'll do that," Mark tells her, says goodbye and hangs up.

"Hello, Thomas," Mark says as his son answers the phone. After the initial greetings, Mark asks, "Could you possibly meet me Thursday evening at the airport and fly home in the jet, rather than driving those five hours? Your mom told me you plan to come down Friday evening. Is there any way you could get away earlier?

"Hmm? Thomas thinks quizzically and asks, "What brings you to Denver? I'll have to check with Annabelle if she could get away a day early. I know I could, and I'd love to ride back with you. Do we get a drink and a bag of peanuts?"

Mark responds to Thomas's question, briefly telling his son that he's on his way back from a brief look at the new Island in the Pacific. Jim is with him, and they're heading to Anchorage to fuel up and stay the night.

Thomas says, "I knew it. You're spying on that island, hoping to move out there someday, aren't you? It wouldn't surprise me. You know I'd be willing to go with you, Dad, camping out under the Pacific moon, snorkeling and sunbathing. Anabele would go in an instant, too. I'll call you later this evening or first thing in the morning after I check with her. What time would you guys get into Denver?"

"Oh, probably late afternoon, depending on when we leave Anchorage. It's a five-hour flight," Mark informs his son, and then, "Call me when you find out, Ok? And about my thinking of moving to that island, please don't say anything to your mother about it, Ok? She's already upset that I took the time to just look at it. Let Anabele know, too, Ok? Thomas, I'll be waiting for your call. Bye for now."

Hearing the conversation over the speakers in the cockpit, Jim tells Mark, "See, you weren't the only one who knows your hidden desires. Thomas knows you better than you do. I knew it immediately, and I believe Susan suspects the same. So, confess up kid. Why are you even thinking about it? What we saw today would in no way be a place where you could set up a permanent residence. It's mostly all rock and cold lava. The lava has cooled down, and lakes are forming for water, but that's it. You would have to import all your food supplies and all the other necessities. I guess you could survive on fish for the rest of your life. We didn't see any signs of vegetation, not even weeds or moss, and good grief, Mark, there wouldn't even be anything to hunt. No deer, not even a rabbit. It may be a nice week's camping trip, but that's it."

"Yeah, I know it sounds crazy. But . . . "

"The UN has a point when they tell us that it may take thousands of years for the processes of nature to do its work transforming the rocks, the lava, breaking down the layers of ash.

Birds, yes, they would come in first, but other land animals? Looking back over pre-historic times, how did animals migrate across thousands of miles of ocean from one continent to another? Deers don't swim. We don't understand how all that developed, as humans were not texting friends what they saw on the way to work. The only existing records are a few sketches in caves, and some fossils buried beneath layers of soil. And that doesn't tell us how they migrated across oceans. Our best and most learned scientists are only surmising how the continents split apart, if they did. Millions of years of earthquakes, they guess. But they can't pin it down to twenty-five million years, twenty-eight million, or six thousand years. It's all guesswork. The animals had to come first, the experts tell us. Are you going to build an ARK to transport two of each animal? Even then, you still couldn't hunt one down for several years as you'd kill off their reproduction. Give it up, Mark."

"I don't know, Jim," Mark responds, "why that Island has my concentration. There's just something about it. It's history in the making. It's a new land formation that came out of the belly of the earth. It's big enough for millions to live on. Eventually, it may be livable, but how long that will take is still a guess. Hundreds, thousands of years, or ten years? Like you say, it's a dream. I was hoping it could support human life in my lifetime, but it wouldn't be much of a life if all of our necessities had to be imported. It'd make us totally dependent on the mainland, and I've worked hard not wanting to be dependent on anyone. Anyway, we got a live look at it, and when I get home, I'll take a closer look at all the pictures. Perhaps in a year, I'll take another look for comparison."

"Give it up, Mark, you're chasing a rainbow. Go find that spot in the Bahamas."

Seeing Anchorage off in the distance, Mark calls the tower for landing instructions and gets the reply to come on in when ready. As he lowers the landing gear, the phone rings. "Jim, answer that for me, it's Thomas," Mark says.

"Hello Thomas, this is Jim. Your dad is landing the plane right now. He can hear you but couldn't take a hand off the throttle to answer."

"Hi, Jim. Dad." Thomas then says, "We can both take another day, and we'd be delighted to fly out of Denver with you. Anabele will take a teacher's day off, and I can get away too, as we're between jobs right now. So we'll see you at the Centennial Airport sometime tomorrow. Call when you know the time of your arrival."

Mark speaks into the dashboard microphone: "That's great news, son. I'll call tomorrow when we take off from here to let you know the time we'll be landing and where in the airport to meet me. Call your mom and let her know too. We'll have a good chat during that trip home. And I'll have a few peanuts for you."

Mark is waiting inside the Centennial terminal for Thomas and Anabele to arrive, having touched down almost an hour earlier than expected. Jim is on his way home, and Mark has opened a conversation with another private Jet owner waiting for his passengers to arrive. Jack Brieesbid transports private parties for a fee, and told Mark he makes a fairly decent living off the charges, as most of his business is from wealthy business owners who have yet to purchase their own plane. During their conversation, Jack tells Mark of one of his clients who wanted to fly over that New Island in the Pacific. "I made a bundle off that trip," Jack tells Mark.

"Imagine wanting to spend all that money just to sightsee a brand new volcanic island five hours out in the Pacific. At first, I couldn't believe it, but he assured me it was. He just wanted a closer look. He said he believes that the UN is hogwashing the world about the near future livability of the Island, keeping to themselves their plans to settle the land, to take it over solely as a UN domicile."

Mark asks Jack if he would provide his passenger's name and phone number.

"I can't do that, Mark. It's against the agreements I have with my clients."

Mark tells Jack, "It's interesting to see a new land being made right before our eyes. It's kind of a peak into pre-historic times." Mark then asks if he saw anything unusual while flying over that island.

"Well, Mark, there was one area of the island I thought as very interesting. On the southern side was a good-sized harbor, a bay that would be sort of hidden from ocean view if one was traveling by ship around the Island. It was somewhat like that lake off New Orleans. You can't see it from the ocean. It had a big, beautiful beach leading up to a plateau and down to a valley where a lake was. I thought there would be a perfect place to set up a campsite. The rest of the island was a no man's land of dead volcanoes separating the north and south sides."

"Fascinating Jack. It was good talking with you, but my son and his wife are coming, so I'll have to leave. Good luck on all your flights, and be safe."

The two exchange business cards as Jack tells Mark, "I've enjoyed talking with you too. Good luck, have a good time with your kids, and be safe." Upon departing, Marks asks Jack if he would contact his client, telling him that he'd be interested in hearing from him about his trip over the island, and if so, you can give him my name and number to call if he so desires.

Mark, Thomas, and Anabele make their greetings as Mark says, "It's great to see you guys again. It was Thanksgiving, right."

Anabele adds, "Yes, it was, and I had a great time with all of you Tebonsons. It was fun, and I'm still telling my friends about that restaurant in town. What a place. Thanks for taking me there, Mr. Tebonson."

"Oh, you're welcome, and we enjoyed having you, Anabele."

She responds, "We would have come down for Christmas, but my folks were having all of us down to Myrtle Beach then. Going to Florida at Christmas, how can one refuse?"

"Hey, no problem," answers Mark. "Let's get going, shall we?"

Mark is taxing toward the runway of Centennial airport when the phone rings, informing Mark of the sudden storm clouds forming over Eastern Colorado and that he would need to head directly south toward Colorado Springs and then around the southern side into Wichita and then north into town from the east.

Thomas says, "This time of year, the weather around here is unpredictable. That could be a snowstorm forming or heavy rain and lightning."

In the air, Mark asks Thomas how the electrical work is progressing.

Replying, Thomas says, "Dad, we're doing pretty good right now re-furbishing many of the older homes, bringing them up to present-day codes, which are a nightmare of compliance mandates—inspections after inspections. But the pay is good, so I can't complain. I'm proud to say that our bills are getting paid on time, and we're actually reducing the mortgage balance quite rapidly."

Mark asks: "How about you, Anabele? How's that teaching jig going? What grades do you have now?"

Responding, Anabele informs Mark that she was upgraded to eighth grade this past year. "My main courses are World and US History. Besides instructing them on the basics of history, I try to get the kids to think for themselves, to ask questions, to reason why certain events happened, and try to get them to connect the pieces of information to the bigger picture. I don't concentrate so much on names, dates, and important events, but more on the whys that led up to certain major accomplishments or disastrous events. At this age, they are full of questions."

Mark tells her that at that age, all he remembers is memorizing dates and names so that they could pass the tests.

"Yeah, testing is difficult, and I have a hard time developing tests that would indicate their level of understanding of historical events. It's a lot easier to ask for just names and dates than it is to ask for what drove Hitler's hatred of the Jews, and how could the people elect someone with that hatred? Why was freedom so important to the pilgrims, causing them to take a hazardous trip to a new land? Why did the leaders of England feel the need to institute a state religion?"

Mark says, "That would certainly make history more interesting, and I suppose the kids get more involved in class discussions too. Do you also connect the past with the present and what the future would hold if and when someone like Hitler came to power today?"

"I try to weave the past into the present. Then there are the kids who don't care. They sit there as zombies, not absorbing anything, nor wanting to, just looking out into space as if they're on medication, keeping them in a vegetative state, alive and moving but unaware. Some are on prescribed drugs, or they'd tear the place apart. That's the sad part, seeing these kids who, through no fault of their own, have been neglected by parents living with a single mom high herself on drugs or being farmed out to grandma as the parents are in jail. The obesity rate among kids in this age group is escalating. Were there many kids around like that forty years ago?"

"No, not that I recall," Mark says, keeping his eyes on the clouds ahead. "It was not the problem as it is now. Well, some were a little bit overweight, but not in this obese category we have now. Then, some appeared to have less intelligence than others, but drugging kids to keep them quiet was unheard of. And our teachers usually handled the troublemakers in the privacy of the principals' office the old-fashioned way. I remember one day, the fourth grade, I think it was when the teacher came by my desk, pulled me up out of the chair by my ear lobe, and took me into the principal's office for the end of a switch. I don't remember now what exactly I was doing that caused that, but whatever it was, I was more respectful, not wanting to see that switch again. The entire school knew what was happening in that office, and nobody wanted to go there. The thought of that humiliation was enough to keep us in line. When I got home from school, the whipping I got from Dad was far worse. Things like that are forbidden nowadays, right?"

"Yes, we can't touch a child, we can't look at them cross-eyed, and heaven forbid we tell a kid he's acting stupid and to snap out of it. No, the kid would go home and tell mommy I told him he was stupid, and then I'd get fired, demoted, and possibly sued. The part of controlling bullies has taken over main stage academics, believing that being bullied is the worst that can happen to a child."

A period of silence, and then, Anabele asks, "Mark, were you ever bullied when you were in school?"

"Well, no, not that I recall, but I was bigger than most kids my age, so I guess I did most of the bullying. That's what kids do. But then, our bullying was usually in the form of calling a kid a dummy, imbecile, idiot, or stupid while we were playing a game and the kid struck out or missed a fly ball. We weren't being nasty; we meant that the kid made a mistake and that he should try harder; they knew it, too, and would try harder the next time. Sometimes, there were fights over it. They did not run home and tell Mommy that I called him a dummy. If they did, then Daddy would tell his son to stand up, be a man, and try harder the next time. That's about it, from what I recall."

"Yes, Mark, it's become way out of proportion, now actually shielding kids from having to deal with problems that life on earth brings," Anabele adds. "I remember being ostracized by the other girls as a frail girl in the ninth grade because mom wouldn't let me wear short shorts. They would call me 'goody two shoes,' which humiliated me. I wanted acceptance by the popular girls, but after telling Mom about those names, she let me have it big time for desiring to be liked rather than doing what I know is right and standing on my principles. I should just walk on by and keep my head up high. I told Mom everything."

Thomas adds his two cents into the conversation saying, "Dad, I don't know if I told you this, but when I proposed to Anabele, she said I'd have to ask her dad first. That's the kind of parents she has."

Mark adds, "I got that impression when we first met at the wedding rehearsals. He told me you were shaking in your boots when you asked him for her hand in marriage."

"Yes, Dad, I was. That scared me."

Mark asks, "Anabele, how are your folks doing nowadays?"

"Ah, they're doing great. They moved to Myrtle Beach five years ago, desiring to escape the cold of western Minnesota. Dad is fishing and playing golf while Mom reads novels and plays bridge. Typically retired, part of that grey-haired bunch. They're a bit older than you, Mark, and their age is catching up with them quicker. I worry about them some, but they're hardy and enjoying themselves. They immigrated to the States from Sweden in their twenties and brought that Viking tough spirit with them. But they still take trips back to Fergus Falls every summer when the seven of us kids try to get together for a reunion. I'm the second youngest; four brothers and two sisters, one three years younger than I. They're all doing pretty good, Mark. But I'll tell you, none of my sisters has a husband as great as Thomas."

"Well, that's nice to hear," Mark tells her. "His mom and I think a bunch of him too. But, Thomas, should I tell her our problems with you growing up?"

Thomas replies, "There's no need to hash over those days dad. Anabele knows it all anyway."

"Ah, come on, Mr. Tebonson, tell me some. I love to hear your side of the stories." Anabele begs, while Thomas gives her that no, no, don't go there look.

Mark says, "No, I better not. Besides, he was a good kid throughout those terrible years of living in Omaha when I was working ten to fourteen-hour days building my software business. I was hardly ever home, but his mom informed me of what the kids were doing to each other. His mom did a fantastic job of raising them without hardly any input from me. I was working all the time, and when I finally got home around nine, they may have already been put to bed. I'd get the quick run down, and then all I'd do was talk with whoever had been naughty that day. I rarely had the time to play ball with them, except on our vacations when we'd go camping somewhere."

"Thomas, you remember the trip we took into Canada that summer? I guess you were about ten, taking our canoes on a two-week circular route down rivers, into lakes and ponds, and back into another stream to a different lake. Two weeks. After paddling all day, we'd spot a site to set up camp for the night, put up our tents, do some fishing, and roast marshmallows over a campfire, after grilling some fish."

Thomas responds, "Yes, I sure do. That was a fantastic trip. I'll never forget it. I was twelve. It was something else when we found that lodge on one of the lakes. I remember going into a steam room, getting hot and sweaty, then running down to the beach and jumping into the cold water lake. Oooh, that water was cold. We couldn't get George to do it."

Mark adds, "No, Thomas, we couldn't get you to jump in the lake. Melody made the jump twice. George, he was the cool one, he had no problem with it, and he'd then torment you by sneaking up behind you, throwing the lake water on you while you were standing on the beach waiting for the sweat of the sauna to wear off, and then you'd jump in."

"No, Dad," Thomas says, "You got it backward. It was George who chickened out, and I threw real ice cubes on him, and then both you and Mom lit into me like gangbusters, saying something about the sudden ice water could cause him to go into shock. I'll never forget it. Ask Melody about it someday. Mom remembers it as I do too. Boy, Melody was a tomboy back then, and could she swim. She loved competing against us. That was a great vacation, and I've told Anabele that when we have kids, and they're about ten to twelve, I'd like to do the same for them. I also remember the portage we had to make carrying those canoes and all our gear, the tents, everything for almost a mile from one lake to another. We were all mad at you for picking out that particular route to take us on. It took us all day."

Mark adds, "It was only a quarter mile long, and we finished it in three and a half hours. That route was recommended to me by the Boy Scouts, as they had tried several different routes, and this was the easiest."

Anabele asks, "Tell me some more."

"Dad, we had another great vacation when we went to Jackson Hole, Wyoming, and climbed up one of the Tetons, camping at national campgrounds. The scenery was fantastic. We met another family camping there with a boy and two teenage girls. George and I were fourteen at the time, and these girls and the two of us would take off walking the trails, having a great time jumping in a pool below some falls, swimming, and teasing each other. You and Mom and their parents got worried that we might do some things that teens sometimes do when left alone. George and I were both too timid, and the girls were not so, having taken their tops off in the water. We enjoyed that, but that's as far as it went. The next day, the girls stayed in the campground,"

"Thomas, you never told me about that before. Fourteen, huh? Come on, what else did you see?"

"That was all. Nothing else happened. Like I said, George and I were too scared to do anything else. We were just fourteen."

Mark then adds, "Yes, I remember now. Your mom and I were sitting outside the tent looking over the mountain range, enjoying the beauty of it all while sipping on a cold beer, when the four of you came walking by. The girls looked at you guys with that mischievous look as they passed us on the way to their campsite when one of them turned back and said, 'can we do it again tomorrow, boys?' Your mom looked at me, and I looked at her, wondering what that girl meant. George then told us you all just went for a walk, found the falls, and went swimming in the pond below the falls. That was it. We didn't question you guys anymore. Should we have?"

Thomas adds, "No, that was all."

Anabele questions again, "Come clean, Thomas. Come on now, two healthy fourteen-year-old boys and two good-looking girls out in the forest by themselves, and you didn't do anything? That's kind of hard to believe. How old were those girls anyway?"

Thomas answers, "If I remember right they were twelve and fifteen."

"Anyway," Thomas, changing the subject, asks his dad what else he remembers about that vacation.

"Oh, I don't know," Mark says, looking out the window and pointing the storm clouds to the north. "We'll have to avoid those, and that's directly in the line we're supposed to be heading. We might have to touch down in Wichita and wait for this storm to clear."

He picks up the phone and calls the control tower, asking for advice. They come back, informing Mark that the storm is huge, is expected to last overnight, and he should avoid it.

"Well, kids, here we go, spending the night in another motel. Your mother will be upset, but glad we're playing it safe. So, Wichita, here we come," as Mark throttles back, shifting into descending mode.

On the ground and booked into motel rooms, Mark calls Susan to let her know of the delay. Mark asks, "So, what's happening there, anything new?"

Susan says, "No, not really. Oh, yes, there was. Two days ago, I was on the tractor plowing up a plot when a shadow flew across my path right in front of me. Looking up to see what it was, I saw a small plane flying over. It was gone over the treetops before I could get a good look at it, but it appeared to be one of those drones we've seen pictures of on the news. Otherwise, just the usual stuff: another letter from the energy department, a call and a visit from two Solar manufacturers, a call from the agriculture department, and another letter from the energy department, again requesting an immediate response to an urgent national importance. Also, the three men you hired for the farm want to talk. Mark, I'm getting very tired of all this. What are we going to do? How can we get these goons off your back? Come home, Mark. I miss you."

Chapter 9

Sitting in a booth at Jeffers Depot, Mark, Susan, Thomas, and Anabele are catching up on each other's activities while admiring the scenery of the old-time railroad restaurant. Thomas and Anabele love this place, captivated by the antiques of days when the railroad was king. Thomas has always been a railroad fanatic since he found a Lionel train set under the Christmas tree when he was just five. At age ten, he had expanded the set to include six engines, numerous cabooses, flat cars, and freight cars on a track the size of his bedroom by saving any money he came into. He threw newspapers while the family lived in Omaha and invested most of those earnings in additional equipment. While he concentrated on his railroading hobby, his twin brother George played golf. Thomas can't get enough of the restaurant and insists on visiting it whenever he makes it home.

Anabele adds that Thomas has taken over what used to be the family room as a toy train hobby room. He's got tracks running around the room and boxes stacked here and there as he slowly puts together the scenery, the tunnels, what looks like a pond, and a small town with miniature people on the streets. It's almost an obsession.

"Sometimes," Anabele says, "he wants to fiddle when I want to go out. Well, at least I know where he is."

As they are being served their choices of desserts by the model train, the mayor of North Platte approaches the booth, greeting them all, especially Thomas and Anabele.

"It's good to have you here again, Thomas and Anabele." Mayor Olsen says. "How long are you in for?"

Thomas replies, "Ah, just for the weekend, and then back to work again."

"Do you mind if I pull up a chair for a few minutes?"

"No, of course not, James," Mark replies.

"Running into you here will save both of us time. You need to know what happened while you were away."

Mark says, "What is it? What's going on?"

"While you were on that trip, two men from the agriculture department came by to see me. They wanted me to know of the recent changes in the pipeline route going through the state. They said they had recently talked with the governor, and his office is working out the details of moving the proposed pipeline route twenty miles to the west right through the middle of your acreage. The line will cross Highway 83 just north of your land. On each side of the line, the government needs one hundred feet of land as maintenance and repair access, with a road constructed out to the state highway permitting direct access for the construction work and future needs.

"They said they would have preferred a more direct route through your runway and old barn, but as a consensus to you, they'll curve it, moving it west of the new barn and your entrance road. As far as the town is concerned, the lines will be crossing the river just east of the airport. And get this, Mark, I'm sure this will send you over the hill, but right in the middle of your acreage will be the junction where the east-west route joins the north-south route. Sorry, Mark, I did not want to lay the bad news on you while you're enjoying a good meal here, but you're hard to pin down. They'll be proceeding with eminent domain soon."

Mark is stunned, but not totally. Thomas and Anabele look at Mark to see his reaction and what he might say, while Susan is visibly upset, twisting the napkin into a rope.

"You know, I'm really not surprised, James; I'm just shocked at the method they're using to punish me," Mark says. "Last fall, a young man came by trying to get me to include a restriction in all of my land leases indicating that all crops must be sold to the selected ethanol producers. And that the new leasor could not sell any of his corn to private food producers. I told him I could do whatever I wished with my land as a private citizen. I was upset and told the guy to leave. On his way out, he said they could condemn my land and that he would be hearing from the department again. I was not pleasant with the kid. Now, this is my punishment. Unbelievable, but yet I do believe they'd do it. Have the men I leased the land to been notified?"

"Oh, yes." Mayor Olsen tells Mark. "The three of them came by my office and asked what I knew about the pipelines. All I could say was that I was informed the proposed line would travel along the east side of 83 and then across the river east of the airport and that the government was working on the eminent domain processes in those areas. They then told me that the Department of Agriculture had notified them that the route was changed to the west of 83, going directly through their newly leased land; the governor had approved it, and they were proceeding as planned.

"They wondered if you knew about this before you signed the leases, as they were provided documents indicating that the changes were approved last summer, and you must have known about it. Anyway, I believe they're going to bring suit against you for non-disclosure. I told them that I seriously doubted you would have withheld that information. They doubted it too at first, knowing you and your integrity. They were stunned that you'd do such a thing to them. They said the government insisted you must have known as their documents show the new route was approved by all concerned parties sometime before you leased the land."

"Now, I'm getting mad," Mark tells the mayor. "Not only will I be fighting the government, but now they step in the middle, and I also have to fight my friends."

"I'm sorry, Mark. You've been good to this town, and I hate to see you or any of our people get run over by the feds. Before you hear of these developments from other sources, I had to tell you myself. Good luck, Mark, and please keep me informed."

"Thanks, James. Yeah, they're giving me a break from the goodness of their heart by not tearing up my runway for six months during construction. Who do they think I am? Some yokel who's never been out of the swamp? Thanks, James. I'm proud to have you as a good friend and Mayor of this town. This adds another reason for us to get away from these tyrants. James, this is for your information only, but Susan and I are heading for Antiqua next week looking for a condo or a beach house, and I'll not let these new developments stand in the way."

The mayor then gets up, puts the chair back into position, and leaves the booth to greet a few people on the way out.

"Dad, what are you going to do?" Thomas asks.

"Right now, I don't know my options except to call my lawyer," Mark replies. "Susan, it looks like we'll have to postpone the trip, so I can relate this to Larry McPherson. He represented us on those leases and handled much of the legal proceedings around town.

Thomas asks, 'Dad, isn't that pipeline built by private companies and not by the government?"

"Yes, it is, Thomas. Private oil companies and their affiliates will construct the entire line, but the federal agencies must approve the route. The Department of Agriculture, the EPA, and the people of Fish and Wildlife are involved. The Clean Air Act must be addressed, and the Clean Water Act must be followed. The animal rights people examine the proposed routes looking for endangered species, as the various State agencies are looking out for their interests. And if a bird poops on the land, the inspections must start again. It takes years to finalize the thing, and the battles over eminent domain rights begin. Lawyers get rich on these proceedings. But the country needs this pipeline, and once it's completed, it will be a good thing for the availability of oil in this country. But the paperwork, the lawyering, and the special interest groups, each with their demands, make the process a gigantic puzzle. Imagine trying to put together a jigsaw puzzle without a picture to look at. Add to that, congressmen must get their pictures in the local papers, and the media will search, finding victims who are hit hard as their land is confiscated, and they all blame the evil oil companies."

Anabele then says, "There you go, Mr. Tebonson. Call the media and let them know what's happening to you, how the government is mistreating you, throwing a wedge between you and your friends just because you did not cave to their demands. Become a victim."

"Anabele, you know my thoughts on the media, and no way will I let them turn me into a victim. I'm not a victim. I consider myself more of a danger to the government, one who could rise up and expose their corrupt operations piece by piece."

"Why don't you run for the Senate?" Anabele asks.

"I have no desire to run for or hold any elected office, anywhere. I will not subject my entire life, or the lives of family members to the scrutiny of politicians, especially the media," Mark says. "They can all kiss my royal behind three times in front of the capital building. I want to fight this the old-fashioned way, but the way things are now, they'd find some way to provide me with blanks while they had live ammunition. All this does is to provide us with a more intense mission of getting out from under these tyrants."

Turning toward Susan, Mark asks, "Susan, are you ready? You've had enough too, haven't you, and you're ready to get out of dodge, just like I am. Antiqua, here we come."

Susan replies, "You know I am. It's tearing you up, and what tears you up, tears me up too, so Mark, yes, I'm ready. I'll have the bags packed for an early take-off Tuesday morning."

Thomas then asks, "How can we help?"

Answering, Mark says, "There's nothing you can do, son. But thanks. Let's leave this restaurant and go home where there is peace. It's seven-thrifty, and I feel like going into the woods, chopping some wood, and sitting around a nice campfire under the stars, making up stories. You guys got to go back home tomorrow, so let's enjoy the rest of our time together."

Susan suggests that they all play a game of cards. They could sit at the table on the deck.

Thomas says, "Mom, that'll be fine, but I'd still like to sit by the campfire for a while. We don't ever get that chance in Denver. Since we were kids, roasting marshmallows around a campfire was special. It was even better than coming down the stairs on Christmas morning. I miss those days."

"Ok, a campfire it is," Susan agrees.

Anabele then adds that one of the things she had always appreciated and enjoyed when she visited here was the campfires. "I'll never forget that first campfire I had with you guys. It was when Thomas brought me here to introduce me to all of you. I was scared. My heart was racing. We arrived in the evening, and you were already sitting by the campfire. George and Ruth were here, and Melody too. But that campfire just put me at ease right away. Thank you for making that time easy; it couldn't have been a more relaxing welcome to the family moment. I appreciate it and remember it fondly."

Susan says, "Yes, I remember that too. Mark and I were apprehensive about meeting Thomas's love and did not want to make it hard on you by being formal. So, we thought a campfire would be a relaxing way of breaking the ice. Thomas arranged it so that you would arrive later in the day, just in time as the sun was getting close to setting."

"Thomas, you never told me that. I thought we had to leave later because of something happening at work and you couldn't get away. You indicated something needed to be arranged, and you couldn't leave until after one. I love you even more." Anabele says, resting her head against his shoulder.

It's a beautiful evening for an outdoor activity. The temperature is expected to drop into the upper fifties at nightfall. The sky is clear with just a hint of a breeze. Mark and Thomas have gathered firewood from the ricks of wood stacked by the barn, put kindling down, strips of pine, and then oak and hickory on top in a teepee formation. They've put another stack of wood on the side to add to the fire as it burns. The fire starts, and the two guys sit in their chairs where the wind blows the smoke away. Soon, Susan and Anabele approached using the golf cart to bring the drinks, marshmallows, and snacks to the campfire in an open area about fifty yards away from the house and barn. They can see a waxing moon rising over the flames of the fire.

'Mark," Susan says, "I'm almost afraid of telling you this, but Anabele thought I should. There was a message on the phone when we got home from Mr. Actkinson from some solar company desiring to see your generator firsthand. That's all he said, besides saying he'll call back some other time soon."

Mark replies, "Thanks, let him call. I've already heard from one company interested in buying the rights to the invention. I told them to forget it; I'd do what I want with it." Looking at Thomas, Mark tells him that the following units he puts together will be going to him, George, and Melody. Then he hopes to strike a deal with the mayor to install many around the town, reducing their electrical costs. I've already talked with Peter Jeffers about converting his restaurant to solar power. Heck, if I'm going to sell it to anyone. I've secured the patent. It's mine for the next 20 years. No way, even though the cash would enable all of us to retire to a condo in Antiqua. I didn't tinker over it for two years thinking of how rich it would make me."

"Dad, why don't you get these calls on your cell phone so mom won't have to relay messages to you?"

"Son, I prefer not to, alright? I don't care to be disturbed by all these nuisance calls when I'm tinkering in the shop. This cell phone is for family and close friends to whom I give the number to, and that's it. Your mom is ok with relating the messages."

And so the four of them had a great time around the campfire that evening, renewing their relationships and chatting about their daily affairs, the conquests, the bad days, the places they've visited, and desires for the future. Every so often, Mark or Thomas would reach over and add another piece of wood to keep the flames hot. A few lighthearted stories were told about the growing up days of each of them reliving some of their past lives. Over the years, a tradition had formed whenever they found themselves around a campfire called storytime. Mark would usually start creating a fictional mystery. Susan would add additional details to what Mark made up. Thomas would add more details from his imagination, Anabele would keep the mystery going, adding more events from her imagination, and the fictional mystery would develop around the circle. Each change either brought a round of laughter from the others, a series of boos, or 'unbelievable.' Where did you come up with such a line as that? Or, that's horrible. You've been rereading ghost stories, or where did you get such an idea, which would bring a response such as, I read about it in Readers Digest. The next in line would then change how the previous one had changed the story to horrible, back to unbelievable and a round of laughter. Story Time required the use of their imaginations. It was entertaining time passing away the hours. It was also revealing in a sense. It showed how they each added their creative fictional events, viewed life, the capabilities of imperfect human beings in an imperfect world, and the sense of justice each had.

Anabele told of how she had introduced the tradition to her family. "We can't make a campfire at my parents' house as there just isn't the room in the backyard, so we make a circle of chairs on the deck around a metal fire pit. It took a couple of years, but now they look forward to the time. You guys don't know how much I appreciate and love being a part of your lives. I'm continually thrilled that Thomas picked me. And, don't go and move away to Antiqua or some other far-away place. I'd miss you." Anabele tells Mark and Susan.

Susan puts her arm around Anabele's shoulders and neck and hugs her, saying, "We're also thrilled that you picked Thomas. You've been a tremendous blessing to him and to us. Now, help me clean up this mess."

Chapter 10

Another year has passed when the chores on the hundred acres Mark and Susan have kept for themselves become hectic, working long hours plowing and planting the seeds. Planting time can be critical, but they've never complained. Watching the seeds grow is rest. They have always enjoyed picking a fresh tomato off the vine with a salt shaker in hand, devouring a couple while placing the rest in a basket to be canned later, and delivering their abundance to a food kitchen for the needy. The favorites that thrive in this part of Nebraska are corn, of course, along with cabbage, lettuce, peppers, cucumbers, squash, potatoes, onions, a strawberry patch here and there, and they even manage to get a fairly decent crop of pumpkins. The automatically timed sprinkler system Mark installed not only waters but also monitors the moisture content of the beds, sensing when water is needed, automatically starting a timed watering, and eliminating some of their monitoring chores.

The past falls festival saw even more participants than the year before, when they were overwhelmed by the local people's support in helping decorate and prepare the barns and land for the children's enjoyment. This October will be the fourth year they've held the event. Remembering two years ago when they were visited by the feds inspecting the Haunted House displays depicting the various federal agencies in a derogatory manner, Mark wondered why the festival of last fall was not inspected.

Mark and Susan have taken trips to Antiqua, Bermuda, and other Caribbean hot spots to investigate the availability of condos and beach homes for possible permanent retirement, but nothing has struck their fancy. Mark claimed that living in any of those areas always seemed to be a negative aspect, while Susan tried to convince him that there would never be a place on this planet that did not have some aspect that he wouldn't like. She's ready to move, but deciding where they could both agree is holding up the move. Mark is also ready to move, as his solar magnifier is manufactured by a company he had previous connections in North Platte, giving him free time to explore other possibilities. His agreement with the local company pays him a commission for each solar unit sold and partial ownership in the company in the form of stock.

His newest tinkering is centered on the thought that electromagnetic waves transmitted downwards could be stopped by having an additional set of electromagnetic waves transmitted against the incoming waves, setting up a barrier preventing the intended destruction. He's gone so far as to create a device that stops a radar detector from checking his traveling speed.

When he's not testing things in his shop, he keeps abreast of the developments of that new island formation in the Pacific. The UN maintains that it will be hundreds, if not thousands of years before the land accepts human habitation. The scientists of the UN declared that the unusual formation of land first, and then volcanoes, happened because the sub-surface area had been slowly rising for many years, which is why the tsunamis were not as damaging as previous earthquakes.

The lawsuit against him by the companies he leased the acreage was dropped as Mark was able to convince them that he did not have prior knowledge of the plans to route the pipeline. After a few calls to his State representatives in Washington informing them of the discrepancies, investigating the agencies' actions, finding that they had changed the dates around. The agency head declared that the system had been hacked into one evening by an unknown adversary; it could have been an interested party to the oil companies, someone who would have benefitted by the eminent domain payments, or someone intent on delaying the project. The head said they are doing everything in their power to determine how the dates authorizing the moving of the previously accepted plans were changed. Three months after the suit was dismissed, the feds reversed the design of the route back to its original acceptance, claiming that environmental factors on Mark's land prevented them from pursuing those plans.

"Yeah, right." Mark muses, thinking of the flock of birds pooping on the land, changing the environmental conditions.

So now the lessors were happy at the turn of events, and their friendship with Mark resumed. Even so, Mark still tells anyone that the change of route through his land was merely a harassment technique by the feds only because he did not initially bow down to their requests.

Mark has convinced Susan to take a trip with him out over the new island to see for herself, and Bruce and Wendy have been invited to accompany them on the exploratory sightseeing trip. They have also been keeping up with the latest developments and becoming increasingly interested in this new land. Is it just Wendy's curiosity, or is it more than a passing fancy? Either way, she too has developed an interest in the new phenomenon after reading a magazine article several months ago describing the unusual nature of the island in these modern times.

Sitting on the deck one evening, Mark is telling his friends about his last trip over the island as he lays out a series of photos on the dining room table for them to look at.

Mark says, "Just like last time, we'll have to fly into Anchorage, stay for the night, take off early the next morning, and make flights around the island as the cameras click away. I've added a camera with a greater zoom focus, hoping to get detailed shots of the ground surface as if I were standing there. The second camera is synchronized with the first, allowing me to have pictures within a picture. All you guys will have to do is look out the window at the entire scene, concentrating on anything that strikes your interest. I see you got your camera. Good, click when ready. That flight out there and back will take most of the day."

Bruce says, "Let's go. All I've seen are the pictures the UN has released to the media, and those few major media photographers snapped on their quick tours. You know, the media. Their shots concentrated on the barren rocks, and the media retrieved some of the original pictures of the volcanoes still spitting out hot lava, showing, no doubt, the worst of the worst. The major media outlets believe it's their job to inform us of the dangers, protecting us from ourselves. Just because one idiot attempted to sky-dive onto the island, desiring to be the first in history, and ended up landing on some lava, hot but not flaming red, they must warn us common folks of the dangers surrounding us, as if thousands of idiots wish to have the first successful landing, getting their pictures on TV. Then politicians will see the need to pass laws forbidding anyone from trying to climb to the top of Mt. Everest because one party of three never made it to the top. And pass these laws in the name of protective safety, protecting everyone because of one's misfortune, or stupidity in the case of the skydiver."

Getting Mark off his rant, Wendy adds, "We've been looking forward to this for weeks, Mark, and thanks for inviting us to come along."

Susan responds, "I'm glad you could make it. As the boys are doing their thing, we can sit in the back enjoying the scenery and each other, talking about purses, while the boys talk about football."

While Mark and Bruce are filing the flight plan in the Anchorage FAA control booth, Susan and Wendy board the jet with their bags of goodies for the day-long flight: sandwiches, chips, cookies, and their favorite beverages. Susan checks the refrigerator, the restroom, and the coffee pot, ensuring each works properly. The two of them settle down, waiting for Mark and Bruce.

In the FAA office, the agent notes the coordinates of the intended destination and tells Mark, "You're one of those, eh? Over the months, we've had dozens of private parties flying out and back. I wonder what's so interesting about this new island. It's just a pile of rocks."

Mark responded quickly, "Thank you, and we'll be back this evening."

Taxing toward the runway, Mark notes to his three passengers that the weather pattern is expected to be perfect throughout the day and that the winds could change. "We'll be heading west with Kodiak Island on our left, continuing over the Aleutian Islands, and then south for 2½ hours. It's beautiful up here watching the sun rise on these clear mornings. These are all volcanic islands, yet over eight thousand people call these various western islands home. Some six thousand permanently live on Kodiak Island. Russian explorers discovered Kodiak Island in the late eighteenth century, while on the east coast, the US declared its independence from British rule."

Bruce adds to the conversation, "Every so often, Mark, I imagine what life was like back then. How could explorers from Russia come across these ocean seas looking for whatever was out there, not knowing if there even was something? Google Earth was not yet, and earth maps had not been drawn. What drove them to risk life and limb, exploring what could be over the horizon and doing it on one old-time sailing ship?"

Mark answers, "Yes, and today, with all of our modern technology allowing us to press a button and voila, we know what is happening on the other side of the earth. How are we any better off? Through the computer, we can talk and see someone on the other side some thirteen hours ahead. I'm moving ahead in time, while the other party is moving back in time. Life is just being made simpler and quicker. This trip we're making today could have been a couple hundred years ago, too, only it would have been months longer and more treacherous. No weather radar to look at. No sonar to determine how deep the water was. This plane ride could also be treacherous. Instead of putting our trust in sails and hulls, we put our trust in those engines and wings. But are we any smarter? Has the technology creating this jet made us any smarter? Has it provided us with a greater capacity to get along with others? Sure, we can send a man to the Moon, but so what? We can send a robot to Mars, but so what? We still have problems getting along with many of our neighbors."

While Mark and Bruce were philosophizing in the cockpit, Susan and Wendy were discussing the reasons they were in the air over the ocean, heading toward a volcanic land that the experts said could not be lived on for centuries to come. Susan asks Wendy, "What has Bruce told you about this Island, and why are you so interested in this place?

Wendy answers, "Susan, there's just something inside, a spiritual thing if you will, telling me to investigate the Island, to take note of its development, to watch and wait. I don't understand it either, but I've been interested as soon as the Pacific started its upheaval. I wanted to know the latest developments. It is similar to what peaked my interest in surgery. Healing people was not what drove me to surgery; I wanted to see the marvels of the inside of our bodies. Watching the heart pump is amazing every time I see it."

Susan tells her that Mark has said the same thing several times. "It's something he can't just let go and forget about. He's driven to explore all the details. He can't get enough. He even told me one day, he felt like Noah must have thought when building an ark in the middle of the desert. Why am I building this thing? I'm never going to able to use it in this desert. I wondered what Noah's wife and kids thought when he told me that. Perhaps she said something like this; 'now, Noah, you've gone off your rocker. You should see a counselor to get psychological help of some sort. And if you think I'm going to stand by and watch you spend all your time collecting these rare woods to build a boat the size of that sand dune over there, you're crazy. You need help, Noah. Get on your knees and get some help. This is crazy."

Wendy chuckled at Susan's comments, linking Mark and Noah together.

"So Wendy, you've been bitten by the same bug as Mark, eh? I did not know that. How about Bruce? Does he have the same intense interest as you do?"

Wendy says, "Well, just about, but he's so busy at the club and making commercials he doesn't have the free time I have. He's interested and keeps abreast of developments but lacks the drive that keeps me going. One day, as I was assisting the surgeon in repairing a heart valve, I caught myself thinking of the cone of a volcano as an open blood vessel spewing out the insides of the earth, and it needed to be stitched and closed. Now, Susan, don't tell anyone what I'm going to tell you next, Ok. I haven't even told Bruce."

"Why sure, of course, I won't," Susan promises her.

Wendy continues, "It was like an outside-the-body experience. I saw myself above the island with a gigantic needle with a rope-sized thread, looking down from above the volcano as my hands and fingers reached into the hot lava, stitching the inside walls of the cone together, preventing any more eruptions. The cone would heal itself, and a lake would form collecting rainwater. A few days later, I heard on the news that lakes were forming in the cones of the volcanoes. Sometimes that imagination of mine goes wild, Susan."

Susan then says, "Well, it seems then that I'm the only one on this plane who has not been too excited about volcanic eruptions and earthquakes forming a new island. Big deal. So what? That's what I thought, and then, when Mark was spending all his spare time looking at the hundreds of pictures he had taken on the last trip, I started getting concerned. You know of my desire to find a beach home somewhere we can retire to and spend the rest of our days relaxing and spending more time together. We took a few trips and looked at some available properties, but something doesn't always fit right. Hopefully, we will be able to go again in a few weeks. Our crops are planted, and the sprinkler system will care for the watering, leaving us time to investigate a few more possibilities."

At that moment, glancing out the window, Wendy notices they are approaching the island, seeing a few volcanic peaks rising in the distance. "Susan, look at this. We're coming upon it. See the volcanoes that rose out of the sea." About ten minutes later, they can see the northern stretch of the land mass.

"It's huge," Susan says in astonishment. "Somehow, I thought it was just a small island, perhaps only a few miles long. But look at it. It's huge, and there are dozens of peaks along the length of it. The beaches are beautiful."

Ever so slowly, Mark turned the jet west, getting a good look at the entire expanse of land, continuing to fly along the northern side with the island off in the distance, yet close enough to see some outlines of the shore. They are high enough to see the ocean on the opposite side over the tips of the peaks. "It's beautiful from here," Bruce remarks.

"Yes, it is," Mark responds, turning the plane to the left on his circular pattern, snapping pictures as he looks toward the island, glancing back and forth from his flight line to the island out the window on his left.

Mark turns on the speakers to the passenger section behind him, announcing his intentions to Susan and Wendy. "As we finish looking at the perimeter, I'll be turning in for a closer look at the beaches and shoreline all around, and then we'll get even closer as we get inside the shoreline to get pictures of the plateaus, the volcano slopes and whatever else."

Through his software program, the camera will print the exact coordinates on each picture, enabling him to compare the same area with the same area of his previous trip, noting any differences that may have occurred during the past twelve months.

Wendy changes her seat behind Susan, having her window to look at the island, hardly saying a word as she takes it all in, noticing how the slopes from the top cones of the volcanoes merge into the plateaus, the shoreline, the harbors, and emerging into the ocean. "Susan, you won't believe what just came through my mind."

"What?"

"Build houses and dwell in them and plant gardens and eat the fruit of them."

"That's from Jeremiah," Susan replies. "What does that mean for us?"

"I don't know," Wendy answers. "Could it be . . . ?"

At that moment, Mark announces, "well, it's time to head back to Anchorage, or they'll dispatch the Coast Guard looking for us. Hopefully, the cameras worked."

Susan then rises, leans into the pilots' position, and asks Mark and Bruce if they'd like a bite to nibble on. They consent, and Susan brings them enough snacks and drinks to last the return flight as they head in a northeasterly direction, expecting to arrive in Anchorage around six-thirty pm. The weather has been perfect for the sightseeing flight. When they head back to North Platte in the morning, the weather is expected to be favorable, allowing them to take the northern route home over Canadian air space into Montana, across eastern Wyoming, and into Nebraska.

After touching down and parking the jet, they find a decent motel for the night, and a local restaurant is not far from the Anchorage airport. The conversations are centered on what they each visualized on the flyover.

Wendy commented on how amazing it was that each of them saw the island from different perspectives.

Bruce was looking for possible locations for a golf course.

Mark seemed to be concentrating on the possible layouts for future communities and their proximity to water resources, with no obstructions to the availability of sunlight.

Even though Susan was still thinking of the beach home in the Caribbean, her thoughts during the flyover were on the beaches, the shorelines and the plateaus next to the coasts for a possible home site, and oddly she was comparing what the island scenery would be like compared to that of the established retirement community in the south Atlantic.

Wendy was looking for sites that would have breathtaking views from the house, views of the mountains, and the shorelines for fantastic sunsets.

They took off at nine-fifteen after a hearty all-you-can-eat breakfast in the motel cafeteria before making the five-and-a-half-hour trip back home, during which they reviewed some of the details of the island that struck each of them.

Touching down on Mark's runway behind his home at two-thirty-five in the afternoon, Mark announces, "Thank you for flying Tebonson Air. Hope you had a pleasant experience and enjoyed the bag of peanuts."

Back in the house and having put their traveling gear away, Susan checks the messages on the house phone. At the same time, Mark is consumed with loading the pictures into the computer as Bruce sits by watching and periodically asking a question or answering a remark from Mark.

Susan exclaims, "Gee, Mark, not one message while we were gone those three days. What say you? We'll head to town and get a good steak tonight. Oh, I know, Bruce, you'd rather go to Jeffers Depot, right?"

"That's Ok, Susan," Bruce answers. "A good thick juicy filet does sound good tonight. We've been to Jeffers several times, so I'll be okay with going elsewhere. How does Wendy feel about that? And for heaven's sake, the meal is on us this time, OK?"

Mark and Susan are in their bedroom getting ready for steak dinners. Susan, watching Mark tie his shoestring, asks, "Mark, are we still planning another look for a Caribbean home next week?"

Mark straightens, takes a deep breath, and slowly answers, "You know, Susan, we've visited several areas down there, yet nothing excites either of us. How many more trips do we need to take? The only difference in any of them is the name of the island. I'm sorry, but I'm of the opinion now that I would prefer staying right here on the farm, taking care of our own needs, and blessing the needy right here in town first, being able to connect with those we help personally. We're comfortable here. We are familiar with the people here. Our farming chores are not that pressing anymore. I'd rather stay right here. We can bless many people down on their luck right here at home with the abundance of our plantings. Don't you think we are chasing a rainbow by looking for that perfect retirement home?"

Susan responds, "I thought so. In a way, it's disappointing, but to tell you the truth, Mark, deep inside, I'm beginning to feel the same way. I enjoy it here, and giving them away is added joy. The festival is expanding. The kids are not far away. We already have our rainbow. And, I've got to tell you this: while flying over that island, I was visualizing the peaceful sanctuary of that island compared to the hustle and bustle of living in an established vacation area in a place like Antiqua, and of those two choices, I could see myself living in peace on that island without the pressure of meeting the standards of others in those retirement areas. Some folks there seem to think of themselves as royalty."

"So, we agree then. No more talk of a Caribbean home, right?" Mark answers and questions.

"You got it," Susan assures.

The four of them, relaxed, rested, and spruced up, are loaded in the SUV heading to a steak house on the outskirts of North Platte when Susan turns toward the rear seat, informing Bruce and Wendy that they have just decided to quit looking for that retirement home in the Caribbean. "We're going to stay here and do what we can to be more closely connected to the local community."

Bruce adds a note, "Well, congratulations! Good news. We won't lose you guys to some Havana way off somewhere."

Wendy says, "Amen to that. I'm happy for you. You've got so much going for you right here."

Susan adds, "Yes, we do. It's a great little town. Having leased out most of the farm to the big companies, we can relax and tend to our little vegetable garden while Mark continues fiddling around in the shop. Perhaps he may even start watching football games again while I read mystery novels."

Sitting down at a lovely, comfortable table in the steak house, they continue their conversations, covering the latest in each other's personal lives.

Mark informs them of his latest project undertakings while Susan tells them more about her change of mind concerning the search for a beach home. Bruce tells a few golf jokes, like when he and a buddy had joined up with two new club members. As the British say, they were having a jolly good time when, on the fifteenth tee box, which parallels a main road, a funeral procession passed by. One of the new members' takes his hat off and stands there silently, watching the funeral cars pass by. After the cars pass, the member returns his hat and indicates he's ready to play.

His friend asks, 'Joe, I've known you for a long time and never knew you were so respectfully religious about a funeral. How come?"

The friend says, "Well, we were married for forty-three years. I should give her some respect, shouldn't I."

Wendy has been telling them of her struggles and triumphs as a surgical nurse in a regional hospital in Omaha. She informs them of how the hospital administration treats them as little children, not knowing when to come out of the rain. "It's frustrating to have to listen to these guys in those meetings upon meetings reviewing every procedure, each step in the process, every precautionary step that we must follow before, during, and after every surgery, and then documented and signed by all the others to be entered in the computer for their review, in case something goes wrong. They tell us it's to protect the hospital and staff if and when a patient or relative gets upset about the result or some other minor complications that might arrive after surgery and then sue the hospital for malpractice. The time and money spent on defending themselves in lawsuits is astounding. Every patient is a suspect. When a surgery was unsuccessful, what did people do twenty, thirty, or fifty years ago? Our bodies are not little robots when a drop of WD40 will correct a squeaky problem." Wendy summarizes her tales by theorizing that modern society expects life to go on without complications.

"Mark, can I bring up another subject?" Wendy asks.

"Sure, go ahead."

"What about that new island in the Pacific? Do you think that during our lifetime, it will be suitable for people to live on?"

Mark says, "Now, this is off the cuff, more from my wishes than from any real scientific information, as I haven't compared the photos yet nor talked with Janet recently. But, from our visit today, it appears that it won't be long before we see vegetation emerging. We did see birds flying all over the lower parts. The cones of a few lower volcanoes are closed and accept rainwater, forming lakes. And the rains are creating other lakes and ponds, streams and rivers. That part is exciting. I did not see any hot lava anywhere on the island. It looks very promising, and I would not be surprised if someone plans to set up a camp soon enough. On the trip Jim and I took last year, the FAA agent told me of several private parties that had requested the same flight plan. This time, he said, there had been dozens. Now, if those are just curiosity sightseeing visits or exploratory trips, considering the possibility of making a homestead out there or not is the thousand dollar question."

Wendy asks, "How many years would that be possible?"

Mark says, "I would suspect five to ten years, but who knows?"

Susan then asks, "Mark, are you thinking of such for us? I thought we just settled the issue, and we're going to stay here."

Marks says, "Well, yes, I cannot lie. I have thought of it. And, yes, we did settle on staying here. But the Island has been in the back of my mind, kind of like a wish we could start our little community where there is no government at all, no code inspections, no rules and regulations to follow, just following our self-imposed codes of behavior, based on old fashioned Biblical morality."

Susan follows that with, "Just as I have suspected. Mark, you do know that we'd be starting all over. It'd be living in a tent and cooking over a camp stove, washing up in a lake or stream, and going to a toilet behind a bush until a home could be built. But then, how would we get all those materials out there? There are no trees to cut down, no Home Depots or Safeways to get our weekly food supply. I just told you I could visualize the peace of living there compared to those retirement areas, but that was just a vision, not a wish. We'd be on our own, but the loneliness would be great, and the sacrifices of giving up so much . . . ?"

Mark replies, "Yes, it'd be tough for a while. Somehow, we'd have to find a way to bring all that stuff with us."

Wendy adds, "You'd have to work on those details for months or even a year or more."

Bruce says, "We could help."

Then Wendy quizzically looks at her husband; "Bruce, are you now getting interested?"

Bruce says, "Well, I guess I am. I like the idea of starting a little village out of reach of the endless regulations already imposed upon us. Marks generator could be available, supplying us with the energy we need. Yeah, I kind of like the idea. Wendy, we've always enjoyed our camping trips, so big deal if we live in a tent for a year while building a home. We'd be free to live according to our moral compass, and we wouldn't get those inferior feelings we often do now when we don't live up to somebody's expectations. I'm always on my tippy toes wondering when a member may get offended because I appeared at a meeting wearing a shirt he disapproved of."

Marks adds, "Boy, this conversation has taken an unusual turn. I'm now hearing from you a desire to move to that island, lock stock, and barrel. Am I right?"

Looking at each other, Bruce and Wendy shake their heads in agreement, together in unison, saying, "Yes, we are."

"Susan," Mark asks. "How about you? It may take a few years of preparation. Would you be willing then? We won't be going off half-witted. We'll be prepared. A year or so of preparing, thinking it all through, making lists of everything. We could do it."

Hesitantly, Susan responds, "Well, reluctantly, yes, I guess so, a couple of years down the road, knowing that we'd have some good friends along to keep us company. It wouldn't be just us alone on a deserted island a thousand miles away from everyone. Yeah, I could warm up to the thought. Two years, five years down the road, anything might come up changing our plans."

"Wow," Mark exclaims. "We've got a consensus. Here we sit, the four of us, in a nice steak house enjoying one of the pleasures of modern life, having what is called the good life, and we're thinking of ditching it all to start over in a brand new inhospitable land. I'm stunned. I'm overwhelmed. I'm excited, and that's about all I can think of saying right now. Pass the ketchup, and I want another beer."

Susan says, "No, Mark, let's have champagne and toast our new adventure."

"Yeah," Mark says, adding, I'll design and make larger tents. Something more comfortable for living in for a year or more."

Agreed, they all say, waving at the waiter and ordering the restaurant's best bottle of Champagne.

Waiting on the champagne to arrive, Mark starts the conversation again, saying, "We've got work to do. We've got to plan this thing down to the minutest of details as there won't be room to re-group if we neglect some item that we'll desperately need, finding ourselves in a pickle a thousand miles from the nearest shop."

Bruce adds, "Let's make our toast, return to the house, and start the process. I did not bring my notebook, Mark, is there an electronics store in town so I can get a USB thumb drive to copy your notes?"

"I got one at home for you, Bruce." Mark answers. "I think we ought to pledge secrecy as I don't want the plans to be interrupted by some bureaucrat somewhere learning of our plans before we even get going."

"You got it, Mark," Bruce assures him. "Are there any other close friends interested in joining us? How about your kids, George and Thomas? What will they think?"

Susan answers, "Whoops, I wasn't thinking of them when I agreed. But, you know, I am almost sure they would join us in an instant. But their wives and what they think is another question. If George and Thomas agreed, Melody would say she was the first. I sort of get the impression from Anabele that she'd be willing to give up her teaching job. Ruth, well, I'm not so sure about, although her job as a secretary means little to her."

"Anyone else? How about Jim Nordingham Mark?" Bruce asks.

Marks answers, "Jim, well, possible, even though he thought I was off my rocker chasing a rainbow when we flew over it last year. He's as upset about the regulations as anybody, but his biggest hindrance is doing something with his company. He's told me that the business does not mean as much anymore as it did when he was building it from scratch. Jim is very resourceful, knowing where to get the best deals on just about everything, and he's got powerful connections all over the country. Now, Janet would be another possibility, and she would be a precious person to have on board with her knowledge of agronomy."

Susan adds, "Giving up careers and jobs to start anew within these States is not quite the same as giving up our entire lifestyle benefits for a land unkind to human occupation."

As the champagne arrives, the four of them grow quiet for a moment, thinking to themselves as the drinks are poured into tall glasses, and when the waiter leaves the table, their eyes and attention turn to Mark to make the toast.

Mark starts, "Let's agree on a code name we will use whenever we discuss this adventure on our cell phones or e-mail messages."

Bruce offers, "Mark's adventure."

"I think it'd be better if my name is not mentioned, as I'm continually monitored. Just about everything I do, wherever I go, is recorded by someone in the government ever since that roil with the energy and agriculture department."

Wendy then offers, "Call it Susan's blessings."

Susan says, "Leave my name out of it, please."

"Ok then, let's name it something neutral to all of us: a place or a name that does not connect to either of us personally," Mark adds. "That reminds me of a Reagan quote; *'While never willing to bow to a tyrant, our forefathers were always willing to get to their knees before God. When catastrophe threatened, they turned to God for deliverance.'* We're in the same boat; not willing to bow before tyrants, but we are willing to bow before God directing us on this venture."

"Amen to that," they all agree.

"How about 'Moses crossing the Nile?" Susan offers. "Whoops, it was the Red Sea, not the Nile."

"Yeah, it was the Red Sea where God split the waters, enabling Moses and his people to escape the slavery in Egypt to the Promised Land," Wendy adds. "Or, how about exiled to Babylon?"

Mark adds, "Oh, that's beautiful, I love the first one . . . Moses crossing the Red Sea. It sort of parallels our plight. To put it briefly, we wish to escape the tyranny, the despotism of government. So, if you all agree, we'll code name our plans 'Moses crossing the Red Sea.' We'll use that phrase whenever we discuss our plans through e-mail or telephone. The rest of them agree, and it is so. They raise their glasses as Mark announces: "to Moses crossing the Red Sea." "To Moses crossing the Red Sea," they each repeat, clicking their glasses together and taking a sip.

Wendy then says, "This is exciting. I can see it now. The four of us and probably others will someday be sitting around a campfire on that island thousands of miles away from civilization, starting our little teepee village unimpeded by rules and regulations too numerous for us to even be aware of, or even count, some so old they should have been relegated to the trash bin decades ago, as the one that recently made news. A town council insisted the police detain an elderly man wading in the ocean beach, who was not wearing a top on his bathing suit."

Susan says, "Drink up. We should get home and start the process. Yes, you guys have got me excited now, so watch out; I'll be taking notes, ensuring you don't forget the feminine side of Moses crossing the Red Sea. We'll need lots of feminine products, lint rollers, toothpaste, mouthwash, hair styling gel, make up, eye liners, dish washing detergent, and many other things. How many tubes of lipstick will I need for ten years before a beauty shop opens? You guys will need shaving cream, razors, deodorants, toothpaste, finger nail clippers, right?"

"Yeah, and I won't have to put up with speed bumps anymore," Bruce states.

They all chuckle at the comments and click their glasses together again, saying: "To Moses crossing the Red Sea." Taking their last sip of champagne.

Mark announces: "Let's go home. Oh, I just had another thought. After a bit, we may need to change the code, as some fed may be catching on to the many notes back and forth and start monitoring every call. We'll come up with other codes to use, perhaps something like Noah has arrived. Ah, Okay?

"Yes, You're right," Bruce says.

Mark asks Bruce, "When do you have to return to Omaha?"

Bruce says, "We'll have to leave early the day after tomorrow, so we still have one day to talk this over and start making the lists."

Chapter 11

Four months have passed; it's now the middle of September, and much has been accomplished, but there are a few setbacks regarding Moses crossing the Red Sea. They have put together hundreds of pages of notes listing items they think they'll need and how much to last a year. What equipment to bring along, the tools and hardware, as well as what to do with their homes and larger personal items such as furniture, beds, tables, dressers, and all the picture frames hanging on the walls of their homes. Mark has offered to sell his jet, the camper, and plans to purchase a sea plane and look at various ships big enough to transport themselves and all their supplies to the island.

They're keeping up with any news over the internet whatsoever they discover about the island. Janet has excitedly agreed to come along and give up her professorship at Texas A & M. Jim Nordingham is holding out as a possibility but is still uncertain. Susan finally received a verbal agreement from both George and Thomas, thinking that the wives were still questioning the wisdom of making such a drastic move at their young age.

At first, George indicated his initial thoughts were that his parents had gone off their rockers, but he was testing their sincerity with his negativity at first. When George was certain Moses crossing the Red Sea was a genuine intention, he gave them thumbs up and told his father that Ruth would not be a problem, as her job is just a job to her. His architectural job can be left easily.

Thomas's reaction was different as he consented immediately, knowing how his father viewed the political spectrum governing more and more details of his life.

Thomas indicated he would not have a problem leaving the electrician field and is already making a list of electrical supplies they would possibly need for constructing new houses and the wires necessary for running the power lines from the generator to the homes.

Anabele had already suggested such an adventure would be right up her alley. She would have been ready last year. She is getting up to date on teaching materials for all grades, collecting some text books and reading material, as she eventually sees herself teaching the children in this new community that is bound to expand. She is collecting every news item for a scrapbook to be used as a teaching aid for the children of the new island.

Mark and Susan's daughter, Melody, was excited at first but has yet to decide to go along, having difficulty with the Health and Human Services Department local office in Denver, as a case worker for abused women, where she has been working since graduation from Nebraska University five years ago. Her case load is extreme, never allowing her to devote enough time to each victim of abuse. The paperwork is astounding. Seeing the women in dire straights, depressed, and often left alone without family, emotional, or financial support is having a detrimental effect on her personal life. She finds it difficult to separate her own emotions from those of the victims. She wants out, but also feels as if she has been called to this field of work.

Susan has been begging Melody to give it up and concentrate on her own mental well-being, knowing that the rape Melody experienced while in high school is driving her daughter to help others, thus somewhat relieving some of her personal anguish and guilt. Melody relents and agrees to accompany her family when she finds that her brothers will also be there.

And so, after four months of engaging conversations, numerous messages, explanations, conference calls, and e-mails,

Mark and Susan have firm commitments from their sons and wives, their daughter Melody, Bruce and Wendy, and Janet.

They plan to be the first to set up permanent residences on that new volcanic island in the pacific. The actual time of departure has still not been decided.

The UN, the US, and Russia have sent numerous scientists, geologists, volcanologists, and agronomists to see the land up close, to examine the rock formations and collect samples, which indicate the full examinations of those samples may take months or even years to comprehend fully. The UN continues to declare the island off limits to human habitation as a safety precaution, providing the mainstream press with official press notifications. You never know when another volcano may erupt, or even the possibility the land may yet sink below the surface of the seas, establishing coral reefs instead of an island. That's their stand, and the various countries are encouraged to support those beliefs.

The media has been relatively quiet about broadcasting new information as it develops, as the island is considered old news and will no longer garner the viewers that recent tragedies will. A few Hollywood producers have indicated an interest in using parts of the island as a backdrop for a new movie production. NASA has indicated it could be used as a training facility for future astronauts' trips to the moon, while a Canadian independent person in business wants to use the harbors as a fishing resort, just as Russia has indicated their interest in establishing the same, a headquarters for ocean fishing expeditions. The US Fish and Wildlife Agency wants the island declared off limits to humans for ever and ever, making plans to transport pairs of wild animals, enabling them to propagate and grow just as in the beginning of time, being left alone by humans. The EPA has declared the island as one of the results of climate change. The NEA is interested in the formational process of the island as an aid in teaching students the evolutionary process the earth went though over millions of years. National Geographic Magazine has already published a story on the island and its formation. Other science journals have written articles about long-term expectations. Oil companies have expressed their desire to explore the possibilities of the below-sea-level rock formations, which could have expansive oil or gas deposits. The UN has declared that the Law of the Sea has given them jurisdiction over the waters surrounding the island.

From the dark side of humanity, an atheist suggested that all Christians should be moved to the island. Muslims are on record as saying the new island will be used as a prison for unbelievers. A homosexual activist was interviewed on a national news talk show indicating that anyone who does not accept homosexuality as genetic should be imprisoned on the island, indicating it could be used as a brand new Alcatraz.

On and on the news broadcasts interviewed every possible ignorant bigot on their thoughts of what would be the best use for the new island, finding one who said all blacks should be moved out there, another who indicated society would be best served if all right-wing extremists were delegated to the island; and the media found some who thought all liberals should be sent there, as well as some wanting socialists, communists, and Marxists to be moved there; and others who wished all lawyers, all lobbyists, all criminals, all illegal immigrants, all journalists, all bankers, all IRS agents, all this and all that be imprisoned on the new island freeing the rest of the world from the degenerates of society.

From the people, the consensus seems to be that another Alcatraz should be built out there, stating that no one would ever try to swim a thousand miles to freedom.

Finally, all of that obnoxious talk has quieted down as other recent tragedies and misfortunes are being given the focus by the mainstream press.

Seeing all of these stories documented on Anabel's list, Mark asked her, "Why are you even saving all this junk? Isn't it enough to just read these accusations from idiots? There will always be these thoughts from people as long as humans live on the planet."

Mark added that if the media ignored people seeking their fifteen seconds of fame on national TV, those seconds in the spotlight would not be a dream to achieve.

Anabele responded to Mark, saying, "Yes, I had the same thoughts too, but storing the articles on the computer is harmless, and they could be used as a teachable subject someday, illustrating how the evilness of society raises its ugly head."

Overall, politicians have been relatively quiet in expressing their thoughts to the media, except for standing by federal agencies' desires, supporting climate change as the reason the earthquake and volcanoes changed the earth's landscape. The national media has provided the liberals in Congress with the air time, emphasizing that we must get control of our carbon footprint and do it now. The US is doing everything in its power to protect the citizens of the various states from the dangers of future earthquake driven tsunamis and volcanic ash pollutants restricting new developments in certain hazardous zones.

The voices of conservatives in congress are not being provided equal air time by the media, except when one of their remarks denies the concept of climate change as being the cause for the eruptions, even though the UN declared the recent rise in ocean water levels by a one thirty-second of an inch was the result of the sea bottom under the islands location had been slowly rising for decades.

The media has also neglected to provide equal air time to the scientists who state the concept of global warming is overemphasized and not a real threat. Since recorded history, there is provable evidence of the earth going through cycles of warmer and cooler average temperatures, the deniers assert, along with the fact that current weather forecasters can't accurately predict the weather two days away, so how can they predict the weather ten years from now?

The average person on the streets of America and the world scratches their heads in bewilderment, choosing which side to support based on which media they mainly pay attention to.

Mark and Jim have had several conversations concerning Moses and the Red Sea crossing. Mark desires that Jim would agree to be part of the group already committed, but Jim is having second thoughts, knowing that it would require him to invest his fortune in a risk he's yet unsure about. They have discussed the various aspects of transporting all those supplies needed to build homes and roads, bringing together a system of utilities to supply water and power needs, sewers, and other structures for safety and protection from the yet-determined weather patterns.

Jim tells Mark that he'd be starting from scratch from day one, working to construct elements essential for comfortable living. It'd be like living in a tent for months and possibly years using rock formations as shields for personal privacy needs. Jim says he's not ready to give up on the comforts he's earned to enjoy and thinks Mark overreacts to isolated federal intrusions in our daily affairs. Mark is not satisfied that Jim is holding back and tells his good friend how much his abilities would be needed and that he'll not give up on working to convince him to forget the fortune. It's just money, and join them in their quest to be free.

Mark reminds Jim of some of his favorite thoughts about freedom, such as: *"Freedom is priceless" "Riches and fortune are like chains binding one to the riches."*

And, from Friedrich Hayek: *"Freedom can be preserved only if it is treated as a supreme principle which must not be sacrificed for particular advantages,"* and this one also by Hayek: *"The freedom that will be used by only one man in a million may be more important to society and more beneficial to the majority than any freedom that we all use."*

And this one from Benjamin Franklin: *"They who give up essential liberty to obtain a little temporary safety deserve neither liberty nor safety."*

Mark reminds Jim that he has this quote form C.S. Lewis framed and hung in his office: *"Of all tyrannies, a tyranny sincerely exercised for the good of its victims may be the most oppressive. Living under robber barons rather than omnipotent moral busybodies would be better. The robber baron's cruelty may sometimes sleep, his cupidity may sometimes be satiated; but those who torment us for our own good will torment us without end for they do so with the approval of their conscience."*

And then one from Ronald Reagan who said; *"Without God, there is no virtue, because there's no prompting of the conscience ... without God, there is a coarsing of the society. And without God, democracy will not and cannot long endure."*

All of those conversations with Jim have not produced what Mark desired, so Mark has no other choice but to let Jim go and let him figure out for himself his real desires. "Dag gone it, Jim, we've been through a lot together over the years. You're one of my best friends, and I had hoped you'd come along, you old stubborn ox."

Jims' final remark to Mark, his good friend from the early days growing up in the Justice Department is, "Best wishes, Mark, and don't permanently write me off. I'll be around, and please, please keep me informed. All communications will stay confidential as always, and if I can help, let me know. I'll do what I can, and I'll miss you."

While Mark has been obtaining the supplies, storing them in his barns, and keeping in touch with his sons and their methods of planning, Janet has been assembling notes specifically related to volcanic islands growth trends: how vegetation begins, how the ashen soil is made suitable for plant growth, how to amend the soil speeding up the process and how the rains and sun nourish the soils changing the landscape into favorable habitats for plants and animals. Her trips (four of them) to the island under the direction and supervision of UN scientists have provided her with up-close observations, noticing that in just a few short months between the last two trips, the land is becoming more livable, even though the official stance of the UN has been drummed into her not to deviate in any of her writings anything but the official stance. The official stance released to the press and other countries maintains that the island must go through its own evolutionary process over a period of hundreds, if not thousands, of years before any habitation would be tolerable to humans. Those scientists on the UN payload point to the historical evolution of the earth's surface, substantiated by empirical data collected by independent scientists from every country of established scientific processes over the past century.

Natural evolution must be allowed to take place.

Janet is tired of all the baloney and secretly gathers her data sets, which could help them as they take their place with Moses crossing the Red Sea. She is also working on her financial end, attending to the details of her retirement funding supplied by the University, enabling her to contribute her due part to securing the list of supplies. Mark has told her it's not necessary, but she insists on helping in her own small way.

Bruce and Wendy are tirelessly gathering data and some supplies while also planning to sell all, giving some of their belongings and furnishing to charities, saving for themselves to take along to the Red Sea crossing only what they'll need. Clothing, rain gear, newly acquired footwear suitable for rugged terrain, personal toiletries, personal photos and keepsakes, favorite reference books, tents, sleeping bags, lanterns, camp stoves, and a supply of oil, propane gas cylinders, several Porta-Johns, as well as Wendy's supplies of medical first aid equipment, their bed, and some comfortable chairs, having learned of the specially designed tents Mark is having made.

Wendy has accumulated a meager supply of freebie pharmaceutical drugs used in surgical treatments, keeping patients comfortable. Wendy continues to add items as they are made available through misuse and discards and some promotional freebies provided by the drug company representatives.

Bruce feels outside the contributing circle as his occupation as golf professional will be useless on the island. His feelings are that he can help the efforts by helping Mark keep the lists current, add his comments, and help Mark pick out the best source for obtaining those supplies. Bruce did have a club member mention his desire to leave the country for greener business-wise pastures and thought the new island could be possible if the island remained neutral. Since Bruce had come to know most of the members, one wondered if Bruce knew of other members who had expressed similar feelings and desires. Bruce told the man no, he had not. He informed Bruce he had been keeping a close eye on the developments and was beginning to feel like escaping the obnoxious federal bureaucracy for freedom somewhere. The taxes and paperwork had become overburdening to his businesses, and there was no way out other than leaving. Bruce related this man's plight to Mark, wondering if he should let it go or inform the gentlemen of their dreams. Mark confirmed his opinion to let it go in one ear and out the other, keeping Moses and the Red Sea crossing to their trusted friends and relatives.

Marks list of items to be acquired is being narrowed down as the barns are getting full of supplies, boxes, and boxes, crates, and pallets filled to weight requirements. Knowing that they'll need to construct a pier from shore to the ship to unload the supplies, Mark has purchased dozens of heavy-duty pontoons to support the wooden pier. Some heavy-duty equipment has also been purchased: another tractor, a ditch witch, and 4-wheel drive jeeps with attachments he thought they would need. He is now in the market to purchase a ship to haul these goodies as soon as the final arrangements are made to sell his jet.

His fortunes are whittled down bit by bit, and he has yet even mentioned to Susan how their financial nest egg situation has been dwindling. He has yet moaned. He continues being unselfish about his riches. Easy come, easy go, believing that riches can become chains binding him to fears of losing those riches, so spend he does, collecting every possible item they think they'll need for a minimum of six months to a year.

As the trucks come and go out of the farm, some of the local people are beginning to wonder what's up with the Tebonsons?

The mayor has been questioned. Peter Jeffers has been questioned. Mayor James Olsen did venture out to the farm weeks ago seeking answers to the rumors flying around town, one of them being that Mark was equipping his barns for a manufacturing facility of his inventions. Another one was that Mark had inside knowledge about a future economic devastation that would hit the country and was building up his supplies. Another rumor was that Mark and Susan had purchased their Caribbean hideaway and were preparing to supply it with goods that could not easily be purchased there. They would be moving shortly.

Mayor James came to the farm to meet with Mark and Susan to discuss these rumors. First, he had a long conversation concerning the affairs of the town, introducing the subject of the Halloween festival coming up next month. Then, the conversation focused on why so many trucks were coming to the farm. James related the rumors he had heard and wondered whether any were true. The two of them have remained close friends through the years, trusting each other explicitly. Mark briefly explained that they were collecting supplies to be used in an exploratory exhibition that could last several months. Mark said he was sworn to secrecy and could not reveal any specific details, adding further that the supplies would soon be transferred to a warehouse in Anchorage, Alaska, and the parties involved would take it from there. That's all Mark would tell him. Mayor Olsen thanked Mark for telling him that much and that he'd try to quell the rumors.

Mark told him, "Hey, people are going to talk. Let it go. The rumors are not bothering me. When the rumors have power behind them, then it can be troublesome, like those borne out of political agendas."

Mayor Olsen agreed. "Being an elected official, I have been a victim of those."

After the mayor left, Mark called Susan, "I've forgotten all about the Halloween festival coming up in a month. Mayor Olsen just mentioned it, and the bell went off: duh, what have I been thinking?"

Responding to Mark's remark, "Gads Mark, I have too. Do we have time to make it? Can we put it together on such short notice?"

Mark responds, "Well, all the supplies we've been gathering are in the barns; they must be moved, or we forget about that part of the festival. Could we do that? How would that affect the festival if we did not have the Haunted House?"

Susan says, "It's been a big part of drawing the crowds we've had. Do we really want to disappoint the adults?"

"Ok," Mark says. "I'll get some trucks and move all that stuff out to another storage area somewhere. We'll have to get it done quickly, like this week, or next week at the latest, so I've time to make the changes for the festivities. How about the volunteers? We'll need to start contacting them to get this thing rolling again, and you know, Susan, this will be our last one. Let's make it a good one for the town. I love this place. I'll miss it."

"Mark," Susan replies. "Why don't you arrange to move the supplies to a storage place in Anchorage? We're going to have to move them there sometime anyway."

"Good thought. I'll work on that." Mark answers.

"I'm sure Bruce and Wendy will not be able to come down, and George and Thomas are too busy working on their end of Moses crossing the Red Sea to take time away from work. The same goes for Melody and Janet too. We're going to be limited to just the town people and their help. Is there any chance that Jim would come over and help out?"

"Hmm?" Mark answers. "Good thought. He'd sure be an aid helping me get the festival ready again, and it'd give me another chance to convince him about coming along with us. I'll call him. Let's get busy."

Mark makes the call, learning that Jim is on a business trip to Russia and will not be home for a few more days. But Jim did leave Mark with the impression that there was a good possibility he could make it over to North Platte for a few days a week or so before Halloween. Mark has contacted some friends in the trucking business who could get over to the house and transport the goods wherever Mark desired. So far, two big semi-trucks should do it, and a couple of flatbeds to move the heavy equipment: the backhoe, tractors, ditch whip, and jeeps. That being arranged, Mark gets on the internet, looking for available storage facilities somewhere in or near Anchorage. Through his searches, he finds that there seem to be none available. No empty buildings the size he needs anywhere within a hundred miles of Anchorage. Making a few more calls to business associates he's known over the years, he strikes out again. Calling a few realtors in Anchorage, Mark explains what he needs, and the man immediately informs Mark that there just aren't any that size that are immediately available, nor would there be any available soon.

Knowing that they'd be loading the supplies to a ship at a port in the area, Mark starts looking at the shipping ports in the Anchorage area, finding the municipally owned Port of Alaska, and is directed to a knowledgeable agent who, after hearing what Mark needs, suggests that instead of using semi-trailers to transport his supplies to Anchorage, he could locally obtain a few of the portable shipping units, which could then be transported on flat bed trailers, and stored at the Port until the time of loading. They'd be secure at the port, and his equipment could be loaded inside those containers. He'd pay a fee based on how long they occupy the space. Mark thanked the gentlemen for his advice and notified the trucking company of his change of plans.

Mark notifies Susan of his plans and assures her that the goods in the barns will be out of there in the next couple weeks, and he can then get to work putting the Haunted House together.

"Super Mark," Susan replies. "A dozen ladies will be out next weekend to help. Mark, I'd like to do something special this year, something we haven't done before, something the kids will not forget. This is our last chance Mark. Do you mind if we go over the budget this year?"

Mark replies, "What are you talking about there? What would you like to do?"

Replying, Susan tells Mark, "I have this idea of creating a maze for the children to walk through, a maze created out of hay bales attached together. When they make it through, they would be rewarded. We could somehow make it a timed event with the fastest time getting a bigger prize. We'd have to purchase the hay, but the ladies and I, with the help of our tractors could do it all, and after the festival, we could donate the hay. We could use part of our garden area. What do you think?"

"Hey, that sounds good. I like it. How many bales would we need?"

"Right now, I haven't the faintest. Some of them would be the large circular ones, and some the old fashioned hay bales before equipment made them round." Susan responds.

Mark says, "Each of those large round bales would probably cost us fifty to one hundred bucks each and the square ones about ten bucks, and then delivery. How big of an area?"

Susan says, "It needs to be big enough to make it somewhat difficult. Perhaps, half the size of a football field."

Mark says, "Go for it. The town has been good to us. You could probably get some of the high school kids to help with the heavy lifting."

Chapter 12

Hearing the phone ring, Susan is the first to grab the cell phone, hoping it's one of the kids. "It's someone named Franklin," Susan says. "Mark, do you know anyone named Franklin?"

"No, I don't," Marks tells her.

"Hello," Susan briefly says.

"Susan, this is Janet. I've had to get a new phone, and I'm using a bogus name. I'll tell you more about it later."

"Janet, are you OK?"

"Just fine, Susan?" And then Janet says. "I have bad news about Moses and the Red Sea crossing. How are you doing, Susan? Are you guys going to have that Halloween festival this year again?"

Susan responds, "Well, yes, we are. Mark and I were talking about it. We almost forgot about it; we were so intense on that crossing stuff that it slipped by us. Is there any way you could come up and help?"

Janet answers, "That's what I'm calling about, and yes and yes! I'm already on my way, but before I got too far, I wanted to call to make sure you'd be home. I've got some important news about the thing. Is Mark there?"

"Sure, Janet, he's right here," Susan says, pushing the speaker button so both could hear and talk.

Mark leans toward the phone saying, "Hello Janet, it's good to hear your voice again. What's up?"

"Mark," Janet replies. "I don't want to say much over the phone, but an important development about the Moses crossing just came to light. I'll tell you about it when I get there. It's not good, Mark. We might have to change our plans."

"Ah," Mark replies, "it can't be that bad. Did I hear right? You're on the way up here?   We'll be delighted to see you again. How long can you stay?"

Janet replies, "I'm on administrative leave, they call it. I've got two weeks at least. Anyway, I should be pulling into your place sometime tomorrow afternoon, and then we'll discuss the latest. Moses can't be stopped from crossing the Red Sea, can he? I'll see you guys tomorrow. Bye for now."

"Susan, I wonder what she meant by 'Moses can't be stopped?" Mark asks.

Susan replies that she has "not noticed anything lately in the news that would prevent us from going there. The UN hasn't changed its stance, and I've not read anything of any other agencies stopping anyone from even visiting the island. It's been relatively quiet the last few months. We'll have to wait till she arrives. Before she does, I'd like to clean her room. Would you help with the vacuuming? And we've got some supplies stored in there that should be moved out to the barn, or the garage. Yes, the garage would be better as those are quite valuable."

"Sure," Mark replies. "I'll get those boxes out. I forgot why we put them inside instead of in the barn."

Susan answers, "They're the pharmaceuticals, the drugs we might need that Wendy had shipped here."

"Oh, Yes, we do need to keep them separated." Mark answers. "I'll take care of that, and then I want to look for any updates about the island. How about dinner? I'm getting hungry."

"Fix your own Mark. I'm not hungry right now. There's that meatloaf you could warm up." Susan replies as she leaves the kitchen area for the spare room.

"Ok." Mark concedes, getting up and following Susan to the spare room. The cases of drugs get moved to a spot in the garage. The room is cleaned, fresh sheets are tucked in, the pillows are ready, and fresh towels are hung in the adjoining bath room. They are prepared for the arrival of Janet, still wondering what happened, causing her to leave on such short notice with several weeks of time off right in the middle of a semester. Those questions kept surfacing throughout the day and evening, but searching the web for articles or explanations about Janet's plight did not occur to either.

Mark is up early the following day, before seven am, desiring to spend some time researching news about the new island in the Pacific. He is sitting on the deck with his coffee cup on this cool mid-October morning. He checks the weather. He checks the new e-mail messages, finding one from Melody asking about Thanksgiving. George briefly relates a news item concerning the oil pipeline construction through Iowa. Mark briefly notes the football scores of the Cornhuskers and Chicago Bears. He sees a headline stating that the World Series may extend into Halloween. Another headline reads, 'Pipeline delayed again.' Searching for shipping containers locally available, he finds dealers in Omaha and Kansas City.

Looking up from the screen, he notes the sun rising for another beautiful day in mid-October, feeling grateful for his blessings, thinking of how he will miss these mornings, and then wondering if he's doing the right thing. Dismissing those thoughts, he searches deeper into the news, looking for anything related to the new island. Only one new item told the story of a group of Alaskan natives who were stopped from boating to the island by Alaskan authorities because their canoe-like boats were too dangerous to travel across thousands of miles of the ocean. They told the police that their forefathers had crossed the big sea hundreds of years ago in these boats. They said, "The spirits told us to leave the land of white men."

Well, he thought, this certainly cannot be what Janet is talking about. She must have something that has surfaced there at the university or through her close connection to the scientists of the UN. At that moment, he notices a shadow moving slowly across his peripheral vision. Immediately looking up, he sees one of those drones slowly disappearing over the treetops. He also notices no marking on the aircraft indicating who the owner is. *Why does the government have the right to fly unidentifiable aircraft when everyone else must identify theirs?* Thinking along those same lines, he begins a search for those laws, finding the language used regarding 'civil' aircraft, which does not apply to state or public aircraft and unmanned meteorological balloons. So, his reasoning leads him to believe that the government can legally fly any aircraft anywhere without identifying itself. 'Oh boy, I feel safer now,' taking another sip of coffee and looking up to see if the thing had turned around and was coming back for another look. *'If it does, I'll give them a good picture to take holding my middle finger up toward the drone,'* He mumbles. Then a quote he recently read comes to mind: The French philosopher Voltaire once said: *"If you want to know who controls you, look at who you are not allowed to criticize."*

His curiosity is piqued now, desiring to know further what the government knows about him and possibly their plans to escape bureaucratic tyranny. He enters: 'Moses and the Red Sea' crossing' into the search box expecting to find only references to the biblical account and those scientists claiming that nothing like that ever happened or could have happened.

Near the bottom of the list was one title to a CIA website linking an article about an agronomy professor at Texas A&M who referenced 'Moses and the Red Sea crossing' in e-mails.

The FBI had previously warned all school administrators to alert them about those code words. Upon further investigation, they found that the said professor had used the same code words that a high school teacher had previously used with her students arranging sexual fantasy parties. A private businessman had used the code name about a planned terrorist attack. Middle Eastern

Muslims had used the name for a planned attack on Israel. A man in Chicago had used the name referencing his desire to do a reverse crossing of the red sea, wiping Muslims off the map. Said professor (name withheld because of privacy concerns) was put on administrative leave pending further investigations by the CIA, and the administrators.

Most mornings like this, Susan would have already joined Mark on the deck, watching the sun rise while enjoying her first cup of coffee, but seeing Mark intently concentrating on the computer, she stayed inside, preparing a few delights for Janet. Unaware that Susan is up, Mark heads inside to refill his coffee. Seeing Susan busy in the kitchen, he greets her with a morning kiss and asks, "What are you doing so early this morning?"

Susan tells him that she decided to prepare a few pies for Janet and to have them ready for her when she arrives later.

Mark says, "Susan, I know why Janet is on the way here. I found something on the web this morning referencing an unnamed professor at Texas A & M. I'll bring it in, and you can read it and weep." He goes out to bring the notebook in and places it on the kitchen table.

Bending over to get a straight-line view of the screen, she quickly reads the brief. "Oh my God," Susan exclaims. "How? What are we going to do now? We thought we had a good way of referencing our plans."

"Remember, I indicated we may have to change our codes periodically. Susan, while I was sitting here, I noticed one of those drones flying over, just like you experienced. We're being watched. Even before our plans were contemplated, the feds were watching. It started years ago, probably even before I chased the guy from the dept of agriculture off the land. Now, I'm beginning to believe that our computers could be hacked also, now that Janet's computer has been."

Susan asks, "How? Now what?"

Mark says, "Well, first of all, let's wait until Janet gets here, and we hear her side, and then we'll take it from there. This is not over yet. We'll have to change our communication method, for sure. We might have to send further messages between us the old-fashioned way on paper, through the mail, or better yet, using FedEx. But right now, I'm going to confuse these guys."

"How, Mark, what do you mean, confuse?" Susan questions.

"I'm thinking of something. Something of a diversionary nature," Mark tells her.

'What would that be? How can you confuse the FBI?" she asks.

"How about this, Susan? A few years ago, Pastor James and I discussed bringing Biblical events into modern-day life so the kids could understand and relate what living during those times may have been like. We talked of several historical events, one of which was building a replica of an ark, another of Moses crossing through the Red Sea, and somehow creating a simulated splitting of the waters. What if I send Janet an e-mail note referencing Moses and the Red Sea as having to do with a demonstration here on our property demonstrating to the children in church how it physically would have happened, asking her for a possible date for her help in designing the event from an agricultural perspective. I'll inform her that I'm just about ready any time she is for digging the trench that will be used by the Israelites to cross over the Red Sea. I'll ask her advice and wonder how we could show the sea splitting. Something like that. What do you think?"

Susan responds, "Well, it sounds reasonable, but let's wait for Janet to get here. After getting the details from her, we can develop our strategies."

"Yeah," Mark responds. "She'll be here this afternoon."

"Mark, in the meantime, check to see if you can find anything else about this. I'll join you on the deck shortly."

Instead of using the popular search engines, Mark goes to one called 'duckduckgo', looking up anything about the newest Island, and finds right there on top a link to the United Nations' ideas to improve the lives of the one million slum dwellers.

"The UN wishes to prepare the volcanic island for those peoples, transporting thousands of them to the new island after the second stage of development. Their ideas call for billions of dollars to be invested in a massive development of sustainable living communities on the new island over the next decade. Trees will be transplanted, the beaches will be made sandy and white, the lakes of clean water, and all crops grown on the island will be organic. All structures will be made of environmentally approved materials and solar and wind-driven energy, and the sidewalks and bicycle paths must be constructed using only materials found on the island.

"It will showcase to the world how communities will be in the future. Transportation on the island will be restricted to publically owned and operated solar-driven machines. There will be no need for private vehicles as people will be housed in units close to their work sites for human well-being and sustainable living standards."

Another headline from Global Cities, a world organization headquartered in Maryland. Their desire is to use the island as building block communities, showcasing the absolute need to eliminate human weakness through proper nutrition and community care initiatives. Each person is linked to a close-knit unit that is trained and equipped to care for each other using resources shared by all.

"Hogwash," Mark mumbles, turning off his notebook.

"Susan," Mark says, "there's nothing new on the web that I can find. It's the same ole, same ole story of idealists thinking that by just repositioning people, they will behave better, and just all of a sudden, the human spirit will be quelled into submission. And life will be grand for everyone. Everyone will be happy, and there will be no need for a police department.

"It's the same old communist deceptive trick," Mark adds, "believing that people develop harmful behavior patterns because they feel left out, they've been isolated, they've been bullied, they've been abused, as they've not been given the same amount of candy as the others. They assume that if all resources are shared, people will not desire more and will be forever happy and content.

'Who can tame the spirit of man?' says the best book ever written about the rebelliousness of mankind, and what can be done about it." Mark says.

Susan says, "the quote is '. . . the tongue can no man tame, it is an unruly evil, full of deadly poison.' Our history illustrates that communism will not work. Why don't they understand? Don't they read history? As much as anyone else, I'd like to live in a world where everyone is decent, hard-working, unselfish, and more concerned about the other person than they are about themselves, living in perpetual harmony as no one ever breaks any commandments. But it will never happen, not on this earth or during anyone's lifespan.

"Well, Mark, if you can't find anything more about Janet's plight, we'll find out when she gets here. She said she was on administrative leave, meaning they suspended her while under investigation.

"Can I fix you a sandwich, Mark?"

"Yes, please." Mark answers. "I've arranged for some of those shipping containers to arrive, possibly even this afternoon. Could we get some high school kids out to help transfer our supplies from the barns? I'd pay them twelve bucks an hour."

Susan says, "Sure, they'd be delighted. Some are always looking for odd jobs. How many? And when do you need them? I'll ask the school to put a note on the board with your number to call. Then you can call them back when you're ready."

The afternoon slowly passed, anticipating the arrival of Janet. The school agreed and posted notes on the boards announcing part-time work for dependable, physically fit teens. After classes were dismissed, Mark received three calls. He informed each caller of the nature of the work; the transfer of supplies into the containers, and helping Susan place the bales of hay for her maze. Mark told them the duration of the work, the pay they would receive each day, and that he would call back when he would like them to arrive.

Susan was busy the afternoon preparing her notes for the Halloween festival preparations. She again contacted the hay suppliers and told them when to have them delivered.

It was four-forty-five when they noticed Janet pulling into the driveway. Excitedly, Mark and Susan hurried out the front door, greeting her as she barely had time to open the door to her vehicle. "Come on in, Janet, we can't wait to hear what happened," Mark tells her.

Janet replied, "Hey, this was a long drive. I'm exhausted and would like a good cold beer first. Ok? Perhaps it's not as bad as I let out to be on the phone. That's something we'll have to wait and see first."

Susan tells Janet, "Yes, you're tired, I'm sure. You get relaxed. We'll go out on the deck on this beautiful evening. Mark could start a fire in the pit. Is there anything else you'd like along with that beer?

"Mark, be a dear and bring her luggage in."

Susan and Janet make their way to the kitchen, retrieving three beers, bowls of chips, and cheese dip and then heading outside to the deck. While Mark is placing the suitcases and the hanging clothes in the spare bedroom, Susan and Janet talk of the trip from College Station, Texas, to North Platte, the weather, the roadblocks, detours, heavy traffic, the motel for the night, her stops and the price of gasoline along the way.

Janet says, "the price in Texas is $4.25, and here in Nebraska, I found one station selling that no ethanol kind at $4.75. We can expect higher prices until they build that pipeline and allow our companies to drill in the gulf again. But nobody expects that to happen again, so we all suffer. I heard that Mark had a run-in with the feds over that pipeline. What happened?"

Susan replies, "Oh, Mark can brief you on that better than I can. Here he comes . . . with some firewood too."

"Mark." Janet starts as he was placing the wood chips and sticks in the pit. "When I see you and your family together, the thought of my own family arises. It's still a desire, but it gets farther and farther away. Another professor and I have been going out some, but there's nothing there for either of us. He's like a cousin. Perhaps some day a guy will strike my fancy, but that time still seems to be over that next hill."

Having the fire started and settling down in his favorite deck lounger with a few sips of beer, Mark says, "Ok, Janet, now it's your turn to tell us what happened. What did you mean when you said we might have to change plans? Spit it out. We've been imagining all kinds of things. I went online and found a CIA document with a reference to an agronomy professor at your school who was investigated for having used our code name. That was you, right? What happened?"

Janet says, "Yes, that was me. I'm surprised you could find that. Three days ago, I was in my office reviewing some research papers I had assigned to my students, when three administrators and four policemen came into the office demanding that I come with them. Hey, I said, what's going on? This is my office. I'm busy, now get out, and we'll talk when you make an appointment. The lady in charge, Ms. Whatever we call her, as she was in charge of campus security. She's a real bitch. Known around campus as Hitler's wife. She insisted I get up from the desk, leaving everything as it is. She flashed a piece of paper at me. Do not touch or take anything, but leave the office right now. She told me she would review the events later in her office.

Again, I demanded to know what was going on. "It's my office; personal items may be here, and you have no right to do this." Then she showed me the warrant to search.

"Well, what choice did I have?" I grabbed my little purse and began walking toward the door, noticing the police officers bracing themselves as if I were going to run them over. Standing in the hallway, leaning against the wall, I could hear drawers and cabinets open and closed, wondering what was happening. Then I thought of our plans, wondering if I had the palm drive in my purse. All communications we've had concerning our exodus were kept on this palm drive." Janet pulled the small device out of her purse.

"The commotion noise had caused quite a stir, as other teachers and research aides started congregating in the hallway. As I was leaning against the wall next to my office door, a professor nearby asked me what was going on.

"Hey, I don't know. Ms. Whatever showed me a warrant to search my office, and told me to get out and she would let me know later. Four police officers observed as I left. Four of them. As if I was a terrorist."

He said I was lucky to have kept my purse. "They usually seize purses, searching it for weapons first."

"Weapons. I don't own a gun, and they know that." He was nice and invited me out for coffee, off campus, where we could talk. I did not know the guy, only having passed him in the hallway. As I was leaning against the wall talking to this guy, I glanced down the hallway at the others, watching it unravel. I noticed a friend shaking her head back and forth. Hmmm? I told the guy no. I was going to wait until Ms. Whatever came out and then get some answers. He insisted that it would be good for me to talk with someone, the sooner the better, saying these things can fester and become psychologically damaging. I told him I did not need a shrink. He then offered that if I needed to talk to someone, he'd be available, to call him, and they would agree on a safe place to talk about it."

"Finally, after what seemed to be an hour of standing in the hallway, the policemen came out carrying my computer and boxes of files. Ms. Whatever told me to come with her to the office, and she'd tell me. My afternoon classes would be held by someone else."

Susan says, "Wow, Janet, you must have been scared and humiliated right there in front of your comrades."

"Yes, I was. And I found out later that that guy who asked me out for coffee was part of the security team. His mission was to befriend a suspect and get them to confess privately."

Mark tells her to continue, wanting to know how our plans are affected.

"In the chief's office, she finally told me why I was being investigated. It seems that one e-mail from Jim with a reference to Moses and the Red Sea crossing was on my University computer, which I knew was being monitored continually by campus security. We all know that, and that's why I have kept all references to our plans on my personal iPad and this palm drive using a private e-mail address. She told me of a high school teacher who was using our code name with certain students for sexual favors. The code had also been used by a terrorist planning an attack in Israel. A Mennonite family had used the code for their planned Christmas party on an island. So, they had to investigate me because of that one reference in one e-mail from Jim."

"I'm sorry. I was neglectful. It was my mistake. I should have been more careful." Janet confesses. "So, while they are digging through the rest of my communications and files, I am on administrative leave until notified, probably the end of the month, I was told."

Mark asks, "What was in that e-mail from Jim?"

Janet replies, "There was nothing specific about our plans, just a note from Jim saying we would get together later concerning Moses and the Red Sea crossing. That was it."

"Are they also investigating Jim?" Mark asks.

"Yes, I think so," Janet responds. "You might want to call him and ask. Since a terrorist and a sex pervert were using the code name, the security chief had to notify the CIA, and that's how it got leaked on their website."

"Yeah, right," Mark says. "The average citizen hardly ever looks at any of the government's web pages unless they apply for benefits. I'm surprised the media has not been all over this. It'd make another hare-raising-tale of the dangers lurking among our college professors, possibly using it as sexual perversity by you since that one high school teacher was. Has anyone from the local media been in contact with you?"

Janet answers, "No, they haven't. The school's policy is to keep these investigations private until the school, in this case, the

CIA finishes their search. So I don't think the media has any idea yet, although leaks in the system have happened."

"Well," Susan says. "We'll have to change our code names. Who would have thought that Moses and the Red Sea crossing would be used as a code by terrorists, a teacher, or anyone else? A Mennonite family? Janet, we're sorry that you had to go through this. It must have been awful."

"Do you think their thoughts of moving to the new Island could affect our plans in any way?"

"No, Mark," Janet replies. "From all I've ever heard, the feds are not interested in Christians, except as possible political insurrection uprisings, or if they would offend Muslims, which they could stop easily using the police force. Nah. They're more concerned with teachers preying on students and then possibly the terrorists, although I believe sexual exploitation is their top priority. So, what do you think, Mark? You're our fearless leader. What do we do now?"

Mark says, "Like I told Susan when we saw the CIA file, any further communications should be by using FedEx. I don't even trust the post office anymore and certainly not any e-mail communications, even though we're using what is called privacy settings and secure accounts. In this day and age, everything we do is monitored. I was stunned last week when I noticed cameras inside Jeffers Depot."

Susan adds, "Yes, cameras are everywhere; the grocery stores, street corners, and all over Pharmacies, going in and coming out, someone can watch every move we make. I've become sick of it, and you know how I used to feel whenever Mark brought up the subject just a few years ago. I'd tell him to let it go, Mark. It's just so they have proof when someone robs a store or one of those flash mobs terrorizing customers, smashing everything, and stealing the store blind."

Mark adds, "I asked Peter about it, and he told me it was for the safety of his customers, a deterrent, and hopefully the rabble-rousers would notice the presence of cameras before they planned to start something. Just a safety feature, he did not want a flash mob tearing up the place, he said. I then asked him about the recordings. He said they were required to keep them dated and locked up in a safe place for a year. Federal regulations, he said."

Mark then adds. "FedEx is it from now on, and always require a proof of delivery letter, nothing through e-mail."

Susan says, "Janet, I'll bet you're hungry. Let's go to town and get something. Ok?"

"Yes, I am, even though I'm exhausted. Being served sounds good to me. I'll freshen up and be ready in ten minutes. A good thick steak with Nebraska corn on the cob sounds good."

Mark then sits by his computer, typing a letter to George, Thomas, Wendy, Bruce, Melody, and Jim. As Janet and Susan enter the office ready to go, Mark prints out the letters, addressing an envelope for each, which he stamps closed with an old-fashioned security stamp, a seal his grandfather used.

"It's sad when we don't even trust the post office to deliver private mail any more securely," Janet says as she watches Mark apply the wax and the stamp image.

And off they go to the steak house, dropping off the letters at FedEx on the way.

Chapter 13

There are four days left before Halloween, falling on Sunday this year, so the festival was moved to Saturday evening. Janet has been fantastic in helping Susan and the high school kids create the maze out of hay bales. It appears the finished size will be about half the size of a football field. One of the parents helping carve and paint the pumpkins had her six-year-old try out the maze. What a time he had, taking 20 minutes to find his way to the end opening. Standing around the perimeter edge, the parents could not see the head of the child moving through the various corridors.

In the middle of the maze, a 30-foot tower was built, tall enough to see the entire maze, the dead ends, and the start and finish points. The coach of the high school baseball team agreed to stay in the tower, shouting directions down to the children: "No, go the other way, not that far, back up, go forward ten steps, take the next left, the next right. Hey, you in the red shirt. You're going the wrong way. Little girl in pink, keep on going, now turn right, no your other right, that's it. Oops, wrong way kid. Hey you with the skeleton costume, turn right at the next turn, then left, then left again. His purpose was to confuse the kids as well as to instruct them.

Mayor Olsen had come out to check on the latest developments and the changes Mark and Susan had made for this year and offered his help Saturday evening. He also wondered if Mark wanted him to say a few words at the campfire. He was so excited about the maze Susan had created he called the newspaper to get a story published on Friday. Peter Jeffers donated candy, other treats, and a church-sponsored children's pumpkin carving contest. This year will be the biggest ever, with hundreds of children and parents, as most of the traditional events around the area had been canceled in favor of attending the festival on the Tebonson farm. Now, the problem of organizing and entertaining many children has become a major concern for Mark and Susan.

"Mark, how can we get many more kids through this maze in just a few hours?" Susan asks. "A few of the women volunteers tried making their way through the maze, and it took them an average of 12 minutes from start to finish. As it is now, we'll never get that many kids through it in two hours in time for the campfire."

Looking at the maze from the tower, Mark says, "Susan, let's cut the thing in half. Make two mazes easier for the smaller kids and one more difficult for the kids over four feet. We'll put a measuring tape at the entrance. We'll let the parents know, but let them decide which one for their children. We'll have to reposition many of the bales. But we got time. I've got time to help with that tomorrow."

"If you can devote yourself to this tomorrow morning, then OK, we'll change it," Susan says.

They ended the day's chores relaxing on the deck as Mark started a fire in the portable fire pit. For a couple of hours, they reviewed more details of their plans to move out to that new island. They went over the long list of supplies they think will be needed. Janet also reviewed her UN-sponsored trips to the island, what she saw, her expectations, and how the UN was using the data.

Janet asked if he had heard anything from Jim.

"No, not yet, and this is not like him. As far as I know, he's still in Mexico, but he always has his notebook and returns a call or an e-mail. Something's up." Mark surmises.

Janet responds, "Yes, that's not like Jim."

Susan says, "You said he was also suspected in that raid you experienced. Do you think that he got detained while on his business trip?"

"That could be," Janet answers.

Janet tells Mark and Susan that she is now happy that events have turned out like they have so she can spend this time with them. "There's something about sitting around a campfire that mesmerizes us all. It's relaxing. It's just wonderful to be here. I miss this relaxed atmosphere and look forward to our extended camp far away from everything. You don't know how excited I am about this move. I wish we could leave tomorrow."

Waking up the next morning to a beautiful day of clear skies a soft breeze with the temperature at seven am in the mid-fifties, Susan and Janet are eager to get busy changing the maze around. Looking out, they see Mark is already on the tractor, moving hay bales, cutting the maze into two. Quickly, they toast a bagel, walk out to the deck, and pour the coffee while sitting on the soft cushions looking out over the farm, quietly enjoying watching Mark work. The project is finished five hours later, so they break for a late lunch on the deck.

"Mark, what else today?" Susan asks. "The volunteers will start arriving mid-afternoon."

Mark says, "It looks like we've just about got it. The Haunted House is ready as most all of the supplies are out. The campfire area is ready. I'll help the men gather the firewood and prepare the parking area. You ladies could do the finishing touches on the decorations, signs, the pumpkin patch, and such, and then I think we'll be ready."

Janet adds, "I'm so glad I could get up here and help this year. You guys should be proud of what you've done for the towns in the area."

Mark says, "We are, and I feel that this year will be the last one, as it appears our escape must be moved forward to spring or summer."

"Did you try to connect with Jim this morning?" Janet asks.

"I tried again, but he's still not answering," Mark says.

Looking at the daily calendar, Susan reminds Mark about the code inspectors' appointment to review the displays at One-thirty. "Be ready for them and be gracious, Mark. Offer them a cool drink. Please, Mark, just show them around and answer their questions politely."

Marks responds, "Ah, they're such jerks, thinking of themselves as our masters, and we're such idiots not knowing that kids can do stupid things, adults too, and we are too dumb to recognize that, be responsible and take the preventive measures. This is our fourth year of doing this, and nothing drastic has happened."

Susan reminds Mark, "They're just doing their jobs. Please treat them with some respect. Maybe you should leave before they arrive and then I can show them around. No, it'd be better if both of us accompanied them. Then I can elbow you if you get out of hand. Ok?"

"Yeah, you're right again. My attitude toward government workers stinks. I know it. Most of them are just obeying the rules set down by people above them, except there's always a few who feel the power and add a few rules of their own." Mark says. "If I could only deal eye ball to eye ball with the one making up those rules, but we can't do that anymore, as it's gotten so big with so many layers between the rule makers and those charged with enforcing the rules. Even the ones enforcing them have no idea who wrote the rules and why.

"Like you said, they just do their jobs and wish to keep the job. But they treat us as trash, and they're our masters, making sure we provide the children with a safe and secure environment according to their safety standards. And their standards include all of the politically correct things, like ah, children deserve the best, and how dare you suggest that two daddies or three mommies couldn't give the attention and loving care the toddlers need."

The phone rings, interrupting Mark's rant. He retrieves the phone from his shirt pocket, not recognizing the number on the screen. Mark gives the usual greeting in such circumstances: "Hello, goodbye. I'm not interested."

"Wait, wait, wait. It's Jim," the voice quickly answers.

"Well, hi Jim, I've been trying to get you. Where are you?"

"I'm home now. Do you know where Janet is? I've been trying to get her."

"Yes, she's here," Mark tells him. "She's helping us with the Halloween festival. I'll have her call you at this number with her new phone. She can explain what happened."

Dialing the number, Jim answers the call. "Hello, Jim." Janet greets. "Mark told me you were in Mexico on business. What have you heard about the events at the university?"

Listening to Jim for several minutes, she answers, "I'm sorry, Jim. Somehow, I had left one e-mail from you on the office computer after I had notified everyone to send all correspondence of the plans to my alternate e-mail account. You wrote something about Moses and the Red Sea that tipped off the administration. The feds warned them to look for references of that code, and that one e-mail was red-flagged. I'm sorry you got involved. I should have known. I'm sorry, Jim. What are you going to do?" Listening to Jim for another minute, Janet says, "Goodbye, Jim, we'll see you tomorrow."

Mark asks, "What did he say?"

Janet tells Mark and Susan how his trip was interrupted by the Embassy in Mexico City, apprehending him for two days of questioning. He said he was treated like a terrorist, being locked up in a padded cell while being questioned by three CIA agents hour after hour, wanting to know his involvement in Moses and the Red Sea crossing. He said he did not reveal our plans but consistently insisted that it was about a Christian event a church was planning to have, demonstrating how Moses would have been able to walk across the bottom of the sea. They wanted to know the church's name and where it was located. He told them he couldn't say, so the questions kept coming, trying to implicate him in the terrorist plans. He said it was the worst two days of his life. Finally, they let him go, informing him that his every move would be monitored. When he got home the other day, he discovered that they searched his office at work, his computer was apprehended, and his home was also searched. He's unsure if the feds haven't found our plans to move to the island, as many records are missing at home. He bought one of those pay-as-you-go cell phones. Anyway, he said he was coming here in the morning for a short visit.

Mark says, "I wish he wouldn't if the feds watch him that close. Now, they'll think I'm in on that terrorist thing."

Janet responds, "Mark, Susan told me about the thoughts you had about constructing a model Red Sea here on your land, and Jim also had an idea to confuse and defuse the feds. He hopes you'll go along with those plans."

"OK by me. I had the same thought." Mark says, "We could get started on it before Jim arrives. If Jim is in their crosshairs, they'll be following him here, and I wouldn't be surprised if the feds don't blend in with the parents tomorrow evening. Let's get busy. Oh, the inspector should be here any moment."

Janet says, "Tell me what I can do until you guys get rid of the inspector."

"Yeah, you know how to run the backhoe," Mark says. "I'll take you to the spot I was thinking about, and you can start digging a trench. I'll call Pastor Allan, briefly explain what's happening, and ask him for any suggestions. He's trustworthy and distrusts the feds as much as we do."

Riding in the golf cart on the way out to the area Mark considered as suitable. He tells Janet of his conversation with Pastor Allan. "He's all for it, Janet. He loved the idea and would contact the superintendent of Sunday school, letting him know of the activity. He said he planned to attend the festival tomorrow evening anyway, and we could discuss the details then.

"Ok? Here we are. If you'd start digging a two-foot-deep and four or six-foot-wide trench about ten or fifteen-feet long, piling the dirt alongside, we would then use the tractor blade to smooth the sides. Ok?

Janet interrupts, "Let's make it wider, Mark. It would have taken the Israelites quite a while to walk across the sea bottom." "Hey!" Janet says. "What about this? We could put hay in the bottom, cover them with blue tarp, and pull them apart by attaching ropes to a winch."

"Yes, good idea, go ahead, make it as big as you think. We'll have something started anyway. Pastor Allan said he would love to introduce the future event: 'Moses and the Red Sea crossing' as a teaching aid for children to be held here on the farm when he makes his comments to the crowd at the campfire, just in case a few feds were in the crowd."

"That sounds good to me, Mark. Now take me to the barn, and I'll get the backhoe going while you placate the inspector."

The local inspector came and looked at every little detail of the planned festivities; the campfire area was OK, the barns were OK, the pumpkin patch was OK, and the only suggestion was to stake down some of the hay bales to keep them from falling in, or children pulling them down. He said that he had to make at least one or more recommendations; otherwise, his supervisors would get suspicious, and he'd be sent to more training classes. He gave Mark and Susan a thumbs up and wished them well, having placed in their hands a completed inspection report by his department that all areas were considered safe and secure, which must be posted at the entrance to the farm. The inspector chuckled when he saw the Haunted House displays and signs: 'IRS: Irritable Revenue Sharing' and 'DHS: Demented Home Safety,' HHS: Healthy Humanoid Safety, saying to Mark, "You're one of those guys, are you? Well, I kind of agree with you."

He also informed Mark that he, his wife, and three kids had attended last year's festivities and planned on being here again this year. During the inspection, some volunteers arrived and immediately busied themselves decorating the pumpkins and corn stalks.

Searching for Freedom

The moods of Mark, Susan, and Janet have changed from near panic to happiness and delight again as the recent events seem to have calmed their anxiety. Again, they feel they control their lives rather than scrutinize objects. The local newspaper journalist and photographer visited the farm, taking snapshots and videos of the various displays while interviewing Mark, Susan, and Mayor Olsen. During the interview, Mark mentioned the future event for the church, hoping the editor would not delete the comment and it would become a matter of public record.

After finishing their day's work, Susan suggested they gather around the campfire and hang out rather than go into town for a meal. They could warm hot dogs over the fire, sipping hot chocolate or tea while enjoying the fall weather and discussing their future on the new island. Janet informed them that she was hoping the move could be next spring, right after school is out for the summer, and she assured Mark that once she has been cleared and is back in the classroom, all communications will be through FedEx. Mark briefly explains his plans to acquire a ship to transport the containers and our sleeping quarters. Three ships have attracted his attention, two of them located in the Anchorage area, where he had planned to visit next week. His shipping containers full of supplies were on the way up there. He expected that once on the island, they would use the facilities on the ship while a dock was built, enabling them to unload the supplies. He also informed Janet the Jet was up for sale, that he had already had several offers, and that he planned on replacing it with a seaplane and the boat.

As always, the campfire was relaxing and informative, erasing any anxieties about the plans to leave America and its blessings behind. The three of them spend much of the campfire conversation around those reasons: why they have decided to venture out on a limb, taking such significant risks, to retrieve their personal freedom in a new world, to an island having recovered from its violent creation.

Mark summarized the reasons, recalling historical events: "The people of Plymouth Rock left security behind. The founding fathers left security behind, risking a war with an established, militarily supreme country. Families left communities in the east to travel westward for months, risking it all for new lives in wild, open territories. Slaves would often risk being caught and hanged just to be free of the tyranny of their owners. Abraham Lincoln chose to defend freedom for all, risking a defeat in a civil war. In the fifties, thousands of Cubans risked their lives crossing the ninety-mile ocean waters in small row boats to gain freedom in Florida.

Mark continues his remarks, "Religious persecution has existed throughout human history, as has tyrannical rulers quenching the dissidents' desire for freedom versus superficial security. The fifty States United was made great by the inherent freedoms that attracted millions of people from all walks of life, rich and poor, from the four corners of the globe to leave what they were familiar with to a life to be re-built in an unfamiliar land."

Janet sums, "The individual is no longer respected, but as an object to be ruled. The order is now reversed as the towns and cities look to the states, the states look to the federal bureaucracy to supply their needs, and individuals look to all three for protection and supplies. America has been heading in the same fascist direction as other fallen nations, spending what it does not have to secure what it cannot. The growing bureaucracy in Washington has slowly eroded those principles of honoring and respecting the smallest."

Susan suggests they should retire for the night as tomorrow is the big day. Jim will arrive before noon, and the town people will bring their kids in for the last Halloween festival the Tebonsons will hold on their farm. However, no one outside Mark and Susan's close-knit family and friends are aware of that. The efforts of Mark and Susan will be expected to continue next year, as many of the visitors will make suggestions and offer to help with next year's event.

Up bright and early before Mark and Susan, Janet takes a trip into town to get some muffins and donuts and picks up a USA Today weekend edition. Arriving back at the farm, finding Mark and Susan still sleeping, she makes the coffee and sits down to scan the paper, nibbling on a blueberry muffin. She reads an article describing a national news organization that had picked up the local North Platte papers story and featured this event as one of many independent Halloween activities around the country. One of the commentators felt the feel of the event was too old, not keeping abreast of the fun of spookiness, ghosts, and vampires that children enjoy, depriving them of the traditional Halloween. Another commentator mentioned the hidden elements of the event, saying she thought the motive behind it all was religious indoctrination as the Tebonsons were creating a demonstration of Moses crossing the Red Sea for a local church, naming Mark as an extremist. The article quoted a volunteer as saying she approved of the festival because of the fundamental Christian message they were promoting as further proof that Mark was a religious extremist. Right next to the article was a headline reading: 'Extremist Islamists beheading unbelievers.'

Susan, awake and ready to fix breakfast, finds Janet and the muffins. "Good morning, Janet. Hmmm? You've been to town already, I see."

"Good morning, Susan." Janet responds and adds, "Yes, I have, and listen to this," as Janet reads from the article about the festival from the paper. "You're famous, but now considered extremists."

"Oh boy, wait till Mark reads this. He'll go bananas. We'll let him have his breakfast first before mentioning the paper,"

Mark wakes up to a breakfast of fresh fruit, scrambled eggs, sausage links, and toast, comfortably sitting around the kitchen table, reviewing the details for the day's activities with Susan and Janet. The weather is cooperating, a sky of broken cumulus clouds and a temperature in the fifties. Susan informs Mark that the latest news from many volunteers is to expect over a thousand people to attend at least part of the festivities. She also tells him of the article in yesterday's North Platte Express featuring various pictures of the farm, the maze, the Haunted House, the hundreds of pumpkins, and the campfire area, interviews with Mark and Susan, and an official endorsement from the mayor.

Mark and Susan were checking off the list of the finished displays, ready and waiting, with those they felt needed finishing touches, while Janet scanned the Saturday morning USA Today newspaper.

"Well, Mark, your interview with the local press has gone national," Janet tells him while sipping on her coffee with the newspaper in hand and getting a nod from Susan. "Not only the festival but the Moses and the Red Sea plot we started was also mentioned. You did it, Mark. Thank you. This may have saved my job."

Mark replies, "No, Janet. We did it, Mayor Olsen did it."

"Mark, there's also this you'd be interested in," she said as she handed the folded newspaper to Mark.

"What is it?" He asks.

"Ah, just read it," Janet replies.

After a few minutes, Mark says, "What a joke. The media is at it again. We'll probably have tens of reporters descending on the farm today wanting more personal interviews, getting some children to say they miss the vampires, zombies, and ghosts, and we'll be labeled again as right-wing extremists clinging to our guns and religion. Let them come. I couldn't care less."

'I've got things to do. Save the paper, though. Perhaps I'll frame it," Mark tells Janet as he pushes the chair back, grabs a mug full of coffee, and heads toward the barn.

The three of them are putting some final touches on the displays when Jim drives his Jeep Explorer into the farm. "It's great to see you guys again," he says as they rush to greet him with the usual initial greetings with hugs and handshakes.

Then Jim says, "Well, Mark, you saved me again. I heard on the news last night that you and a local church would be hosting a Moses Crossing the Red Sea demonstration. Thanks, buddy. How did you pull that off?"

Both Janet and Mark brief Jim on how it all came about.

"So now, Jim, you can help us right-wing extremists get ready for this evening. Did you bring any work clothes? How long can you stay?" Jokingly, Mark asks, "Do you have any guns in that car of yours?"

"Nope. You've got enough in your closet for both of us four times over. I can stay for the weekend, but on Monday, I need to head back to the office." Jim tells them.

The volunteers for the festival started arriving at five. Peter Jeffers brought the candies out, and they were ready to begin the maze challenge at six pm. A dozen high school kids showed up to help with directing the traffic and parking. The maze challenge was a delightful time for almost everyone as each child was timed, and the winner of each age group was rewarded with extra goodies. The school kids kept a count of the visitors, informing Mark that they had counted one-thousand-forty-five. Yes, some national media did come out with camera crews filming children going through the maze and interviewing the children and parents. They also took pictures of the Haunted House displays, capturing the signs of IRS, DHS, HHS, and ATF along with the Roman soldiers, as reporters took notes. Some of the locals were put off by the media's insistence, desiring interviews, shoving microphones and cameras in their faces, and wanting names and personal information to interrupt their enjoyment of the activities.

While Jim and Mark were preparing the campfire, the reporters filmed them, and that's when Mark got upset. He told them all to leave and that their welcome had terminated. He would not let them stay to intrude any further. Mayor Olsen had arrived and was also telling the reporters to leave now. A few said this was a public event and they had the right to be here. The public had the right to know, and it was their job to inform them of events such as this.

Mayor Olsen insisted and threatened to call his entire police force to have them removed from private land. His confrontation with the reporters was all captured on video. They finally relented and left the grounds as the campfire was underway. Pastor Allan made the opening remarks and introduced Mark and Susan, who received a standing ovation. Tears were flowing down Susan's cheeks.

Most people had left about eleven pm, yet some stayed on offering to gather the trash. One man remarked that he had seen the tremendous amount of waste left on the Washington Memorial grounds after a political hip-hop event, noting the difference between rural homespun events like this, where hardly any trash was thrown on the ground.

Worn out but thoroughly satisfied, Mark, Susan, Janet, and Jim lean back in the living room sipping on drinks when Jim says, "Mark, I wish I could join you on your move to the island, but the business just demands too much out of me right now, and I don't see it improving any time soon. I've got to be there. Too many depend on me; I'd feel guilty satisfying my desires first. If only I could find a worthy buyer who'd stay the course, I'd be out of there in a minute. These last few days have put a burner under my butt, and I'm warming up to the idea. If only"

Mark says, "We're sorry too, but tomorrow, we can talk some more, and I can pick your brain for any ideas you have. But now, it's time for me to hit the sack. Good night, Jim and Janet. I'll get up when I wake up. No alarm clock for me tomorrow. Pretend you're at home. Good night." Susan also bids Janet and Jim to be comfortable and stay up as long as you want.

Sunday morning comes, and Janet and Jim announce their plans to leave later that day, Jim to Omaha, a four-hour trip, and Janet on her two-day drive back to Texas.

Chapter 14

"Mom, you've been staring out that window for five minutes. What's so interesting?"

"Mel, look at that," Susan tells her daughter. Melody puts the potato smasher down on the counter, looks out the window, and sees Mark, George, and Thomas with their bows and arrows shooting at the target. "Mel, now that you're looking for a man to come into your life, you'd do well if he had the qualities of any of those three."

"What do you mean, mom?"

"Looking at them got me in one of my reflective moods," Susan answers. Hearing the remarks Susan is making to Melody sparks the curiosity of Ruth and Anabele, who stop their part of preparing the Thanksgiving meal and crowd around the window, peering out at the three guys with their bows and arrows.

"They're hunters and gatherers, as the saying goes. It's built into them to hunt, to put all their energies into finding the best deal and gather them together for his use and the use of his family. Watch them. Right now, they're competing with each other. They're serious about putting that arrow right in the middle of that red dot, beating out the other two. It's that competitive drive." Susan relates as she admiringly watches them practice their archery skills.

"I feel safer and more secure about this trip."

"Is Dad bringing his bows and arrows to the island?"

"You bet he is, and he's bringing his collection of guns too, even though there won't be an animal anywhere, but the guns and bow will be there anyway. He's bringing that target, too, so I imagine he's thinking of practicing out there sometimes. And the guns will be available if and when he needs them."

"I asked Thomas if he was bringing his guns, and he said, "Of course I am. Why wouldn't I?" Anabele adds.

"Yeah, and George, too. Well, that's one of the first things he put on his list: that collection of arrows, his bows, and the paper targets." Ruth adds her part.

"Did Dad go hunting this fall like he normally does?" Melody asks.

"No, he missed it this year. He's been too busy preparing things for our adventure."

Still gazing out the window, Susan says, "Mel, your dad doesn't need me, he could make it on his own anywhere, but he wants me, and that's true of George and Thomas too; they want Ruth and Anabele, but they could just as well make it without you. They'd miss you, but it wouldn't stop them in their innate quality of toughing it out. Watching the three of them now makes me proud to be part of their lives. With those three around, I feel very comfortable and safe."

"Now, there I go again. I'm getting all teared up with gratefulness."

Susan pauses and then adds, "You know, I couldn't care less what the elites and the feminists are saying that the only difference in male and female is biological. That's baloney. It's a bunch of bull crap that's been fed into this modern life of ours. It's right out of that feminine mystique garbage. Just another deception. There is a big innate difference. It's built in us. We've got different qualities right from the beginning. As little girls, we wanted dolls, and boys wanted trucks and guns to play with and went around pointing those toys, saying bang, bang, you're dead. God put into Adam the desire to subdue the earth, and after the fall, we were cursed with pain, and our desire was made to please our husbands." Turning to wrap her arm around Mel's shoulder, Susan looks into her daughters' eyes, "Mel, don't you go chasing after a man. Let him find you."

Turning away from the window and looking around the kitchen, Susan says, "Girls, let's give these guys the best Thanksgiving meal ever. Where are we? What needs to be done? Mel, you're just about finished with the potatoes. Anabele, you're still working on the apple pies. Ruth, it looks like all the vegetables are ready to be put on the burners when the turkey is ready."

"Did we forget anything?"

An hour passes, the table is set, all the vegetables are in place, a couple of tall candles are in the center, and the big roasted turkey is ready. "I think that's it," Anabele announces as she lights the candles. "Call them in, and let's eat."

Opening the door to the deck where she could get their attention, Susan yells, "Hey guys, we're ready. Come and get it."

"Wow," Mark says as he enters through the deck door.

"Mark, the turkey is in the kitchen," Susan tells him.

Mark carries the big roasted turkey from the kitchen and places it in the center of the table as the oohs and ahhs finish off the ritual. The traditional blessing is said with each holding hands around the table. Mark stands to make the first cut into the breast and carefully places that piece on Susan's plate.

"Thank you, Susan and Melody, Ruth and Anabele, for your hard work. It looks delicious." Mark states his appreciation.

They dig in and fill their plates as the sides are passed around, taking a bite of each, commenting on the food, giving thanks for it all, laughing at some remarks, a few jokes told, and then the conversation gets down to the preparations for the big adventure.

"Dad, have you started the process of selling this place yet?" George asks.

"I just signed the paperwork last week with a local broker I've known over the years, so the house will officially be on the market soon, along with the hundred acres." Mark answers.

"You're going to miss the farm, the barn where you've been working late into the evenings, and everything else about the place," George states.

"Yes, we will," Susan responds. "It's been a great life these past twenty-five years on this farm. We're planning to slowly move some of our favorite furnishings to storage in Anchorage, the items we hope to be able to take to the island."

"I'm going to miss this house," Melody says. "It was so much fun living on the farm, chasing the boys through the trees, spying on them as they went nudie in the pond."

"You did not." Thomas quickly answered.

"Oh yes, I did. I saw you guys throw your shorts into the wind and run like crazy into that pond. Don't you remember coming up looking for your shorts and you couldn't find them? Na, na, ha na na, I crawled on my belly, grabbing them, then hung them in a tree, making it look like you threw them in the air, and they got stuck on a branch."

"You guys thought you were so much smarter than I." Melody adds.

George and Thomas look at each trying to remember the occasion as Melody does, and Thomas answers, "You must have been dreaming, Mel. First of all, that pond was a mess most of the time. It smelled, and the water was always dirty. We even took the old tire swing down and moved it to the grove of Oak trees. That pond was miserable just to look at."

"Well, you went in there anyway just to show yourselves that you could. Mom could smell you trying to sneak in through the garage when you came back."

Susan answers, "Yeah, I remember that smell. I was doing something in the garage when you two approached. The smell. You guys looked horrible too. I had you outside spraying you with the water hose. That was when your dad thought he'd like a few pigs around, and they lived by that pond."

"Do I need to fill the coffee pot?" Ruth asks.

"I'm fine." Mark answers as the rest agree.

Anabele says, "Thomas has told me many stories of his favorite times on this farm, but that was not one of them. Thomas, how come?"

"You're right, as some of the things George and I did as stupid kids are never to be repeated. But I know of one that concerns Mel that would be interesting."

"Don't you dare?" Insistently looking at Thomas, Melody says, "If that's what I'm thinking of, forget it, Thomas. Remember, I've got a few on you too."

"Oh, come on," Ruth says, "spit it out."

"No, let's not go there."

"George, you tell it then."

"No, we better not," George responds, taking another sip of coffee.

"Well, I'll tell one on myself if the boys are chicken to relate some of your misbehavings. Dad was teaching me how to run the tractor to plow a field. He pointed to an area he wanted plowed, showed me the straight lines, and told me to get to it. He watched for awhile and then left. That was so boring after a short period of making those straight lines. I started turning the tractor in small ways, leaving gaps, turning it, wanting to write letters in the ground, and then running the thing in circles for hours going farther and farther out.

"Dad came out and saw that and blew a stack. He made me go over the entire area again, or I'd never drive a tractor again and wouldn't get dinner until I finished."

Mark responds, "Mel, it wasn't as bad as you put it, but I did have to make you understand."

"Anyway," Melody says. "We had a great life here on the farm, and I'll miss being able to come back here periodically,"

"I will too," Susan agrees. "We've been blessed over and above anything your dad and I had hoped for. There are lots of fond memories. I think I'm going to cry just thinking about how great we have had it, and now, we'll be leaving it all." Susan reaches for the napkin to wipe away some tears.

"Mom, don't," Melody says, as a tear drops from her eyes.

Mark says, "Yeah, It's been a blast. I've loved it and will miss this farm forever. We had a great time here. The town has been wonderful. We've become friends with some wonderful people, but now, we're being moved to a new land to develop new memories. These will always be in our minds, and I'm sure they will periodically return so that we can give thanks again for these times."

"I know that, Mark," Susan replies. "But since we've made the decision, I still get homesick thinking about being in a place without trees, a barren land without a store, without a friend to visit, without the church we love, and all the conveniences we take for granted, and at times, I question whether we're doing the right thing.

"Are we?"

"I know we are," Mark assures her. "Boys, how do you feel about it?"

Thomas is the first to answer, "I'd have difficulty not going through with the move. It's as right as it could be."

George says, "Mom, at first, I was somewhat apprehensive about leaving all of this to start over on land that the UN declared uninhabitable. They had been there several times, seen it up close. Going there, like on a camping trip, would be fine, but to pull up complete stakes and make it our home forever and forever did seem outrageous when I thought about it. But then, reality hit me."

"What do you mean reality hit you?" Mark asks.

"The reality of continually being subject to rules and regulations imposed upon us by someone else, and the only ones obeying those rules are responsible people who could make it on their own wherever they are. We don't need the regulations; we get them anyway, and being adults, we submit to them as our obligation to obey those who are in authority over us. The ones not submitting to the rules are the troublemakers, the criminal element, and the idiots who spoil it for the rest of us. Then, some new rules get passed to control the criminals and idiots, and parts of the rules affect us too. But many still find ways to get around those new rules. At the same time, the majority of responsible people quietly go about their daily lives submitting to the new rules, and on and on it goes, each decade and year getting overwhelmed.

"That's the reality of modern life." George finishes.

During their conversations, they decided to simplify why they are leaving the States for a new land, and writing it down in black and white, something that could be released to the press if they desired.

<u>Our Reasons Why</u>.

When America was becoming great, immorality was shunned, but now immorality must be accepted as normal, as genetically driven. In America's prime, people sought harmony through a sense of belonging to a country that honored its citizens and encouraged and welcomed their hard work and ingenuity, a government that stood on the sidelines cheering the accomplishments. The greatest generation, when people sacrificed for the good of the country, has given way to the now generation, when people are demanding their rights to blissful happiness now, no need to memorize anything, with the government acting as coach, referee, nurse, equipment handler, sideline marker, water bottle runner, whistle cleaner, down marker movers, ball cleaner, usher, food preparer, and sensitivity enforcer."

"Yes, those early settlers would rather live in a tent knowing they are on their own, responsible for their own lives, accountable only to each other while acknowledging God as their ultimate enabler. They are willing to take on the uncertain rather than living in luxury being regulated and monitored by bureaucrats nearby and those a thousand miles away deciding for them which of the industrial products they

should use and which must be banned for the sake of sustainable living, as well as demanding they accept a new civil personal happiness morality.

The list is endless. The intrusions are formidable. One either fully submits or faces the wrath of penalties or even jail time as a common criminal. America is on a collision course. It's dying. Just as a loved household pet is put to sleep when it gets sick, American society is sick and on the verge of being euthanized.

Signed by us ten.

Thanksgiving would be celebrated next year on the island.

George and Thomas have put their homes up for sale, knowing they may have to take a loss as the real estate market hasn't yet recovered from the disastrous economic turmoil of previous years when Government mortgages failed, and foreclosures flooded the market. Melody has been an apartment dweller. Bruce and Wendy have been living in a home as part of his compensation plan with the country club. All he needs to do is quit his job, move his personal belongings, and the house returns to the club to be occupied by the following professional. Janet has yet to make arrangements concerning the sale of her small condo near the University, knowing that it will go quickly, suspecting that the University may still be monitoring her comings and goings.

The communication plans of using FedEx between the group have been working without flaws, keeping everyone updated on recent developments, new changes, and recommendations. Mark and Susan have desired to have another gathering at the house before the great getaway and have established the coming Easter week as most beneficial to all.

The latest developments about the Island have been put aside as unimportant for media coverage, while the UN is continually monitoring the minute changes the landscape undergoes as the rains, sun, and nature bring life to formerly dead zones. Trees have been sprouting. Wildflowers are blooming. Birds have migrated. The volcano cones have filled with water. Rivers and streams are nourishing the flat lands. Beaches are being transformed as the stones and ashes dissolve into sand. The UN has secretly forced the US government and other major developed countries to take a back seat stance, meaning wait and follow the direction of their esteemed scientists.

Jim has also learned of other small independent groups having intense curiosity about the island becoming an oasis for them; one of them was of the apocalyptic Jim Jones type, another is a group of white separatists, a group from Russia wanting to escape religious persecution and one from as far away as Afghanistan desiring to establish an Islamic state.

Political unrest has hit the United States. Numerous protests across the land have been the focus of the news as political action groups are demanding more and more rights. Big labor is demanding more, and big business donates more. The riot police were called out to quell one of the riots in New York that violently broke out, destroying stores and government buildings. The Department of Homeland Security went on alert in every state and large city, monitoring Americans.

Jim wonders if America will go the same way as other great countries have done previously. His business has also suffered over the past few years, feeling the burden of regulations and the fears of an uncertain future for growth. The demands on his time to forge new opportunities are overwhelming. He knows where he would expand if the business climate were more positive, but that remains elusive, so until those positive economic influences return, he must hold onto what he has. He can't leave. He must remain and hold tight.

Mark is in the perfect condition to leave, and Jim is jealous of that, now wishing he had sold out a few years ago when he was approached by a mega-conglomerate offering him the chance of a lifetime, but he hesitated, and they withdrew the offer. Now, the company is uninterested and holding back on expansion plans.

The end of the year comes near with the Christmas holiday celebrated on the farm with just Melody attending, as their plans to visit Bruce and Wendy were canceled when Susan's parents called and asked to spend Christmas there on the farm, driving across the Midwest from Indianapolis.

George and Thomas are spending Christmas with the families of their wives, Ruth and Anabele, knowing that this would be the only time they would have to enjoy the relationships. George and Ruth traveled to St. Louis, and Thomas and Anabele flew to Florida. Melody was able to get home to North Platte for Christmas.

At her modest childhood home in western St. Louis, Ruth and George were relaxing in the living room the evening after Christmas when the conversation touched on the direction of US politics. Her father indicated he had heard of rich businessmen leaving the country and finding more favorable tax havens elsewhere. He also was upset with how half as many Americans could feel good about being on welfare, and how the feds encouraged people to get on the dole, making it easier by redefining the terms and finding more reasons to seek federal help. Feeling double guilt about releasing information of their plans and not informing her parents, Ruth was unable to keep silent; she opened up and told her parents of their future move, despite the objections from George.

"Mom, Dad, I've got some news for you." Ruth starts.

Ruth's mother, Megan, excitedly questions, "You're pregnant?"

"No, Mom, I'm not, and that's not the news. George and I …
"

George interrupts, "Ruth, we shouldn't, did we not agree?"

"No, I must, as I may never see them again."

Her dad, Ralph, perks up and says, "Now you got my full attention. What would cause you to say that you may never see us again?"

Ruth starts, telling them of the move to the new island in the Pacific. When, who is going, why, and what they expect. "It's an adventure I'm looking forward to, and, yes, I'm in my right mind, and I cannot be talked out of it."

Both her dad and mom were upset, thinking of the dangers and that they might never see their daughter again, questioning how she could give up their comforts for uncertainty on a volatile island. Ralph blamed George and his father. No amount of reasoning persuaded her parents that their daughter had not been overwhelmed by the riches of the Tebonsons. Her father agreed that the country's political atmosphere was terrible, but to throw away everything was insanity. "Surely, it couldn't be that bad. It was just one of those political phases that will pass." Her mother was overwhelmed with emotions, leaving the room and retreating into the privacy of the bedroom.

Ruth and George continued to explain to her father the safety precautions they had taken and, in detail, the preparations they had already made, the supplies they would bring, and that they felt they would be more secure and safer there than here in the States.

On some areas, Ralph agreed but was still in fear for his daughter.

Ruth tried again to relieve her mother of her fears, when her mother yelled angrily, telling her, "Leave now. I lost my daughter. How could you? I didn't bring up a daughter to run away? Get out now?"

Packing her bags, Ruth was in tears as she said goodbye to her dad, making him promise not to reveal to anyone what she had told him, and then loudly, through the locked bedroom door, said, "bye Mom, I love you."

Driving away from the home, George tried to console Ruth, when she told George, "Just drive and get me home, please."

In Florida, at the retirement home of her parents, Anabele and Thomas had a fantastic time, as all of her siblings were able to get home for the holidays. There were nine of them, plus six spouses squeezing together around the large dining room table, contributing to the lively talk as the grandchildren played away in an adjoining room. Anabele has reasserted over and over again that a big family is a blessing. However, she is convinced that two children would be enough for her, remembering her parents' sacrifices while she, her brothers, and sisters were growing pains. And sometimes she grows cold to the idea of having any children. There was always some sort of turmoil. Does she really want a big family? Her father asks if there was a chance that a holiday in the future, there could be forty-nine grandchildren running around the house. It is easy for him to wish, as he gets to see them come and then see them go.

On telling her family of the upcoming move, she declared to Thomas that she trusted her family but was unsure of their spouses, so she determined that she would not indicate to anyone that they were moving to an island in the Pacific. She kept that promise but wanted to get her brothers and sisters together and inform them. She hesitated, yet she was unsure that the plans would be kept secret. Anabele is hoping that she would have one more chance sometime later this spring before the big day. Either way, she is preparing a letter explaining everything that would be mailed to her family members the day they left the harbor in Anchorage.

Janet spent the Christmas holidays with her parents in Omaha, arriving two days before a significant sixteen inches of snow fell on Christmas Eve. Janet was the only child, as her mother was diagnosed with MS shortly after her birth. Her father has worked as a reporter for the Omaha Times newspaper for forty years, retiring two years ago, but still writes articles on subjects of special interest to himself. Christmas day found the three of them having a Turkey dinner catered in the day before, warmed up that morning and served with wine, as the conversations went from her trips with the UN to the island to whether or not she will ever get married again and her classes at the university. Janet notices her mother's worsening effects of MS compared to their meeting last year. She now uses a walker to go anywhere. Janet tries to engage her father in political talk. Still, as a journalist, he has kept his political thoughts away from personal relationships, saying it's best to leave politics at the office. During his years as an on-site reporter, he has seen the worst of humanity. Reading his articles, Janet knows that her father is a staunch liberal. He dismisses any opinions she offers as immaterial, and rarely do they get into a discussion of political matters.

"It was nice to get home again," Janet tells her parents as she is packing her bags for the drive back to Texas, wishing them a Happy New Year and saying she will see them again this spring after the semester.

Before leaving town, she called to check in with Bruce and Wendy about their Christmas holiday. "Come on over." Wendy invites her. "We've had a quiet Christmas here, as Mark and Susan couldn't make it."

"Sure, I'd love to see you guys before I head back to school," Janet responds. "We can catch up on each other's plans. This snow is still causing problems on some of the highways, and I'll need extra time going south to warmer weather, so I can't stay long."

"Welcome to Omaha." Wendy hugs Janet, entering their home of the last ten years. Comfortably seated in the living room, the conversations quickly go to the plans each has made and is making. When they are away from Mark's radar, they also wonder if they are doing the right thing for themselves. Bruce will be giving up his golfing career, which is satisfying and fun. Wendy will be sacrificing her medical career, which she knows will only expand as more and more people are having various surgeries performed. Janet will be tossing a lucrative and promising educational tenured professorship out the window.

Janet added that the prospects of meeting someone to love again on an island with only her friends would be nil.

Then Wendy adds, "Yes, but. Sure, we'll leave this good life behind us, our comforts, and the many friends we've established. Still, we also realize that if the political atmosphere does not change, and in all probability, it won't, then the chance of our comforts continuing unabated is also bleak. We've seen the signs. I see it in the hospital. Janet, you've experienced it firsthand. And Bruce, too, has had run-ins with the bureaucrats and code enforcers on those golf course projects he designed and helped develop."

Bruce tells Janet that on the last planned project on previously used farmland, the EPA declared half the property as wetlands, shutting down the planned community. Bruce adds, "I'm now wondering if any new courses will ever be approved considering the environmental decrees. Twenty years ago, none of us saw this coming, but since 9/11, the government has grown by leaps and bounds. We're not the only ones predicting the demise of America. There's the move to regulate talk radio and put the entire news network under the direct control of PBS, telling the public that the lies and misinformation put forth by the independents are not in the country's best interests. They've become divisive."

"You've heard it before," Wendy continues. "We have two choices, maybe three: submit and go with the flow, keeping to our little world, hoping our lifestyle will not be affected. Or move to the island starting under our radar, and the third choice does not appear very promising either; we stay and fight the system."

Janet tells Wendy, "Well said. That summarizes our situation. I've got to get on the road, wanting to get a couple hundred miles behind me today. It's always good to visit you guys and keep the FedEx coming. See you sometime this spring."

"Bye Janet. Be careful on the road. There's always some idiot out there who's paying more attention to the cell phone than the road," Bruce warns her.

Two days before Christmas, Mark, Susan, and Melody, who just arrived from Denver, are pondering over the photos of the island detailing several of the most promising spots to set up camp and build their little community. Over the past few weeks, they have been piecing together the hundreds of pictures taken of the island into a three-by-six-foot puzzle, taping together the adjoining pictures according to the coordinates of each so that he could hang the panorama on a wall, photographing it. Comparing the two side by side, they notice the differences nature performed.

When Melody arrived, Mark and Susan had just cleared off the dining room table, placed the panorama on the table, and looked at the various areas of the island that appeared to be the ideal location to land and start building. They agree on one that seems to be the most diverse: a harbor located near the southeastern edge of the island with a plateau easily accessible from the beach where they predict the homes could be built overlooking the beach with a peninsula jetting out and shielding the harbor from the ocean. They each remember noticing the area on the last flight. The width of the harbor is over a mile. A valley north of the plateau looks suitable for growing their crops. A couple of volcanoes rise forty-five hundred feet north of the valley, appearing as flat-topped mountains.

"It looks like the perfect spot," Mark exclaims. "From the plateau, a road could be built sometime in the future to other parts of the island, one going north between the two volcanoes and one both east and west along the shoreline." Mark affixes a star-shaped sticker on the spot, noting its coordinates as identified by the cameras. "What do you think Mel?"

Not answering the question, Melody shifts gears in the conversation, sharing with her parents that she is sometimes unsure if this is the right move for her. She confesses that she has made peace with the experience of the rape and has been noticing some men. She tells them she started dating recently and is ready to enter a relationship when the right guy comes along. Her dates were OK, but there was no connection, no desire to have a repeat. Both of the guys were from the singles group at church. She wonders if moving to the island would remove any chance of meeting a guy and falling in love.

Susan says, "That's wonderful, Mel. We're happy for you."

Mark reaches across the table, grabbing his daughter's hands, "You've just made my day. I love you."

"Mom, Dad, what am I to do now? I want to go, but that nagging thought about being out there where there will be no opportunity to meet any men, and I'll end up as a single woman who will be all alone for the rest of my life is driving me up the wall. I had to tell you."

Susan asks, "How long has it been since you made peace with it?"

Melody answers, "Oh, it happened just after Thanksgiving. A minister was invited to speak to us singles about the church and homosexuality. There were about thirty of us in the meeting. I had chosen a seat in the back of the room where I could exit without much disturbance. In his talk, he related some stories of other singles, their troubles, and their turmoil in dealing with previous hurtful events. At first, I was bored and sitting there, not paying too much attention, but then something in his remarks touched me. His message penetrated my heart, and all of a sudden, I started weeping and then crying.

"After the end of his remarks, as everyone was leaving, the minister approached me while I was wiping tears away. He said he noticed that I was crying during his talk and then asked if I had been dealing with same-sex attraction issues. I told him no, never had, that's not it. Then I found myself telling him about my rape experience, and the crying started again. He listened to it all and held me until the crying abated. He prayed. Blessed me.

"And then, walking out to my car, joy suddenly came over me. I jumped and kicked my heels together like a kid joyfully playing. Several times. I was free again. Joy just swept over me. I felt like I could look in the eyes, the dirty rotten kid who tore me apart and ruined my life for years, and say, 'God loves you. I forgive you.'

"Oh, mom, it's been fantastic. I've never felt so peaceful."

"Ah, Melody, that's great," Susan says as the tears start falling down her cheeks. "Your dad and I have been concerned about this for some time now, and we're so happy for you. I'll always remember this Christmas as the year my daughter was set free."

Mark continues holding Melody's hands, looking at her as if he was seeing a new person, the life in her eyes radiating out.

Melody started crying, "I've wanted to tell you this since I walked in the door an hour ago, but you guys were so intent on looking over the pictures of the island that I couldn't break through until you had picked the perfect spot."

Mark says, "I'm sorry, Mel. Before you arrived, your Mom and I had just retrieved the pictures and laid them all on the table. Then you came, and well, I assumed you'd be very interested in helping us search the pictures for clues."

Susan says, "We didn't even give you a chance to say anything. We brought you to the table as if you had been here all week. Sorry, Mel."

Controlling her tears, Melody says, "That's all right, you didn't have a clue that anything had changed. But now that you know, what are we going to do? What am I going to do?"

"Hmmm?" Mark ponders. "I don't know. This changes things for you. Yes, you're right, there won't be any men on the island, just your brothers, Bruce, and I. Janet, is in the same boat as you are, if that's any consolation. We want you to come along, but that's your decision. I've also tried to make that known to your brothers, and I hope they're not coming along to please us. You'll have to make that decision, and, Mel, whatever you decide, you'll be loved and missed if you stay here, and we'd be blessed by having you join us."

"I know, Dad. You have not pressured me. I want to govern my own life. I feel more in charge now than ever."

Susan adds, "Mel, you will make the right decision for you. You do what you know is right for you. You've got your whole life in front of you, as you're only twenty-eight, whereas your dad and I have lived most of our lives. It's behind us, and we're sliding downhill now, just eight years shy of that proverbial retirement age."

"Dad?" Melody asks. "Do you think that sometime, not too far in the future, other peoples will come and make the island their home?"

Mark ponders, "Well, of course I do. When and who are the unknown. From what I've already heard, a church pastor in Atlanta, I think, is on record as desiring to move out there. If there's one, there'll be more, is the old saying about human behavior. Sometime in the future, thousands will be living there. That will happen if, and here's that big IF, if the various governments, specifically the UN, do not quarantine the island and physically prevent anyone from visiting. Or any other scenario could happen. We don't know what's in store. The UN does not know. No one does. We are taking that risk. It could be disastrous for us. I've kept a positive attitude, wanting to be the first to build something, a home on the island, claiming possession. We haven't gone off half-cocked about this move. It's been planned, researched, and examined from just about every conceivable angle we thought about.

"We're ready, Mel. We're just waiting a few more months to accomplish a few additional details, so once there, we can start and will not have to return to gathering additional tools or supplies we forgot. We've planned this well enough to last us at least a year. To answer your question, Mel, other people will make the island home too, but when and who, is the sixty-four-dollar question."

"Thanks, Dad, I was thinking the same thing," Melody responds. "I'll have to come to grips with one or the other soon. If only I had made peace with the rape right afterward, then things would be different now. Perhaps I would have found my love and been the first to bring you a grandchild. I always wanted to beat George and Thomas at everything."

Susan says, "Mel, take your time. There's always that IF. Yeah, Hey. We did not get to tell you, but Grandpa and Grandma are coming over. I think they'll be here later today or tomorrow.

Melody says, "That's great. How many years has it been since I've seen them? Three, maybe four years? How are they doing?"

Susan says, "They must be feeling pretty spry to drive that distance from Indianapolis. Physically they're in good shape, no diseases, no major health problems, nothing crippling, just what is known as old timers hindrances. They left three days ago, saying they would take their time. I've been expecting a call anytime, but Dad can be stubborn, not wanting to let on that he can't make the trip like he did in one day. Mom, well, she's getting stubborn too and does not want anyone fussing over her, and sometimes the two of them fuss with each other over fussing over each other. He won't call until he can't find the right road off 83 to get here. Mark offered them a GPS device for the car, but Dad said paper maps would do just fine."

"I'm so glad I came home for Christmas," Melody says. "This will always be my home. Thank you for being the best. I've not always been the best for you, yet you kept being there for me when I needed you, even when I pushed you away. And now Grandpa and Grandma are coming. What a perfect Christmas. I can't wait to sit down and listen to his stories. Now, I'm going to cry again."

"You're going to have me bawling too," Susan tells Melody. "Here, let's you and I get busy baking a few pies and a cake for them. And Mark, You should put those maps away, as we don't want to hurry to get them out of sight if they suddenly drive up."

"Ok, yeah, and while you are baking away, I'm going to print out copies of these maps to FedEx to the gang," Mark responds.

Several hours have passed as Susan and Melody have worked away in the kitchen baking a chocolate delight, a favorite of grandma, an apple crumb, a favorite of grandpa, and a three-layer coconut cream cake. Mark has been busy on the computer printing out the maps on eight-and-a-half-by-fourteen-inch sheets, which he has taped together, forming a three by six-foot map folded and inserted in the FedEx pre-postmarked envelopes ready to go to Bruce and Wendy, Janet, and to George and Thomas. He has also written a letter explaining his reasons for selecting the spot, placing a star on the map as the location of their proposed landing and settlement area. He also seeks Janet's thoughts as she has been to the island several times with the UN crews.

Entering the kitchen, Mark tells Susan that he noticed the weather forecast predicts another snowstorm approaching from the north due to arrive later that evening, possibly dumping another foot on top of the sixteen inches" already on the ground. He asked Susan if she wanted to call her dad and see where they were and when they expected to arrive.

"Thanks for the update. I will." Susan replies.

Dialing the number, it rings and rings, and finally, her mother answers, "Hello, Sue."

"Hello, Mom, where are you guys?"

"Oh, we're just around the corner. We would have been there, but Bernie missed the turn-off again, just like last time, and we had to turn around. But right now, I can see you in the kitchen window. Come on out and help Dad. He's had a hard time driving among all the idiots out here on your roads."

Rushing to open the front door, they run out to the car, waving their arms in total glee. Mark goes to the driver's side, opening the door for Bernhard, while Susan and Melody greet Grandma Sophia, who is already out of the vehicle.

"Come on, let's get inside. Mark will get your luggage." Susan announces. "You must be tired. Have you eaten yet?"

They arrived at four-thirty, leaving Indianapolis three days before, right after breakfast. No, too bad, considering that most of the area was covered in snow, slowing Bernhard down from his usual seventy mph highway speed, making it to Urbana, Illinois, the first day and St. Joseph, Missouri, the second night.

"You can discern a lot about a State driving on these highways," Bernhard says. "Illinois was the worst, just miserable compared to Missouri and Nebraska. It was three days after that big snowstorm, and many miles of the highways had only one lane of traffic open. We saw four snow plows sitting in a rest area. Broken down, perhaps, or just taking one of those union-mandated breaks."

Sophia tells Bernhard to quench it. "Don't get off on a rant right away, Bernie. We just got here. Say hello first."

"Hey, you say hello, and I'll sing Hell-O Dolly. I was sure they'd ask how the roads were, so I just beat 'em to the punch."

Chapter 15

Sitting comfortably in the living room with a fresh cup of coffee and a slice of pie, Sophia brings up Bernhard's latest physical exam. "The doctor said your father is in good physical condition, and I'm not too bad off either, Susan, but I'm beginning to wear down quicker than before. We might make it another ten years, but these long trips are hard on us. We wanted to see you guys, so here we are. We only drove four to five hours a day when we had the camper. We made it, and I'm glad I insisted on coming."

"I'm the one who insisted on coming. You wanted to play it safe." Bernhard responds.

"Well, Mom," Susan says. "We're glad you came, but I was worried about you making the trip, especially in this weather. There's another snowstorm approaching us for later tonight. We will have a White Christmas."

Sophia congratulates Susan and Mark on the beautiful Christmas tree. "So fresh looking." She says. "You must have cut one of your trees."

"No," Susan replies. "We get our trees from a local tree farm each year."

Turning to look at Melody, Sophia says, "Melody, you're as gorgeous as ever. I'm so glad you are here. Have you fallen in love yet?"

Responding, Melody says, "No, Grandma, love is still out there somewhere. But I'm thrilled to see you again. You're looking good. You two haven't changed a bit."

"Ha," Bernhard replies, "You ought to see us when we're relaxed." And then he asks, "Melody, are you still working for that government agency taking care of the helpless?"

"Yes, Grandpa, I am. They're not all helpless. Some of them have had a horrible time of it, getting beat up continually by a drunk or drug addict, a boyfriend, or husband. It's a depressing job as all I see all day long are those who can't make it on their own, and then, there are the ones who won't even try, and those are increasing dramatically. Discerning the true hardship cases from the perpetual self-victim is difficult. My supervisor tells us, 'don't even try as we might get one lousy case misjudged,' and then the crap will hit the fan. Process quickly and move on to the next case. I'm looking in other areas for work, and when something comes up, I'll be out of there."

Mark announces, "Bernie and Sophia, we're going to take you to town this evening for a great meal in a great historic restaurant you haven't been to yet. Ok? So, if you need to freshen up a bit, let's plan on leaving in an hour. And don't give me any back talk."

The four of them were comfortably seated in Jeffers Depot when Bernie took leave from the table to walk around peering at the pictures, the antique signs, the miniature trains, looking inside the caboose and the dining car, stopping to read some of the framed news articles from the twenty's to forty's about trains. While he was off on his own, Sophia reminisced of her experiences taking the train to and from college and the trip she and her parents took to California from Indiana. When Bernie rejoins the table, he tells of how his father worked the evening shift building the freight cars at a factory in Pennsylvania while, at the same time, an early shift at the local newspaper running the presses to save enough to buy one of the first Fords.

"Today's generation has no idea what it was like back then in this country," Bernie says. "They're a bunch of spoiled rotten no goods, throwing a fit if the school-provided lunch lacked a little mustard. My parents and Sophia's folks, too, spent a month on a ship together to get here from Germany right before Hitler became popular in the mid-thirty's. They arrived with little to nothing but the clothes on their backs, knowing little English, and dag gone it, no cell phones to text back and forth to their friends back in Garmisch. Somehow, they made it to western Pennsylvania, picking up English as they worked. Then, the stock market burst a few months after they got settled. Imagine how young people today would handle the situation if they were suddenly put in my parents' shoes."

Mark says, "Now, that would make a great survivor show for TV. I'd like to see one based on that."

Sophia adds to Bernhard's account, "Yes, Bernie's parents and my parents stayed close during those times, and they both eventually moved to farming territory in Indiana, where we were born and raised. Those were tough years, but we didn't know it was tough. It was just life. We made it, and the tomorrow was always considered to be better than today, and look at us now."

Sophia then adds, "I went to a tattoo shop, and the artist couldn't find any unwrinkled skin."

Surprised, Susan says, "Mom, you're joking, right?

"Of course, dear," Sophia responds. "I see these young girls who've gone and had tattoos on their ankles, their necks, arms, back sides, and who knows where else, and I picture them sixty years later in a nursing home stretching their skin to show the others. Why do they do it?"

"I think they call it liberation," Susan says.

Melody asks, "Grandpa, tell us the story of your experience in the army in the sixty's."

"Well, since you asked," Bernhard says. "I enlisted right out of high school. I had just turned eighteen. I did so many dumb things back then. I was messed up and did not know what I wanted to do. Somehow, I thought like a meaningless, unprincipled, indecisive hippie, so I enlisted to get away. I gave the responsibility of my life to the Army. After basic training, I was sent to Nurnberg and then to Berlin. Berlin was enclosed in East Germany, half of the city under Soviet control, the other half under the Allies as a consensus to the West. I was on patrol one day when some Soviet tanks and troops appeared at the gate, closing it, and then started building the wall separating the two parts of Berlin. For those fifteen years under Soviet control, so many people had left the east communist side for the western side of Berlin; the Soviets were losing their workers. They blamed 'the fascists of the west,' so they constructed the walls to keep people from leaving East Berlin. I saw people jumping out of their second and third-floor windows to escape, risking life itself. I saw people cutting through the barbed wire to make a dash across the fenced in area to freedom, risking getting shot by guards in the towers. Some did. At the time, I didn't understand why people would do that, except that communism was bad. That's what we were told.

"But what was so bad about communism? I was just a kid back then. I didn't know anything. Sharing resources seemed like a good idea then, as no one would go to bed hungry. When I got out of the army, I went back to college, choosing a major in sociology and psychology. I almost enlisted in the Peace Corps, wanting to save the world, not realizing I was the one needing to be saved from stupidity."

Bernie further adds, "During my tour, I was able to see where my parents came from. A town called Garmisch, right at the base of the Alps. What a beautiful town that is. My cousin is still living there."

Melody adds, "Throughout history, countries have built walls to keep people out, as protection from invaders. The US is being invaded, and our leaders stall at building a wall. Our leaders must have flunked history."

"No," Bernie says. "Our leaders think they are smarter than history. Think of how illegal immigrants are now rewarded. No special privileges were provided to my parents. They worked hard, and they had to learn English fast. Heck, now the feds have even encouraged firearms to be shipped across the border, and one of our own border agents got killed by one of those rifles."

"Bernie, let's talk of something else besides politics all the time," Sophia says. "Susan, you know we sold our camper."

Susan answers, "Yes, I heard that. You had some wonderful times camping all over the country. Do you miss it?"

"Yes, I do. At times, I wished we still had it. We saw it all, and this really is a marvelous country." Sophia responds. "We met a lot of wonderful people wherever we stopped. Bernie would play golf, I'd sit back and read, and the evenings were around a campfire. But we can't do that kind of traveling anymore. It's become too tiring for both of us. We want to settle down."

Mark asks, "Bernie, are you still playing golf?"

Bernie says, "I play maybe once a week during decent weather, sometimes more. My game is not like it used to be, but I still enjoy getting out there with the guys. That camper life was a dream of mine for years. I tried to plan the trips from one golf course to another, never driving more than two hundred miles a day. In those five years, we drove over a hundred thousand miles. Maybe more. And I've played on over fifty golf courses in almost every state. But, dang it, I missed Iowa, Mississippi, Alaska, and of course, Hawaii. Played some in Canada too. I saved all of those scorecards."

As they were about ready to leave the restaurant, the train brought the picture of them and the bill, and Peter Jeffers approached the table to greet Mark and Susan.

Susan introduces her father and mother. "Mom, Dad, this is Peter Jeffers. He created this restaurant. His grandfather was with the Union Pacific railroad company."

"You've got a fantastic place here, Mr. Jeffers. We've enjoyed it. The pictures and signs have brought back many memories of the past. My dad worked building trains when they first arrived in America." Bernie says.

"Yes, trains were a very important part of America's expansion into the west." Mr Jeffers says. "Thank You for coming. Mark, when are you guys leaving?"

Shaking his head back and forth, indicating to Peter not to say anything more about the future, Mark says, "Peter, are you going anywhere for the holidays?"

Bernie picks up on the subject, asking: "Mark, You're leaving?

Susan then says, "Hey, let's go home and relax. We've had another great time here, Peter, but we need to get home before the next snows."

Peter then says, "I just looked at the weather, and that storm is expected to arrive in a couple of hours. Thanks for coming, and it was good to meet you, Sophia, and Bernie."

As they stand getting ready to leave, Sophia asks Susan. "Where are you going, dear?"

"Come on; let's get home before the storm," Susan responds.

Whispering to Mark, Peter apologizes for the question about the move, saying, "I'm sorry, but being Susan's parents, I assumed they have been informed."

"It's Ok, Peter," Mark softly responds. "Not yet, they haven't."

Arriving home, they all sit down to a fresh cup of coffee and slices of pie and cake, chatting about previous Christmases and the updates about what George and Thomas have been doing when Bernie asks again, "You're leaving? What? Where to?

"Mark, they should know," Susan says.

"Yes, they should." Mark answers. "Go ahead."

Susan starts informing her parents about their plans to move to that new island, who is going, and why. She also briefly explains how they have stocked up on supplies, hoping they'll last a year or more.

Bernie and Sophia listen intently, and after a few minutes of the explanations, Bernie interrupts his daughter with questions;

"are you sure about this? When did it all start, why, what do you intend to accomplish, and why not stay here and fight the system?

For each question, Mark or Susan filled in more details. She injected the reasons the kids were joining them, trying to reassure her parents they were not going off half-baked, that they had researched the island, that Janet had been there several times, and trying to assure them that they would be fine.

"Mark, get the map out and show them your pictures," Susan tells him.

Laying the map out in front of them on the dining room table, they look it over, and Bernie says, "Mark, I think you should stay here and fight the system. One person can still do wonders in this country. You could get the media to help get your message out. The church could help, and a few representatives in Washington realized the country is going downhill fast and needs to reverse the tide. Mark, you guys are giving up. I'm surprised you want to give in and not fight here at home."

Mark responds, "The days of fighting the system are over Bernie. The media, entertainment industry, and big corporation lobbyists run things now. They've got their special relationships and a direct hallway to the Oval Office and the back rooms of Congress, getting their special deals worked out. If anyone gets in the way, the media will pounce on them. Remember the guy who asked the president a simple tax question that exposed the wannabe president as a socialist? Sure, the guy became a hit with the conservative movement, but the media tore into his background, exposing him as a liar. But the question he asked was legitimate. The media tormented him as a lunatic. He was hung out to dry on every media outlet around.

"When a lie is told over and over by the media, people begin to accept it. That's a big part of the problem now. The people are not being leveled with and don't even know it, don't want to know it, and don't even care as long as they have their toys to play with. Only fifty-four percent of Americans made the effort to vote."

"It's not the same anymore. In your generation, the average American read the daily newspapers and the weekly magazines, which you can't find anymore. The only magazines I see in the stores are women's gossip and beauty magazines, men's body-building magazines, those about cars and hobbies, and those girly magazines, too."

Sophia adds, "Yes, you're right about the reading material. It's aimed at supplying the interests of tenth graders. Bernie bought me a Kindle to use, but the materials put up front to read are geared to the younger crowd, and I'm not interested in the e-books available through the library, so I don't use it much. It's gathering dust. I still prefer paper books. We go to bookstores, and I buy what interests me, mystery novels and some history."

Bernie adds, "I'm still disappointed that you won't stay and put up a fight. The country needs people like you to make a stand."

Mark responds by informing them of his run-ins with the bureaucrats over the leases to the acreage, over the Halloween displays, his personal jet, his software business, his inventions, the solar magnifier, his radar nullifier, over the dispute while working in the Justice department, about the drones, even his recent investigation by his local representative seeking to stop the camp fires. He tells them how the politicians demanded that his solar invention must be for the public good, that it was wrong and selfish to keep it in private hands, picking and choosing who would get to use it, rather than equally sharing it, allowing the poor to enjoy the usefulness of such an item.

"My defense went on deaf ears. They did not want to hear that I do not choose who gets to use it, but private customers would choose by paying for it. To them, private contracts are selfish, and lawyers have made them so complicated that they're easily broken.

"I believe America is too far gone; it is being destroyed from within by our passivity. I'm tired of it all, and we're getting out." Mark says. "That's final, and we'll be leaving this spring sometime. We'll have our cell phones and computers so we can keep in contact. And, did not your parents escape the despotism of Germany by coming to America for freedom?   We're doing the same."

Susan adds to these comments, saying, "Mom, Dad, yes, I wholeheartedly approve of this move. Look at the map; it's going to be wonderful, a bit physically rugged at first, but so what? We can handle that. We have plans to grow the food we need, and we're taking some chickens along for eggs, and eventually to eat. The weather will be somewhat like it is in San Francisco on the southern side, while on the northern side, we expect weather similar to that in Canada. We'll be fine. And with Mark's seaplane, we can return to the States in less than five hours."

Sophia responds, "Well, if your mind is made up, then we'll support your adventure. We'll miss you. We've been miles away all these years; another couple thousand miles won't make it seem much further. Is there anything we can do to help?"

"I want them to stay and fight," Bernhard adds. "I can't hide my disappointment. This country needs people like Mark to stand up, to speak out, forcing them to take the original documents seriously. Do as some of our great statesmen have done in the past, Mark. You could make a difference."

Mark asks, "Would you like to come along with us?"

"No!" Sophia quickly answers,

"No, I don't desire to start over," Bernhard loudly says. "To live in a tent for the rest of my life, wondering where the next meal will come from. No, I like to sit back in my recliner, watching football and baseball and reading. You guys are making a big mistake."

"Well, you guys could fight over this for days," Sophia tells them. "I'm tired, and I'm going to turn it."

"Good idea," Susan says. "Santa is coming soon, so let's be good children and go to bed."

The snow starts to fall during the wee hours of Christmas morning, adding another six inches of white fluffy flakes by the time they arise, with more big white flakes still falling.

"I'm dreaming of a white Christmas' Bernie hums as he looks out the patio deck door toward the row of tall trees with their branches gently bending toward the ground under the weight of fresh, wet snow.

"It's beautiful here," Sophia says, joining Bernie at the door. "Look at it. There's something magical about a snow-covered landscape on Christmas morning. I want to go out there and make an angel. Come on, Bernie, Let's do it. Get our coats, and let's be kids for five minutes."

Overhearing her parents' plans, Susan retrieves her jacket and camera to capture the moment standing on a chair on the deck, focusing downward to catch the full images of the snow angels side by side. "Fantastic, Mom, I'll be taking these pictures with me.'

Mark is busy in the office searching for news concerning the new island, finding zero updates, this being a holiday time all over the world. The major headline story was of Santa Claus finishing his delivery route and returning to the North Pole.

Another headline read, 'Santa missed these children,' a story of children in parts of America who woke early expecting to find presents wrapped in beautiful paper, tied with bows, but finding nothing. 'Millions of children get nada' is another headline on a popular media site. 'Happy Holidays' takes up a major news organization's website's central portion. Another headline reads, 'Christian's heap presents on each other.' Tired of seeing negative stories about Christmas, Mark closes the computer and joins Susan outside on the deck, saving the moments on her digital camera.

Standing behind Susan, holding her around the waist, Mark says, "They're acting just like we did when the kids were all here." Running through the deck and jumping in the snow next to Bernie and Sophia, Melody is forming another angel. Then she leans back, her arms reaching out for a handful of the fresh snow, throwing the ball of snow toward her mom and dad, calling, "Come on, let's have a good snow ball fight. Sissy, sissy, sissy."

Mark reaches down and tosses one in Melody's' direction, and the fun begins. Bernie is quick to send one at Melody. Mark at Bernie, another toward Melody. Melody at Bernie, and a soft one toward Sophia. Bernie at Mark, and then a quick one toward Susan, still on the deck. Mark tosses a soft high ball at Sophia, and a hard-liner hits Melody in her left thigh as she escapes around the corner, starting to roll snow together, assembling a snowman. Sophia gets up and walks toward the deck, getting a direct hit from Bernie on her backside. She turns, shouting at Bernie, "That's enough, boys."

Susan snaps more pictures, shielding the camera from the oncoming snowballs, and then calls out, "Breakfast, anyone?" Turning to enter the kitchen, she calls back, "Leave your boots outside, please."

"Come on, Mom, let's do breakfast together."

Refreshed by their enthusiasm for a white Christmas, they enjoy the full-fledged breakfast of scrambled eggs, pancakes, sausage links, and toast with orange juice and coffee.

While enjoying the huge breakfast, the conversation shifts back and forth from Mark's solar magnifier, to Melody's work with DHS in Denver, the island in the Pacific, and more details of Bernie and Sophia's camping trips in the national forests and campgrounds.

After breakfast, Mark and Melody get excused to work with the tractor backhoe bucket to remove the snow from their driveway, creating a pile at least twelve feet high, and then plow the half-mile gravel road, where they meet another farmer plowing his road out to the thoroughfare gravel road that leads to highway 83. The snow is still falling as the local weather forecast predicts an additional six to eight inches before nightfall.

"Finished with round one," Mark, entering the house, announces: "A farmer's work is never done."

The afternoon is spent around the dining room table putting together a thousand-piece jigsaw puzzle and then looking at family pictures.

Whenever Bernie brings up another question about the island and what Mark and Susan expect to accomplish, he again challenges them to stay put and work to change the system. Susan quickly changes the conversation back to a previous family event, like when she was in high school leading the cheerleaders and becoming sweet on a football player. They started dating to the objections of both Mom and Dad.

"You were only fifteen, and that kid was a senior." Bernhard tells Susan. "We felt all he wanted was an evening with you in the back seat. We were right, too. Weren't we?"

"Yes, you were," Susan responds, adding that during nursing school, she wasn't interested in guys, and it wasn't until the summer internship at the resort that she met Mark during a justice department convention, and here we are. She also tells the story again about Mark's proposal on the sidewalk in front of Grand Central Station in Washington DC.

Mark adds his version, "I had planned on taking Susan up to the Lincoln Memorial and propose there at the feet of Lincoln, but as I watched her park the car and walk up to me, I said to myself --- what the hell --- and got down on one knee and asked her right there, as a tour bus unloaded."

Melody enjoys hearing those stories, as does Sophia. Melody asks her mom for more but then says, "Grandma, remember the story you told me of your mother and her ball of string?"

Sophia adds, "Oh yes. Back in those days, Mom saved everything; nothing was thrown away. The only trash that went to the garbage trucks was containers. No food was ever thrown away. We had to eat everything on our plates before leaving the table, and if there was anything left in the bowls, it was saved and used again to be blended into a hash of some sort. The ball of string started out marble size and ended up the size of a softball. She would save any length of string. It could be just a five-inch piece coming off a hem of a dress or a five-foot piece left over from wrapping boxes to send to the military boys in Europe. She would wind them all together on the ball. It was just that everything had to be saved and used again when needed."

Mark says, "I love that illustration. It shows just how the government has grown and grown into a huge bureaucratic ball of twine, one piece of legislation on top of another until it has become a monstrosity that no one could unwind. Someone said that a government program is the nearest thing to eternal life on this planet."

So goes the Christmas holidays for the five of them. Family stories, both good and the other ones too, and some remembrances were questionable.

Two days later, the roads are clear enough for Melody to make the trip back to Denver, but the roads to the east are still snow-packed and icy; too risky for Bernhard and Sophia to leave, so they settle in for a few more nights and more time to discuss the move to an island out in the Pacific. Filling them in on more details, Mark still cannot convince Bernhard of the wisdom of such an adventure, so he changes the subject whenever Bernhard asks an additional question.

Mark asks, "Tell us some more of your travels from one campground to another."

Bernie says, "We really enjoyed the people we met along the way. We've met some fantastic folks, some we still keep in contact with, and we have had great times chatting over the campfires. But you know that the Forest Service banned campfires now, claiming that they've got to do everything within their power to stop those forest fires, claiming that it's possible that people like us could have been responsible for the California fires. Yeah, right. People like us. Of all the people we've met in these campgrounds, not one of them would have been irresponsible in leaving the embers of a smoldering campfire unattended all night, nor would they build a fire so big it could get out of control. We have encountered those who would have though. They come and go in the pick-ups, usually with large dogs and even pit bulls in the back. They leave their site a mess of trash, beer bottles, and other stuff. At night, they play their rock music so loud the rangers can hear it in their homes a mile away. I confronted one of those once about the loud music, and he told me to mind my own business, Grandpa. "If you don't like it, tough."

"One day, we pulled into the campground at Yosemite National Park, and a Hollywood film crew was filming a scene," Sophia adds.

"The actors and actresses stayed in the lodge while the crew had these big motor homes right next to us. This was before the campfire ban, so the crew joined us a couple of evenings over marshmallows. They were very nice, just doing a job. But you should have heard the stories they told us about certain actresses and actors, about how self-righteous they are or how they expect to be treated as a celebrity or queen. During the day, we got a chance to view the filming, the behind-the-scenes work moving lights and fixtures in place, and the fuss made over the actress. She had to have a carpet laid down as she walked to the set fifty feet into the woods. I thought of how the queen is treated, and the presidents of some countries, who get bowed down to as kings or Pharaohs.

"After two nights there, we canceled the rest of our reservation and moved on. To a state park. The state parks are not as restrictive as the federal parks, but they also have more local rowdies occupying the campsites over the weekends."

Bernie says, "Remember this: state parks during the week and national parks on weekends."

Bernie adds, "It has changed dramatically over the last five years. Susan, do you remember the times we took you camping? It was more fun. We could relax, enjoy ourselves more, and know we could leave our supplies out while we spent an afternoon at the lake, knowing they'd still be there when we got back. Not now; you've got to lock everything up if you leave for a few hours."

The house phone rings, and Susan, the closest, picks it up to see on the screen 'William Manwalker.' Telling Mark who it is. "Well, go ahead and answer it." Listening for a bit, she hands the phone to Mark, saying: "A journalist and camera crew want to come out and interview you."

"Yes, this is Mark. What can I do for you?"

Holding the phone close to his ear for a short time, Mark responds, "It is none of your business what I do, and I don't care if thousands would be interested. I don't know who your sources are since you won't reveal them. Tell your editor to stick it. What I do is private. None of it is any business of yours. None of it, and I'm not interested in having my face on TV. It's not the business of anyone else, either. Leave us alone and go cover a hurricane somewhere. Good bye."

Mark proceeds to tell them what the journalist told him. "He said he represented News First and Always. They had been informed by someone they would not say. I was taking a group of family members and close friends to that new island in the Pacific, and they wanted to interview me about it. They said it would make great evening news and make me famous. They were interested in the reasons why I would risk everything to move out to an uninhabited island. It would be a great human interest story, and they could do it right here on my farm tomorrow morning. The segment could lead to future talk show interviews. Then, after we were on the island for a year, they would love to feature us again."

Mark then says, "Now, there's an example of our media sticking their nose into the private affairs of private citizens. Many people fall for it, thinking that having their face and name on national TV would improve the situation. But all they get is the kick of saying, "Look, it's me on TV."

Bernhard questions Mark, "How many of these calls have you had?"

"That's the first from the national media, and now I wonder who was their source, who told them because they had some details that have not been released that I know of. Susan, do you know who could have called the media?"

"No, Mark," Susan responds. "Unless that guy who got upset at your Haunted House display. Or, it could have been the local reporter who covered the festival."

Mark says, "Oh, yes, that local reporter. But, we did not reveal our plans to either the reporter or the guy who left in a hissy fit. Remember afterward, the attention we got from the national media. It was just the Halloween Festival that they covered. This will not change our plans, except possibly moving the date up a few months."

Taking a deep breath and settling back into a more comfortable position in the recliner, Mark continues, "I better let this rest, or I'm likely to return the call, invite them out, and then when the camera and mike are on, let them have it good, letting them know how the country would be better off without an invasive national press."

"Gads." Mark continues getting off onto another rant of his. "What business is it of mine that a gang in Detroit ransacked a convenience store? Or, a homeowners association fines a man for parking his boat in his driveway. Those are local issues, not national news, for heaven's sake. News stories like that make us all paranoid. We've got enough on our minds to worry about our next trip to the gas station."

Quickly picking up on Marks's attitude, Susan changes the subject back to the camping trips saying, "Dad, I remember the time we went camping in Canada. We spent an entire week at one site overlooking a magnificent lake of the woods. You rented a small boat, and we did some fishing, rowing, and swimming off the boat far out in the middle of this giant lake. You caught some muskies and trout, which we ate every night. That was fun. You and Mom had a one-room tent, and you bought a pup tent for me, and I got sick of marshmallows. They were so sticky, but you said I ate too many. I also remember a trip we made to New Hampshire. Remember that one?"

Bernie says, "Sure do. We couldn't find a camping site, and it was getting late. Mom was tired. We were all tired, and there were no campsites available for us. Everything was full, even the small hotels were full. We were told the next closest camping area was seventy-five miles away. Driving would have been another couple hours, and the sun was going down fast. Those days, before the internet enabled us to check availability online before heading that way. We stopped in a local café for a bite to eat before taking off for the other campsite. A local farmer heard Mom and I discussing what to do next; he interrupted us and invited us to set up our tents on the shore of a small pond on his 160-acre farm. We stayed there for three days, and he did not charge us one penny and even invited us to enjoy an outdoor Bar-B-Q with his extended family. His sons had girls your age, and you played with them on the tire swing hanging from the big oak tree."

"I remember that," Susan says. "It was one camping trip I wanted to do over, and I begged you to go there the next year."

The phone rings again, indicating it's the mayor, James Olsen. Mark answers, "Hello, James, how are things around town? What can I do for you?" Anxious to hear what is said to Mark, Susan quietly tells him to hit the speaker button so she can listen, too.

". . . a high-rolling News First agent just left the office stating that many people around town are wondering what's going on with you, as the trucks have been busy coming and going into your place over the past months. They said a resident contacted them, suspecting you were planning a trip to that new Island. You had already leased your land, your house had been put on the market, and you were getting ready to move to the new island. The reporter dropped by the office to see if I knew anything. Of course, I told them that any news of any resident in North Platte is private business; in all cases, I hold their private lives as more important than being exposed on national news. I told them I do not divulge any information about my citizens. If any desired national attention, it's their decision, not mine."

"Thanks, James, I appreciate it. But who was the person who called the media?"

"He would not say." James adds, "Yep, the journalist implied that if they could get the broadcast, it would put the town on the map, increasing business and our tax revenues, that he could guarantee that my name would be part of the broadcast, and that would help in the local support I would get. Imagine that. I laughed in his face, and he did not like that much, telling me they could swing the news in the opposite direction. That's when I called my secretary to bring in their coats as they were leaving."

"Thanks, James, and if you ever find out who the informer was, please let me know. No, I won't do anything violent against the guy; just go over and have a nice conversation. You're a good friend, James. Thanks."

"Mark, just like I will not divulge your name to anyone, I can't give you his name either, if I had it," The mayor informs Mark. "Good bye, have a great New Year, Mark."

Chapter 16

New Year's comes and go, and Bernhard and Sophia seize upon a break in the weather, loading up to head back to Indianapolis, tearfully leaving their daughter, knowing that this was probably the last time they'll see Susan and Mark. Bernie indicated he was going to take the northern route home through Iowa, over to Chicago, staying there a few days, as they've got tickets to watch the Colts play the Bears in Soldiers Field, and then south to Indianapolis.

Mark addresses another FedEx letter to the group encouraging them to update their passports and tells them of the call from the media, cautioning each to be careful in all their proceedings. He seeks their input on the best date to leave for Anchorage, offering his opinion that the first of April would be best. The sooner, the better.

The weather on the Island on the first of April would be somewhat like April in southern Oregon: light jackets, cool evenings, and sweatshirts during the day. That would be ideal, as they'd have seven to eight months to prepare for the unknown winter months. Two weeks go by, and Mark receives all the replies with two objecting to the April date: Janet and Anabele, indicating each would prefer to finish the semester. Anabele said she would make that date if necessary, just disappearing, faking a sickness, or some other excuse. Janet said her retirement funds would be downsized if she left under unfavorable conditions. Mark hears from Jim, who is still interested, but the timing is off. He can't possibly make it by April, but he advises Mark to open it up to other people to join the group. In his travels to Russia, Japan, and Hong Kong, he's heard rumors that groups from those countries are interested in setting up communities on the new Island. The UN, he informs Mark, is planning another inspection for the coming summer months. Business associates have asked him what he knows, seeking his advice on whether the island offers opportunities for future expansion or as an escape from the bureaucratic intrusiveness they now face out of Washington and the EU too. Millions have mentioned it on blogs and Facebook pages. In the letter, Jim tells Mark that thousands of people are sincerely interested in escaping the tyranny of large governments, seeing the island as another young free America.

"They would be thrilled to join you." Jim writes back to Mark.

Over the next month, Mark and Susan tend to many details while enjoying their comfortable home. Several times, as they are packing memories to take along, Susan mentions how much she will miss these comforts they secured for themselves. Mark agrees that they've had it well and have been blessed. They could call the whole thing off, relax and live one day at a time, travel, continue with the festival, and take their abundance to local charities.

Then, something on the news reminds them why they are moving. Every so often, a story of local control gone mad makes national attention. One is about a small-time farmer fined by a local council for selling her farm produce to local citizens, even though she had the license to do so, it was just not updated, including the new permits and restrictions, which are very vague as to what percentages of vegetables must be organic. One of the restrictions required her to divert her water from the crops to relieve dusty driveways. Rural areas are usually gravel roads, and dust is considered a nuisance. The country wants farms to be dust-free. Dust has been determined to be an environmental hazard, contaminating water, adding sediment into storm waters, causing health problems for some, and on and on. This lady was also demonized for hosting a private birthday party for less than a dozen local girls without getting a gathering permit beforehand.

When Mark was reading this article, he thought of what could eventually happen right there on his farm for hosting a Halloween festival when some local busybodies get in a position of power. He felt that sooner or later, the festival would be shut down. Sooner or later, he could not donate his abundant veggies to local charities. Sooner or later, he would have to pay fees to operate his solar magnifier. Sooner or later, he would be required to pave the two-hundred-foot gravel entrance to his home. Sooner or later, he would have to buy licenses to operate a business out of his barn, even though it's just a workshop. Sooner or later. It'll be submit, or else.

The freedoms that made America the world's most prosperous country are slowly being removed. One step for man has now become a giant leap for government.

The last week of March has arrived, and it's getting close to their departure, to the time when they will all meet in Anchorage for the loading of the ship and the sound of engines taking them on the adventure of their life. The house was sold to one of the farmers who leased acreage. His equipment has been shipped. Everything has been moved to containers in and near Anchorage.

Mark and Susan have made their last visit to Jeffers Depot. They have said their goodbyes to the church, to the mayor, to their friends and neighbors, hosting a final party of parties on their land, building one of the greatest campfires ever for the thirty-some close friends they've made over the years on the farm.

Would they tell them of the secret move? Mark and Susan have debated this issue over the past few weeks as the time drew close. Let them all in on the secret, or lead them on knowing of the guilty feelings they would have later. They feel an obligation to their close friends, all of them having the same feelings toward the creeping despotism over the past few decades, friends who would possibly desire to forgo the present comforts for freedom just as Mark and Susan are doing.

The weather pattern for this time of year could provide a reasonably warm evening for a campfire, or it could be one of those last blasts of snowfall. Uncertainty plagued them as they contemplated the event. Even the forecasters, with all of their technology, are mute in predicting what's in store a week ahead. Mark remembers his subscription to the Farmers Almanac he has consulted over the years, opening the page to North Central US, the prediction for the week in question says: 'Mostly fair through the week-end giving to light snow the following week.'

"We're on," Mark tells Susan. "Let's do it this Saturday evening, and then the following Monday, we'll be heading out."

"You're sure?" Susan questions. "Melody indicated she was planning to be here that week-end."

"Yes." He answers. "Let's start calling, OK, telling them we're having the campfire to bid adieu, and we'll make an announcement at that time. It's going to work out just as we hoped."

They made the calls; the responses were favorable as all their friends indicated they would attend, bringing their chairs and promising not to spread the word to anybody. That Saturday morning, Mark busied himself gathering the wood and cleaning up the area. He also prepared the barn, which they could use if the weather turned opposite.

Mayor Olsen came early, expressing his appreciation to Mark and Susan for all they've contributed to the town over the years, briefing Mark on what he would say in his short introduction. Pastor Allan James will also be speaking. Mark and Susan would each spend some time telling their friends of their plans, the whys, how it came about, where they were going, who was going, and their hopes and desires of starting a new American experience. Mark was now feeling that he couldn't care less who knew. He was certain that the plans could not be stopped, that his precautions were secure, and that their announcement could not hamper the plans. The time was too short.

Melody arrived on Friday, saying she informed her superiors two weeks prior she was leaving the department for untold reasons. Her associates hosted a brief lunchtime party for her, showering her with best wishes, a few vases of flowers, and gift cards for Wal-Mart and Kohls. A gentleman superior expressed sorrow, saying he was getting quite interested in her romantically after having had dinner dates with her. He questioned Melody about where she was going, what she would be doing, and how to contact her. Brushing him off was easy, she told Mark and Susan. "No one in the department has any idea that I'm leaving the States for good," Melody assures her dad.

Just as the Farmers Almanac predicted, the weather on Saturday was clear skies, the mid-fifties during the day, the evening decreasing to jacket-type forties, a perfect time for the first of the year outdoor campfire gathering. The fire was burning hot, the hot dogs and sausages were ready, portable grilling grates were in place over the side embers, and marshmallows, coffee, tea, and beer were plentiful when the friends arrived, all twenty-two of them seated comfortably around the fire.

Pastor Allan officially started the evening with a short prayer and blessings to the Tebonsons. Mayor Olsen then took the stand and briefly told of the many times that Mark and Susan had blessed the town and that they would be missed, among interruptions desiring to get on with it and let us know what was in store. Where are they moving to and why?

Susan took the front next, telling them of her fond memories of life in North Platte and how much she would miss them all, again, with interruptions, wanting explanations and clarifications as to where to and why they were picking up their roots, leaving all behind.

Then Mark explained in no uncertain terms why they were leaving it all behind for a rugged life on the new island in the Pacific.

"We'll be starting in an unfamiliar territory for a life of freedom, the expectation of creating a new community, a colony with Judeo-Christian moral laws that have been the foundation of

American society from the start but are slowly removed for politically correct reasons. Our hard work will determine our future, with no guarantees of success or expectations of failure, just diligence and determination to live free on our terms.

"We leave a life of comfort, a life filled with the blessings made possible by our previous determination and hard work. But as you know, the political climate in these once-free United States is no longer concentrated on the individual but on a collective as determined by those in power. That which is corrupted by their perceived power, expanding their reach into regulating and policing the affairs of the individual. The FBI has already implemented a program of face recognition technology in cahoots with a major airline manufacturer using the cameras, with audio, from drones watching who the FBI says may be enemies of the state. We've had those drones flying over this very campfire during those Halloween festivals and other times. And I would not be surprised if one of those drones is now monitoring this conversation. But, as you see, I don't give a flip anymore."

"Bureaucrats have determined that we must accept what they say is the politically correct way to think and speak, and we must conform. We all belong to one body, one platform, one belief system, and a politically correct way of life. Our religious faith must be mixed with peoples of other faiths, as each faith is as worthy as the other. Muslims rioting in the streets defending Allah is equal to Christians donating time and money to those in need, in the name of Jesus. Our family life must be subordinated to the whims of those who hold no basic moral principles, that a child is best raised and educated by the State, protecting the innocent from the biases and phobias of parents.

I recently read an article from the UN indicating that future women having just given birth, machines would milk her new baby, as the bonding a mother makes with her baby during breastfeeding makes it hard to separate the two. The business life for entrepreneurs is precarious, and the financial support could be undermined any time a bureaucrat determines it best. The rules of operation govern what each business owner must adhere to. His sales cannot be determined solely on a mutual basis between seller and buyer, but on what the bureaucrats determine is best for the community."

"As the old saying goes, I'm sick and tired of it, I'm worn out and disgusted that politicians have slowly and methodically dismantled the one thing that drew disgruntled peoples from around the world to emigrate here: freedom."

"The average citizen is too busy supplying the needs and desires of their families to keep abreast of the political maneuvering, and the politicians know it and use it to their advantage. And the media, well . . . it's become disgusting."

"That's why we are moving, giving it all up just as our forefathers did when they arrived at Plymouth Rock, just as early Americans moved into the west seeking riches in the unknown regions west of the big river. Sure, the government offered plots of land to those who would live and work the lands for a period of time, encouraging the hardy to risk the unknown, while at the same time, the feds violated the treaties they previously made to Native Americans. Sure, we can trust the government. The government is not guaranteeing us ownership of our plot on the island, and in fact, the feds and the UN may inhibit us in our endeavors, but I say, bring it on, I'd rather die trying than be forced to live under their socially and medically correct functions as determined by them. We say good-bye and good-ridance to their collectiveness."

Concluding his remarks, Mark tells them, "Your friendship has blessed us. We will be leaving shortly, and this meeting is our way of thanking you. Thank you. Thank You."

Questions from their friends started to flow as several asked how they could join them and what would they need to do so. How soon could they join? Do you have any special financial requirements? How soon do you expect to have homes built and the basic infrastructure, such as water supplies, power lines and roads, schools, hospitals, and police? One of the friends said he read that pirates have set up a base of operations on the island. Another said he read about a group of Russians who have already settled in. Are these accounts legitimate or faked by the authorities?

Trying to answer those questions, Mark could only definitively answer the one about electrical power saying, "I've arranged with the manufacturer that any units of my solar maximizers I desired would be available. I'm taken several along to get started, which I could hopefully install within the first few weeks if the weather conditions allow. The hard part will be burying the cables in the rocky soil. These generators could supply our limited electrical needs for our five homesteads since we will be without most of the comforts we now take for granted. Our friends Bruce and Wendy are already in Anchorage, loading the ship. The rest of your questions are unanswerable."

It's now past midnight, and most of the close friends have left for home, each of them hugging and blessing Mark and Susan while saying their last goodbyes along with a final 'God bless, wish we could join you. Take care.'

Mayor Olsen and Pastor James Allan have hung back, desiring to spend a few additional minutes with Mark, Susan, and Melody. Inside the house, Susan brings out her apple pie, a scoop of vanilla ice cream, and fresh cups of coffee as they gather comfortably in the living room.

Mark informs them they will take their final jet trip to Anchorage early Monday morning.

"It has been sold to a buyer in Anchorage. Susan and I will fly the new seaplane to the island, while Bruce will pilot the ship. I'm beginning to feel sad leaving you guys. Are you sure you couldn't join us?"

Mayor James says, "Mark, you know I cannot now. The future, though, is always uncertain. You'll be missed tremendously. You've blessed us beyond our hopes and dreams, and the blessings of God are with you."

Pastor James then turned quiet, sadly reflecting on how much Mark and Susan have inspired him to continue to speak the truth in love over the years. The church split a few years back as half and more members got offended at his directness and political stances, nearly destroying his desire to pastor a congregation again. The denomination's superiors wanted him to step down. Still, Mark and Susan stayed and encouraged him to continue preaching the truth as the scriptures reveal, and to leave the denomination to establish an independent church. The following year's attendance expanded and has grown ten times over that small group that stayed with him. He is now seeing over seven hundred for the Sunday morning services, with one hundred fifty children attending the daily after-school activities.

Pastor James concludes his remarks saying, "Mark and Susan, even though I cannot go with you at this time, I will be working to gather a group to join you sometime in the future. The entire church might go as much as they all love you two. You've blessed us, and now our blessings go with you. Somehow, we'll try to keep in touch. Please, Mark, I know how you are about keeping that cell phone handy. You'll be so busy building something there that it'll be easy to forget about us, but please don't shut us out."

Mark says, "As far as our financial obligations, I've arranged for the bank to automatically send you our tithes and offerings for the next year. We will not forget you, James. You have blessed us as your teachings have touched our hearts over and over. We're the ones who will feel empty not having you around."

Melody also tells the pastor how much she was ministered to during her high school days, the weekly fun fests, the summer camps, and how she was ministered to after that horrible rape. She then tells James of her experience at the church in Denver and that she is now free again, having made peace with it.

"That's wonderful, Melody. I'm so happy for you."

"That young man is now in the Navy somewhere." The Mayor says.

Mayor Olsen excuses himself, saying, "I don't know about you guys, but this dude must get home, so this is it folks. Hopefully, we'll see each other sometime down the road. Good luck and blessings to you." The hugs lasted a bit longer than usual, and Pastor James also said he must go as the church service tomorrow. They each drive off waving through the side windows, leaving Susan and Melody on the porch with tears on their cheeks. Mark puts his hands in his pockets, holding back his tears as he turns, quickly entering the house.

Monday morning, the three of them were in the air by seven-forty am, heading toward Anchorage to meet up with Bruce and Wendy. As the jet left the home-built runway, Mark turned it to get another nostalgic look at their farmhouse, the barns and land that kept them busy for years.

"Goodbye, you've been good to us, and sorry, Dad, if you had other thoughts of keeping the farm in the family for a few more generations," Mark says. He then aims the jet over the town, taking another look at memorable buildings and crosswalks, the railroad museum, the rail yards, and Jeffers Depot, while thinking how neat it would be to see Mayor Olsen looking up and waving.

The weather throughout the day was perfect for flying, not even some of those fluffy white clouds off in the distance anywhere. Susan and Melody were more intent on viewing the land below as they passed than on previous flights. "It's so beautiful. What a country of beauty everywhere.

"Susan and Melody," Mark calls back to the passenger area, "we're approaching Mount Rushmore."

"There it is," Susan says to Melody. "I've never seen it from the air before. What a sight." Peering down at the heads of the four presidents, Mark turns a few degrees for a full frontal view of the monument, telling Susan and Melody, "It was almost a century ago that a dynamite blast started shaping those heads out of granite. I look at it in amazement at what was accomplished in those days, thinking ahead to today, wondering if the country could even start such a project under the present political atmosphere.

"Environmentalists would never allow it. The Forest Service and the Fish and Wildlife Agency would prevent it. Politicians would never agree as to which presidents should be honored. The Occupational Safety and Health people would insist on untold safety features for the workers. Yet, using primitive safety measures, there were no fatalities during its construction."

The Jet makes its way north over Montana, turns westward, flying over Idaho and into Washington State, and then up the coast into Anchorage, arriving six hours after leaving the farm. Bruce and Wendy meet them at the airport. They arrived two weeks ago to prepare the ship and load the containers. The first order of business was a quick lunch, and then Mark arranged to transfer the title to his jet and secure the title to the seaplane.

Bruce informs that all is well with the ship; it is loaded, the tents have arrived, and they are ready to hit the waves as soon as George, Ruth, Thomas, Anabele, and Janet arrive.

"We're ready to go, Mark. We heard from them this morning, and each expected to be here this evening."

"Tomorrow morning, then, we can head out?" Mark questions and informs. "Super, I'm ready. In the next few hours, let's get together and review it all, the route we'll take and where on the island we'll park, and also double-check the supplies again."

Bruce adds, "I don't foresee any problems. The news about the island has been quiet, which could be something of concern. The UN hasn't made any new announcements. And if other people are inhabiting the place, it's not been covered, so we're free to go. We've triple-checked the supply list, so if we discover we missed listing something, that's just tough. I've got my clubs and five dozen balls, so what else can there be? But, do you think we could get along without chewing gum?" he adds.

Mark asks, "What does the weather forecast look like for the North Pacific for the next week?"

"Mark, it looks fairly decent. The winds should be almost calm, and no storms are appearing." Bruce says, "We're in good shape."

"Great! Let's hit the road. I'm feeling a bit of anxiety as the day approaches. No turning back now. We've invested too much. Moses is going to cross the Red Sea."

And so it went: the kids arrived just before dinner, and Janet appeared at the motel just before eight pm. In the morning, they all shared their sleeplessness and anxiety, knowing that when they woke up, the work ahead of them would be entirely different than what each had become accustomed to over the years. Breakfast was quick as the eagerness to get going was also present.

Janet said it the best: "Well, my friends, here we are, tossing away the technologically easy life watched over by strangers for a life we inwardly seek, a life based on our own merits as individuals in cooperation with those of the same mindset. I thought I'd feel a great relief, but I'm a bit uneasy and at the same time excited."

All except Mark and Susan headed for the ship, parked, and ready for them to load with their final belongings. Mark informed Bruce of the time he would take off, looking down in the harbor as Bruce maneuvered the ship into the Pacific. "We'll get to the island and park the plane near shore, looking for you to pull in tomorrow morning."

In the air, Mark circles around the ship a few times, radios Bruce, "Ok buddy, it's all yours. See you soon." Then he heads directly toward the new island, telling Susan, "Could you have thought that by marrying me, you'd be leaving these states after 35 years for a life of hardship, living in a tent hoping to build a new colony?"

Susan says, "Mark, if you had told me 35 years ago that we would eventually move to an uninhabited brand new island in the Pacific, I don't know what I'd done. Probably looked at you and thought, 'he's off his rocker, he's been reading too much science fiction.' But, I would have still said yes, thinking I could get your reading habits changed. Now, here I am, willingly and of a sound mind accompanying you on this move, you never told me about back then. Leaving my parents was the hardest part, Mark. Everything else was fun and exciting. I'm looking forward to it. Sleeping in a tent with you has always been romantic."

Mark says, "You're the best. I would not have believed it myself, thinking I should see a psychiatrist. But here we are. We've had it easy. God has blessed us, and now I feel He is taking us on a journey into the unknown. It's His Island we're going to.

Susan adds, "This could be the making of a Hollywood movie."

Chapter 17

The ten safely arrive at the island, parking the sea plane and the ship in the harbor, using a pontoon boat to move their needed equipment and supplies on shore. The first few days were spent on exploration trips around the area: up the plateau, down the valley, partially up the side of the nearest volcano, down the beaches, around the lakes, beside the streams, searching and getting familiar with their new landscape. Mark assured them that when they arrived, he flew over the island, inspecting it all before landing in the harbor, satisfying their curiosity and desire that they were the first to settle.

There's always been a thing about campfires with Mark, ever since his days in the Boy Scouts, and so one of the first items Mark insisted on having enough was ricks of wood. A celebration of liberty was held the first evening on the plateau, burning up an entire rick of wood. They sang songs. They reminisced. They prayed. They joked. They planned. They hoped. They sanctified the island to the Lord.

Over the first few weeks, they've built a pier out far enough so that the ship could pull alongside, making it easier to unload more of the heavier equipment, a jeep, the trailer, and the tractor they use daily. The barrels of fuel have also been placed close to the shore and easily accessible to the jeep and tractor.

Knowing that it'd be months or perhaps even years before adequate homes could be built, Mark had tents specially made out of heavy canvas material overlaid by heavy-duty vinyl, according to Mark's plans submitted to a company in Omaha. He got five tents, one for the couples and one for Janet and Melody to share. Each tent measures an overall twelve by twenty feet. One enters the tent through a screen flap into an eight-by-twelve-foot living room with four-by-four mosquito net windows on each side. Next is the kitchen area, containing a propane stove, a portable sink, a few book cases used to store cans and cans of food, and utensils and pots and pans.   Next to the kitchen is a four-by-four-foot restroom with shower, LP hot water system, and one of those portable toilets. The shower head is connected to a fifty-five-gallon drum outside, enabling it to collect rainwater.

Push aside a canvas flap into an eight-by-twelve-foot bedroom area with mosquito net screened windows on three sides. The tent Janet and Melody share has two bedrooms. Janet brought a Quonset hut tent she acquired from the UN, which they use to store additional supplies.

Progress is being made. A larger canopy, somewhat like a revival tent, has been installed to store supplies, tools, and equipment and used as a meeting area, keeping everything dry during the rains.

They're enjoying themselves. They're working together as a tight-knit team. They continue taking walks along the beaches, the plateaus, inspecting the rocks, the emerging vegetation, the streams, and the creeks forming while thinking and planning future uses. Anabele started keeping a daily journal.

Annabel's first entry relates to what Susan told her about their arrival on the island ahead of the ship.

"Susan related to me that when she and Mark arrived on the island, they first flew over the entire island just to check if anyone else had occupied any part of it, then touched down in the harbor, anchored the seaplane, waded ashore and sat on the beach for a few moments looking at the beauty of the sun shining down upon them. They then

took a walk up the rocky path leading to a plateau, where they found some vegetation starting to stretch out.

"Standing there looking over the area, we looked at each other and spoke in unison, "this is it, we're home.""

The eight of us arrived in the harbor at eight-twenty-three am, April 2nd; I'll call it year 01.

A beautiful day, the skies were clear, the sun was bright, a soft breeze blew from the west, just enough to ripple the water, the temperature at 62. Nature had bestowed upon us a fantastic reception.

Bruce navigated the ship as if he was on a green, sizing up the speed, the slope, the distance, and surmising the power needed to get us to the target.

During the 25-hour trip, Wendy, Janet, George and Ruth, Melody, Thomas, and I relaxed in the cabin, trying to play cards while chatting about our desires, our wishes, our dreams of the new life we would together create on the island.

The games could hardly start as our thoughts were centered on those future events and the anxiousness we each felt about finally pulling into the harbor to see Mark and Susan excitedly waving at us.

Marks's first words as we reached shore were: "Welcome to this new island. Your home."

Many times, Janet has said she imagined that camping out for this amount of time would be tedious and would get tiring. It has. But the freedom she feels makes the tedious worthwhile. They all agree. The freedom they enjoy every day has been refreshing, even though they sometimes feel lonely for the hustle-bustle of modern-day life in the States. When those feelings come, they've learned to take a deep breath of the fresh air, looking out over the cliff into the wild blue yonder of ocean waves or up in the skies seeing the massive bright stars without any surrounding artificial lights dimming the view.

Mark and Susan had what they thought at the time was a perfect peaceful view into the heavens on a clear night at the farm, but now, what a difference. Near North Platte, there was still the distant view of city lights forming a haze under the deep midnight blue sky; the lights and sound of a plane flying overhead and traffic on the roads were always there. Here, a thousand miles away from modern life, the only disturbance to the quietness is hearing the exhaled breath of the person next to you.

The fishing has been unbelievable. They enjoyed snorkeling among the reefs after a hard day's work moving rocks and preparing an area to grow their vegetables. But that stopped one day when George was gathering equipment from the ship, noticing shark fins gently moving about not far from the stern. Swimming was moved to the lake.

They've become like a close-knit scarf. Susan has thanked Mark over and over again for this experience. Being the shutterbug, she has captured most of their activities with her ever-present camera. She captured far-off shots of island scenes, close-ups of the installation of the tents, the insides of the tents, and portrait shots of each of them: some smiling, some just playfully acting dumb, some unaware shots of each deeply involved in a project. Some shots of vegetation expanding over the rocks. These are transferred to her computer, and then e-mail attempts are sent to her parents and the families of the girls, along with Pastor James, but connections to a satellite are troublesome.

So far, they've been visited only by a US naval ship inquiring about their safety and one UN ship concerned about their intentions and safety.

One evening as Mark and Susan had retired to their tent lounging back on their comfortable chairs reading a book, Susan looked at Mark with a look of appreciation, "Mark, I know you've been amazed at how all of this has worked out, the kids coming along, Janet, Bruce and Wendy all agreeing to make this move, but have you recognized the hand of God upon your intense desire to build a solar magnifier for our farmhouse, and now we are on this island where we absolutely need it."

"Yes, Susan. I've been amazed, too. Little did I know five years ago, as I was spending all that time perfecting it to provide an alternative source of energy on the farm to reduce our dependence, that we'd be using it to light these tents?"

"Yeah, when I get somewhat stressed because of our lack of gadgets and how physically easy they made life, I'm reminded that we're here because God made it possible, and He's got the future, our future," Susan replies.

Mark answers, "When we gather together on the beach looking up at the stars, I'm filled with peace. When I look at how this land is transforming, all the anxieties and questions about future food supply and the unforeseen weather, those negative thoughts vanish by looking at how the rains and sun are transforming this land."

"We've got nothing to be anxious about, Mark. You've got that ability to follow His lead even though you don't immediately recognize it," Susan finishes, putting the book down and moving closer to Mark, laying her head on his shoulder as his arm reaches around to pull her close.

Periodically, they have taken a trip around the island in the sea plane, inspecting and satisfying their curiosity that they are the only ones who have set up camp. Janet has led them to prepare an area down in the valley, big enough to nourish the fruits and vegetables from the seeds they brought. Hopefully, enough for the ten of them and then some. All kinds. Many varieties. Early tomatoes and late tomatoes. Squash. Wheat. Potatoes. Peppers. Beans of every kind. And corn, of course. Onions. Cucumbers. Beets. Lettuce. Spinach. Cabbage. Celery. Collard greens, and then spices too. Fruit trees. Not having a historical weather data for the area, they know it's wait and see what will adapt to this weather.

They're besides themselves with excitement. The Coleman stoves and ovens have been fantastic. Susan surprised them all one evening with the coveted pies she had scratched together, baking them in her propane oven. There is just one area that gets to the ladies now and then: the primitive restrooms in the tents. The shower is powered by a hand operated siphon pump on a tube running outside to the 55-gallon water barrel. Squeeze a few times, and the shower releases a flow of cold water to get you wet. Squeeze, soap down, rub, and squeeze, squeeze. Squeeze, Soap down, rub, and squeeze some more.

Ruth commented that after the pumping shower, she had to jump in the lake to remove the sweat from squeezing the tube. Her forearm muscles were growing stronger. A bar of soap in knee-deep sea water or the lake also refreshes for awhile, but the salty water is not the same as a long one-hour soak in a sudsy-filled bathtub. The hot running water to the bathtub is missed, but they wouldn't trade anything they now have for those comforts.

Another area that gets them reflective on modern conveniences is scrubbing dirty clothes and hanging them on lines to dry, remembering grandma's tedious chores of keeping the clothes clean. Susan has been after Mark to use his ingenuity to give them a modern way of washing his duds. When they get fully electrified with running water and a sewage system, then the washing machines and dryers will come. In the meantime, keeping their clothes clean by scrubbing over the washboards in lake water is a weekly event.

One afternoon after being alone on the island for two months, Mark, George, Thomas, and Bruce were unloading supplies from the ship when Bruce suggested they splurge and have chicken roasted over a campfire to plan, reminisce, take stock, and relax.

Mark asks Bruce: "Have you ever prepared a chicken before?"

"No, but we can do it, one step at a time."

"Mark, we'll still have twenty-three chickens if we sacrifice five for ourselves for a celebration. We've been enjoying the eggs; let's indulge in the meat. We could use a break."

"Sounds good to me," George quickly agrees.

Thomas adds, "Yes, I can just about taste it now. Fantastic. Emphatically, he yells in the air. "We're going to have a party!"

"It does sound good," Mark replies. "Run it by the ladies and see how they feel about sacrificing a few prized egg producers."

Bruce starts walking toward the valley where the ladies are tending to the seeds. Bruce tells them, "Let's go have a party." When the ladies heard of the suggestion, they threw down the tools, shouted, jumped with glee, and ran toward the ship

Bruce finds the guys still in the ship, separating supplies needed on the plateau. "You should have seen Susan, Mark. Her face lit up like a Christmas tree, and Melody went wild too. Ruth almost started to cry. Mark, we can't get second thoughts about roasting a few chickens now."

"Well, good. Let's unload and transfer this stuff, and we'll get the party going. Bruce, you got the honor of wringing the neck of the chickens, and we'll pluck the feathers. OK?"

As they were approaching the tent with the supplies, the ladies appeared, stopped long enough for Wendy to shout: "we're going to clean up, put on our best cocktail dresses, and then we expect you guys to get into your tuxedos," and then they disappeared just as quickly down the path toward the ship.

Thomas questions, "tuxedos?"

"My god, we started something now," Mark responds.

Bruce adds, "Well, I guess I did. The rain last week drove me into boredom, and this week has been a drag on all of us. I was thinking of having this break last week, but then the rains came, and I forgot about it.

Bruce chose five of the biggest hens out of the pen and proceeded to do what must be done to get them ready, remembering how it shocked him one day. He was about six or seven when he saw his grandfather in the backyard placing the head of a chicken on a tree stump, holding it there under the pressure of a forked prong, and with a swing of the axe, the heads fell to the ground, and the body runs freely around the yard spurting blood out the neck, wildly running until it can't no more.

"For a six-year-old city kid to see that was traumatizing. I couldn't eat chicken for a long time after that." He tells the guys while he places the first one on a piece of firewood, having carved a strip of wood into a fork. "One down and four to go," Bruce announces. "Now you guys get busy and pull those feathers and whatever else. OK? I've done my part."

After cleaning up in the ship quarters, the girls are dressed in their best clean shopping jeans and shirts. They're relaxing around a campfire, watching the boys. The chickens, soaked in a special Wendy's sauce, are on rods over the fire when Anabele asks, "What are we going to have with the chicken? Something special, I hope. We should have baked a pie?"

"Girls, should we play one on the guys?" Susan questions. "I think it's their turn to eat humble pie. Let's do something, shall we?"

"What?"

"Remember a few weeks ago when the boys were snorkeling along the reef while we sat watching, when George shouted, "Sharks, Sharks, scaring the daylights out of us. George and Bruce then went under the surface, splashing about and throwing water all over the place, while Mark and Thomas rapidly swam toward shore. All we could do was stand there panicking, watching in disbelief." Susan adds. "We owe them one. Come on, we can think of something. There are six of us versus four of them."

"Yeah, that was mean," Wendy adds. "I let Bruce know about it later, too."

"So what is the one thing that would get them panicking?" Susan questions.

"Dang it, here they come. Keep this in mind, as we owe them big time. We've got to get even." Susan quickly adds.

"Yes, we do. We can't let that mean trick slip by. Their time will come." Wendy says, and the rest agree in unison.

"Oh, look at 'em. They're wearing white tee shirts with a black ribbon tied around the neck," says Anabele, looking at the four guys slowly proceeding toward the girls, heads high as if they were entering a ballroom.

"Where did they find those ribbons?" Susan questions.

"Ahh? That's the best you could come up with? Where are the tuxedoes?" Janet asked the guys as they approached.

"Where are those cocktail dresses?" Bruce asks in return.

"Hey guys, what are we having with the chicken?" Wendy inquires. "This is your treat, we hoped you'd have it all planned out and be ready to serve us."

"Just wait," Bruce announces. "This will take awhile."

The chickens are cooking over the campfire. Pans of canned vegetables are slowly heating as they all sit back, relaxing and enjoying the late afternoon on the beach. Knowing it'll take a few hours for the chickens to slowly roast, they sit back, relaxing as the sun slowly dips toward the horizon. Their conversations take several turns, bringing up the subject of their security, the weather, the plans next, and even a name for the island, as the cooking is monitored by Bruce and Thomas, slowly turning the whole chickens over the fire embers while basting them with a special barbecue sauce.

"We're blessed," Anabele announces. "This is fantastic. I'm glad Janet thought of having this break."

Bruce looks at Anabele and Janet. "Yes, thank you. It sounded like a good thing for us to do today."

"I think the chickens are ready," Bruce announces. "Let's eat."

Mark and George proceed to pass around the plates, the utensils, and inquirers as to what each would like to drink, as Bruce removes each chicken from the rod, cutting them apart, and then Thomas places the breasts, legs, wings, each into separate pans on the camping table. The pots of vegetables, green beans, corn, broccoli, and peas are on the table. The guys did not forget the jars of seasonings, either. Napkins are there too.

"Ladies, come and get it," Bruce calls out.

Marks grabs Susan's hand, and they all hold hands in a circle as he prays a blessing over the food and themselves. They then fill their plates and position the camp chairs in a circle.

"Oh, this is terrific. It looks good. Thank you." Melody announces as she is the first at the table when Janet, right behind her, picks a breast, a leg, and some of each vegetable on a separate plate.

Then she asks, "Are there any rolls?"

Susan says, "Thank you for this. We needed something like this," then she raises her voice, thanking the guys for their efforts to bring them all an evening of joy.

"What a meal, what a terrific idea this was. Thank you." Ruth says while holding a fork full of chicken. "This is fantastic. We've got to remember to do this more often."

Susan then adds, "The next one is on us."

Somehow, the news of them homesteading on the new island made national news, making them the talk on Facebook and other internet blogs. CNN has interviewed their friends. Each of the major networks has sent reporters to interview acquaintances to expose the groups' foolishness. BBC has broadcast their rendition of the imagined hardships of living on a barren land thousands of miles from anywhere, painting them as lonely mountain people of the Middle Ages.

In spite of the negativity, thousands of politically disenchanted freedom-minded people are getting interested, and wondering how to make the move themselves. To most, it's just wishful thinking, a wishful lust with possibilities at first, but then reality knocks.

Anabele made an entry in her journal after being on the island for forty-three days relating this account:

"We had all assembled early evening on the beach on this beautiful May 12th. comfortably laying back in our lawn recliners relaxing and just starring out. first at the sun setting below the horizon and then up at the rising moon surrounded by uncountable stars. and several shooting starts. The beauty of it all was breathtaking to enjoy. The sky was as clear as looking through a window without the glass.

The psalmist said it first: 'The heavens declare the glory of God; the skies proclaim the work of his hands.'

We dared not speak to each other for fear of breaking the rhythmic sound of ocean waves creeping up the sandy beach. But I could not keep what I was seeing to myself. and so I nudged Thomas. whispering: 'honey. look over there at that cluster of stars. it's as if God is smiling down on us.' Susan noticed it. as did Bruce and Wendy. and soon the ten of us were down on our knees worshiping.

Chapter 18

Mark and Bruce have started to set blocks of rocks in place for the first of their homes when Janet drove up in the jeep with news that another ship was entering the harbor.

"We'll never get anything done the way they keep on," Mark shouts out.

"Hang on there, Mark, there is something different about this one. Go back to work, and I'll see what's up and let you know, OK? I just thought you'd want to know. I'll handle it," as Janet turns the jeep around and heads back toward the sea harbor, a ten-minute ride down the hill on the rough rocky two-wheeled path. The ship was stationary in the harbor, lowering down a lifeboat as Janet approached the hill's crest. The boat made its way to shore, and as it was about to be beached, Janet yelled out: "Whoa now," Janet shouted, wheeling onto the beach in front of the boat and the two strangers. "Stop! Who are you, and what do you think you're doing?"

"We're here to help." Said a tall, muscular hunk somewhere in his forties, riding in the front. Another man dressed in fatigues, with his cap pulled down over his eyes, was operating the small engine, steering it onto the beach. The first man steps out of the boat into a few inches of water, taking a couple steps to dry land, his right hand pulling the rope and the boat onto shore.

"What'd you mean to help? We have not asked for help. Who's in charge of this ship?   Where is he?   Please, just stop where you are, turn around and get back on that ship of yours and let me talk to whoever it was who brought you here. Where's the captain of this ship?" Janet shouts out.

The man sitting in the back of the small boat with his hand on the outboard motor shouts, "Where's the leader of this renegade bunch of wannabee George Washingtons?"

Janet turns, recognizing it as the voice of Jim Nottingham.

"Jim, is that you?" as he steps into the water to walk ashore. Janet steps into the water, meets him halfway, and gives him a great big hug. "Boy, it's good to see you."   They embrace for a full minute, rocking back and forth as they each pat the back of the other.

"God, this is great," says Jim.   "What a beautiful harbor you've got here.   Look at this beach.   You know you guys are all over the news."

"Yeah, I know. I've seen a few accounts of what's happening States side, not that we care anymore. Jim, I've thought of you often. It's so good to see you. But why didn't you let us know you were coming? What do you have in that ship? Oh, Janet, this is Mike Galloway. He's one of the best hands-on construction professionals." Mike reaches out to shake her hand and warmly caresses it with his left hand.

"Hi, Mike." Janet greets him, captivated by his eyes. "How did you get connected with Jim? Oh, forget it. I guess we'll have time for that background stuff later. I'm still shocked."

"Janet," Jim says, "I've been trying to contact you guys for weeks."

"Come on, Jim, we'll catch up on all that stuff later. Mark will be thrilled to see you. They got started building our first home."

"Over three hundred folks are on board, ready to get to work." Jim says, "I've brought enough lumber to build a small town. I thought you'd need some."

"What? Did you say three hundred? Who are they? What were you thinking? Oh, Jim, this is too much for me to comprehend. Lumber, too?"

Janet takes a deep breath, looking out at the cruise ship and seeing lots of people leaning over the rail, waving in her direction.

"Come on. Let's go get Mark and Bruce," Jim says.

"Mark will be jumping in his boots and peeing in his pants when he sees you," Janet adds. "But then, learning about all these strangers. Gads, I don't know what he'll do."

"Now, don't worry about the little things, Janet, as this ship is loaded. They can sleep in the quarters until we get homes built, or if they prefer, sleeping bags and tents. Now, take me to Mark. I've brought along a great bunch of right-wing renegades, Janet, and I'm sure Mark will be thrilled after he gets past the shock of it all. I sure hope so. We've got the makings of a town here and nothing but a lot of time to take care of all that other stuff."

"Mike, We'll be back shortly," Jim tells him.

Jim and Janet climb on the jeep and head up the hillside. "It's about a five-minute ride, but hold on as this path is as rough as a city street."

"Where are they?" Jim asks.

"Oh, you know Susan," Janet returns, "She and the kids got the tractors down in the flat land area over there," as she points to her right.

"How are they doing?"

"Oh great. They've been helpful and co-operative."

"Hey, how about we pull something on Mark? Got any ideas?" Janet quizzes as the jeep bumps along at five mph, rocking from side to side, almost throwing Jim off at one point. "We'll get to building these roads in due time. We've got tractors, but we need cement. "

Jim tells her he has six bags on board.

"Six bags? Gads, we need six thousand."

"Joking, Janet."

Jim's hand reaches into his pocket and pulls out a bunch of firecrackers, one of those packets of fifty pops. "Where did you get that?" Janet asks. "They've been banned in the States for fifteen years now. If you set that off on this side of the crest, Mark and Bruce will go crazy, dropping everything and running to get their guns."

"That's the idea, Janet. I need an entrance that'll get their attention."

"He'll wrap his shovel over your backside when he sees it's you," Janet says to Jim over the noise of the jeep. "And Bruce, he'll just stand there looking at you and say, "did you bring any Shiner Bock?"

The firecrackers start exploding, and Mark and Bruce look at each other for a few seconds, wondering: What was that? Then the instincts take over, and without a word said, they both drop the tools and take cover behind pillars of basalt rock standing twenty-feet high, fifty yards from the shelters. Mark is on one side, and Bruce is on the other.

Janet comes running down the hillside in their direction, shouting, "Help, Help! The jeep got away from me, and I haven't been able to stop it." In front of Janet, the jeep appears to be driving itself. Mark and Bruce each run towards the runaway jeep as it wobbles from side to side on the makeshift path, bumping into the rocks and forcing it in the other direction. Jim shouts above the steering wheel when he's ten feet away, "Help, help, I've fallen, and I can't get up."

In amazement, Mark and Bruce, Recognizing Jim, look at each other, then at Jim and Janet standing next to him.

A few seconds later, the three of them run towards each other, giving each other jumping chest bumps, then a high five, a knuckle bump, and a good old-fashioned handshake. "Jim, what are you doing here? I thought we'd never see you again."

"That's a long story, Mark. How you doing? And it's great to see you guys again. You don't know how much I've missed you, and thought about you so often. So here I am, for good, to make it or break it to the end with the only man in the world who could pull this off."

Janet gets in the Jeep, turns it around, and says, "I'm gonna tell the others."

Mark quizzes Jim, "How did you find us? You didn't know what side of this island we'd be on, and this land is 42 miles from one end to the other, and we thought we had found the perfect cove to keep the ships and my plane hidden from the coast. But, I know you, and if the Navy and the UN can find us, you would too. Oh yeah," he remembers, "I sent you a copy of the map."

"Mark, you may not know this, but the UN has had their drones circling this place for two months, taking pictures so sharp that you can see the labels on the bottles of beer you guys tossed aside. I just clicked on that UN web page and found a picture of this harbor, the location concerning the rest of the Island. They got the distances detailed in meters. One of the pictures looked like two people were getting it on behind the rocks. Was that you and Susan, Mark?"

"You got to be kidding! Well, I should have expected it. But we've been so busy working on things and enjoying the peace. Oh well, they'll do their thing. It's the UN.   It'll take years for them to move beyond the meetings and conferences."

"This is it, Jim. It doesn't look like we've accomplished much, but progress is being made." Mark informs Jim.

"So, how did you get here? A canoe? Plane? Did you bring anything?"

"A cruise ship, full of stuff we'll need."

"Oh, my. Let's see that ship of yours, and we can all get together and visit."

"Yeah, Mark, I even brought you some ricks of firewood so we can sit around the campfire just like the old days. But first, hold your pants on. I've got three hundred like-minded folks wanting to do what you've done.?"

"What! Did you say three hundred? Why? Who are they? Seeing you here is great, but bringing, what did you say? Three hundred people, strangers. What were you thinking? We were enjoying our little world here. What possessed you to go overboard?"

Jim tries to calm down his friend, explaining how just a few interested people had contacted him when the word got out that he was gathering supplies for a future move to this island. The word spread, and the number of interested citizens grew and grew. He tells Mark of the thousands turned down or changed their minds. He informs Mark of the interest that has spread across the country like a wildfire.

After a long pause, a deep breath, and a sigh, Mark says: "Well, here you are and, well, Jim, I've been through many surprises in my life, some welcome and some downright disturbing, and this one is both. I'm not ready for this. Couldn't you have warned us somehow? The suddenness of this shakes me."

"Mark, I tried to, many times."

"Well, you could have made the trip by yourself first. Then we'd have a chance to discuss it."

Mark sits down, looking up at Jim, and Bruce. While taking a deep breath, he asks: "Now, what do we do?"

Looking at Jim for direction but seeing nothing but perplexing heaviness, then to Mark, Bruce says, "We can't just sit here and pretend it hasn't happened. In the past, we've discussed the possibility of hundreds, and even thousands, wanting to join us and what we'd do if they suddenly showed up. We did not think it was something that could be planned; they would just come. We contemplated sending them off to another part of the island but did not want to create animosity between us. We did think that it'd be smaller groups, not hundreds at once, even though we knew that could happen too. Mark, it's not like enemies are invading us. Jim says these folks want the same things we want.

"Mark that time has arrived."

Looking back at Jim, Mark says, "Oh well, here we go. We've been enjoying our little world here so much, and now, suddenly, all that changes instantly. Jim, you don't know how peaceful it's been, just the ten of us. We've gotten so close, we're comfortable, there's not a care whatsoever, it's been fantastic, and now all that changes."

After breathing hard and slow, Mark finally says, "Give me a few more minutes, Jim."

"Well, Mark". Bruce says, "We talked about something like this happening, so that time has come. Sure, it disturbs our peace, but we did not have that feeling of serenity when we arrived. We had to work to earn this. It came, but there was a struggle at first. We'll get it again, Mark. We've had our heated discussions too. Melody and Susan got into it, as have you and I. Remember, we agreed that when the time came, we would get to know them first. It's here, Mark. The time has come."

Reflecting on those words, looking again at Jim, back to Bruce, Mark takes a deep breath, letting that settle, another deep breath, a sigh, and then, "OK. Well, I guess that time is here. Let's get this over with. Knowing Jim, he's done what he considered best. Let's get back and see what we can do to greet these people, make them feel welcome."

"All of that other stuff aside, It's great to see you, Jim. But next time you want to surprise me, let me know first, as I'm not as open to firecrackers popping off fifty feet. You scared the jeebeeze out of us."

Looking around the area, Jim says, "This place is beautiful. I'm amazed the closer I see it. Trees emerging, moss growing, and wildflowers too, oh my. It looks like you were right, Mark."

Bruce tells Jim, "Just wait, and we'll take you for a spin in the plane and let you see the entire Island. It's fantastic. It's a beauty, God's creation. Nothing else could quickly transform these limestone rocks and lava into soil suitable for vegetation.

Janet, Wendy, and Susan have been working the soil in the valley down there (pointing towards the east) into land for crops. Janet brought along desalting material, and part of the land is ready for seed already."

"Where are they? They should have arrived already." Mark wonders why Janet and Mike have not arrived with Susan and the rest.

"Oh," Bruce responds, "You know Janet, she'll be informing them, talking until the class bell rings."

Mark continues, "Jim, we're on the southern side, so the prevailing winds from the south keep this side warmer, while the northern side is cooler with the winds coming from the Aleutian area, the North Pole, and these mountains separate the two climates, as the winds converge creating storms mostly on the northern side of the volcanoes. It's almost like being in Hawaii.

"Mark was right all along," Bruce tells Jim. "It's a New World."

"Jim, the best thing I did was give away the jet and buy that sea plane. . . . and the ship. God, I loved that jet of mine, but it went to a missionary organization in the Philippines. Can you imagine that? Americans giving up their good life in the States to see to the needs of a group of people who have no idea what it's like to be free, to live in a land of opportunity, to have the opportunities that we've had, even just to be able to walk around inside a football field size grocery store and get any food that fits their fancy. When I see the pictures of those in need, I feel guilty. We're not here to help others, only ourselves. Those missionaries in the Philippines gave up their luxuries to benefit the needy. And here we are, escaping the life of plenty for a dream of freedom. And, freedom we have."

Mark adds, "You know all that, but, why didn't you let us know first?

Jim responds, "hey, we can sit around the campfire and rehash our lives later, but now you need to greet these people and . . . well, heck . . . I don't know what we're going to do with them today, … or tomorrow. We'll have to discuss all that."

They arrive on the beach.

Mark looks at the ship and stares at the passengers waving and shouting down at him.

"See. They're excited. They want to get with it, now! So Let's get to work building a new world. That's what they've been told," returns Jim. "Where do we start, Mark? What do you want us to do?"

Susan runs to Mark and Jim, who are standing together near the shore.

"Jim, What a surprise."

"Hi, Susan. You look good, just like a farmer should."

"Honey, Mike, and Janet briefed us all on this surprise, or it's more like a big gift we'll enjoy unwrapping. Melody and the rest are right behind us."

"Mark, I want you to meet Mike Galloway. Mike is our construction guy. He can do anything with a hammer and a wrench, and if he doesn't have a hammer, he'll use his hand or teeth."

"It's great to meet you, Mark. I've heard so much about you. I'm ready to do whatever. We all are." Mike tells Mark, reaching out to shake his hand.

"Mike, this fine lad is Bruce Wilcox. Bruce is a golfer, so you two will get along very well." Jim finishes the introductions.

"Mike, but do you know what you're getting yourself into?" Mark questions.

"I know what I'm getting into, Mark. Jim has briefed us and briefed us until I told him to stop yakking and let's get on with it. So here we are ready to build . . . you're . . . our New World."

"Hells bells, Jim, this is too much. Pinch me, I'm still dreaming," Mark says. "What changed your mind? How did you arrange all this? Where will we put 300 people? We're still sleeping in our tents?"

"I tried to call you several times," Jim answers. "I'm sorry, Mark, but there seemed to be no other way than just showing up. I was anxious. These people sold all and wanted to get on with it."

"We've been here over six months without a word from anybody," Mark says. If we knew you were coming, our plans would have changed, and we'd be better prepared to take on additional people. I'm not adjusting quite yet. We might need more time to comprehend what happened and what to do about it."

Mark breathes in, and agin, and then says. "We've often thought of what we'd do if a bunch suddenly showed up. But that's it. We're not wondering anymore. It has happened."

Talking to himself, Mark says, *'Get it together, kid. Come on, you can handle this, so get with it.'*

Then George, Melody, Janet, and the rest run down to the beach, and they all excitedly greet Jim, and then look up and wave at the crowd waving and shouting.

"Now what, Jim?"

Jim responds, "Get in the boat and shut up a minute. Janet, as you can see, this boat is small. Let me take Mark and Bruce up there first into the captains room. So, if you ladies would like to freshen up a bit before meeting everyone this evening, go. My chef will prepare a wonderful meal for you all. And Mike can help you climb aboard when you're ready.

Jim leads Mark, and Bruce to step in the water and climb into the small boat, looking up, seeing the strangers leaning over the railing waving at them. Climbing up the walkway, Jim leads them past the front deck to inside the captains' station, where he leans against the window, pausing a moment, looking out around the harbor and taking a breather.

"Mark, these people come from all walks of life," Jim starts informing Mark and Bruce. "There are doctors, nurses, engineers, lawyers and accountants, preachers, historians, cooks, electricians and plumbers, business people and ah . . . did I mention we've got great mechanics, and teachers, gads, we've got teachers, some retired, some college professors leaving their years of tenure, all of them just fed up with the feds. There are some recent college graduates, a couple of dropouts too, some over-the-hill professional athletes, and . . . well . . . it seems that every one of these renegades has had enough of the unneeded intrusions and regulations, and, fed up to the ears with how things are progressing in the States.

"Did I mention there are some young families with children? They all hated the system. The schools are being dumbed down. There are a couple of families from Detroit. They wanted out as only three percent of eighth graders are proficient in reading. As parents, they feel society is working against them. They all knew they'd just have to accept it and go on pretending to be happy and satisfied.

"But then thousands heard of you and what you are doing. I want to briefly introduce you to who's onboard. Come on, let's go meet them. Are you ready?"

"Jim, I still haven't processed all this yet. I feel like a fish out of water. I'm flapping away, trying to get into my own little habitat. Let's slow things down a bit." Mark tells Jim as Bruce quietly sits there, knowing their lives have just changed.

"Mark, we'll have plenty of time to figure out what to do next," Bruce says. "Let's go. You can say a few words. Like you said, let's get this over with. The time has come, Mark. As Jim has told us, these folks have come this far to escape, just as we did. Ready?"

Chapter 19

The three of them exit the captain's area, walking along the front deck's side and continuing to the passenger area. Jim opens a door, entering the room first, with Mark and Bruce following when a loud thundering applause breaks the silence. The people rise to their feet, clapping with all they've got and shouting, "Mark! . Bruce!. . Mark!" More and more thundering applause.

Jim slowly makes his way to the center platform, raises his arms, and a slow quiet comes over the crowd. "Ladies and Gentlemen, Meet Mark Tebonson and Bruce Wilcox."

The applause erupts again. Mark and Bruce, overcome with emotion, surprised and bewildered. The two of them stand there looking over the crowd, back and forth to each other, to the crowd, to Jim, and back to the crowd of over three-hndred. Mark thinks to himself, taking a deep breath. *Yesterday, we knew what we were doing, and now we're overwhelmed."*

Someone yells out from the crowd. "Speech!" "Speech!" as Mark and Bruce stand there, surprised and bewildered. Jim speaks out loudly to Mark. "Come on, Mark, say something. Bruce?"

Mark slowly takes a few steps forward, looking like he'd be ready to tear into Jim, as Jim hands him the microphone. Mark looks at Jim with a look that says: we should be back over the hill placing rocks.

Holding the microphone in his hand down near his waist, Mark starts, "Ah . . . well . . . I don't know what to say. I'm shocked and overwhelmed. What are you all doing here? Why? Not that we can't use you, but . . . Hey, I don't know what's going on . . . this is . . . well, I'm dumbfounded. I've barely accepted the fact that my best friend has just surprised the . . . well . . . you know. I owe so much to Jim, as he's been my trusted confident since those years with the Justice Department. But this? And so many of you here, here in a no mans land far out in the Pacific. I couldn't imagine that so many people would throw away their comfortable lives in the States to forge a brand new existence on an uninhabitable Island in the Pacific." He pauses. "Or, is this one stop on your trip to Hawaii?

"No, No, Hawaii," a Man shouts.

"This land, all the experts said," Mark says. "Ah, yes those experts say this island could not be usable by humans for another thousand years or more, while some other experts said it could possibly be millions of years. And here you are. I'm not an expert, but I'm . . . ah, we took a chance that we could do it, and we've done it for the past six months, and now you're here, and I'm told you want to do it."

"Yes. Yes, We want to do it too."

"I don't know what Jim has told you about this island, what to expect, or how you can contribute. But he did briefly say that he's assembled the best of the best and that I need not worry about you one bit. I have no idea how he gathered such a distinguished-looking crowd, but if anyone could have done it, it would have been Jim. Thank you all for that very emotional welcome. I'm overwhelmed and, yes, confused too. I wish Susan would have been here to witness it. She'll be here shortly. Mike and Janet went over to get them. They're working the land to harvest some of the seeds we planted months ago. We must be self-sufficient here, as there are no Safeways, Krogers, and Sam's club down the street. There's not a Wal-Mart anywhere. No restaurants. We're starting from scratch, and it may take years. We don't have a sewer system . . . yet, nor running water. We're just camping out, folks. Yes, camping.

"Thank You, and we'll be getting to know each other in due time, I'm sure, but first I've, er . . . now it's . . . we've got a lot of figuring out what to do next. This sudden surprise has me surprised as I'd never been. Thank You. Thank you."

Another rowdy sound of applause as Mark steps back, and Jim takes the microphone and mentions for Bruce to come forward. "Ladies and Gentlemen, meet Bruce Wilcox, the heads and tails of this new world island."

The applause keeps going in pulsating highs and lows as shouts of "Bruce" "Bruce" ring out above the applause. Sheepishly, he looks down and gathers a couple of big breaths, overcome by the rousing welcome.

"Speech . . . Speech"

"Oh my God," Bruce says softly, slowly taking the microphone from Jim. "I think I now know what a celebrity feels like when they first enter the stage. This is ah. I'll find out later, and yet, well, a sudden surprise. We thought that it'd be just the ten of us for possibly years." Bruce pauses, looking down at his feet, away from the crowd, gathering his thoughts together.

"I'm just an ordinary guy who was ready to start something new. Ready to go to work to build a new town, to construct homes, a church, a meeting hall, and roads, if we want to, on our own terms this time, in a new world, a new way, a new thing . . . if you will, something that has not been done since the beginning of America." Bruce pauses.

"This island is amazing. It's forty-two miles long and thirteen miles wide, with mountains, newly formed rivers, streams, and lakes; Yes, freshwater lakes. The vegetation is beginning to emerge all over. The rocks are breaking down into sandy beaches, and we're harvesting some vegetables.

"God is so good. I believe, with everything I've got, that the earthquakes and volcanoes came out of the hellfire belly of the earth to wake-up millions of people as the tsunamis raced toward shore. But then, the winds blew against the waves, and no lands were devastated while a new island was in the making.

"Mark was the first to see it. It's because of something God put inside him, and that his vision was not allowed to die, but festered into where we are right now, right here, already at work, beginning a new life, a life free of oversight, free of hindrances by people assuming they are our masters and know what is best for us. We're free of safety regulations, free of housing codes, free to erect a cross wherever, and free to shoot my rifle or fish in the bay any time I so desire. And let me tell you, the fish in these waters are great. No deer or bears yet. Not even a squirrel. But there are ants, and how mosquitoes could get here, I can't imagine. We've seen birds of all kinds flying over and searching the area, doing their thing. I'm so excited about this venture. Nothing could sway me to move back to the States and have to listen to the media tell us how backward we are, that we are nothing but right-wing extremists, clinging to our guns and Bibles."

"Yeah, preach it, preach it." Shouts echo out from the audience.

"Embracing freedom is the greatest test, the greatest challenge, the greatest energizer, and the greatest high all at the same time. Hopefully, you'll soon experience the same feeling of serenity we have come to know. From what I understand so far, you're of the same mentality and are willing to give up modern life for the greatest gift of all, your right to choose, your right to your life, your liberty, and your pursuit of happiness. Thank You. I bow before you as you have made my day. Can I say . . . with the greatest gratitude . . . Welcome to this new island world."

"I think I just heard Wendy Susan and the kids come aboard. Ladies and Gentlemen, let me introduce my backbone: Wendy, come up here, please; Melody and Susan, greet these wonderful people. These ladies have started working the land so that we can become self-sufficient, not needing help from Washington of all places, nor having to listen to those so-called experts. Those two good-looking guys are George and Thomas, twins of Mark and Susan, and gorgeous Melody, their daughter. The ladies at their side are their wives, Ruth and Anabele, and here comes Janet Studebaker, a college professor of Agronomy at Texas A&M. Well, she was."

"This is us folks, all ten of us. We've enjoyed our freedom here, and now I hope you will learn to rest and enjoy your freedom too. Thank You."

Mark takes Susan's hand, and the two of them approach center stage, with Wendy joining Bruce, all of them looking out at the crowd, when suddenly a group at the back of the auditorium start playing a marching melody. The crowd rises to their feet again in loud, thundering applause. Mark, Susan, and the others look over the crowded hall from one side to the other, smiling and waving, and patiently wait for the crowd to quiet down.

Still holding the microphone, Bruce speaks up over the chatter. "These ladies are as shocked as I am, and I'm sure they'd prefer to absorb it all first. You'll get to work with us shortly."

Turning back to the crowd, he continues: "Thank you all for coming. Thank you."

"Jim, come and get the microphone and take over. Please . . . these people are bored with my ramblings. Did you bring us something to eat? I want a rib-eye steak."

Jim calls out. "Bob Tuit, where are you? Come up here."

A large man in his fifties approaches the stage. Jim bends over and says something to Bob.

"Folks, The time is now four-forty-five here in this part of the world, and it's about time we had something to eat. Dinner will be ready at six-thirty, and then fre'll party. We are making history. And, No! We are not going to Hawaii. This is it. We've arrived to build our wonderland. Thank You, and dinner will be served then. We need some volunteers to rearrange the chairs and set the tables."

Jim looks at Mark and says: "How was that? But you guys better clean up and come back here for dinner. Bob will have one of his best meals waiting for you."

Mark looks over to Susan. "I guess if we're going to a dinner party, we'd better get ready. Look at me, and you too. We need a dip in the lake. Eh?" The ten of them exit the auditorium, walk down the ramp toward the loading door, and climb down to the boat to get ashore.

"Jim, we're taking the boat ashore, and hopefully, we'll be back for dinner. Thanks, Jim, you've made my day. Give me time to absorb what just happened."

"See you then," Jim says. "Need any help with the boat?"

The kids take the pontoon while Mark, Susan, Bruce, and Wendy get in the row boat. They were all speechless on the ride back to shore. Not a word was said as they each sat there looking at nothing in particular, just staring out into the distance as if someone were to begin talking, they would wake up, and the dream would be over, or the nightmare would end. Bewildered. Confused. Surprised, anxious, and frightened too. Upon reaching shore, Bruce anchors the boat and proceeds toward the dock, each of them instinctively knowing that the somewhat dressier clothes are still in the ship's quarters.

Mark sheepishly says, "OK, lets get cleaned up and ready to party, and we'll be eating something other than fish, tuna, or Spam" as they head toward their ship and quarters. The silence continues inside Mark and Susan's quarters as Susan undresses and proceeds to bathe, while Mark sits down on the side of the bed, lays down softly with his arms and hands folded behind his head, the pillow covering his ears. Closing his eyes, he thought he would go into a deep slumber, knowing that he shouldn't. *This is too much,'* he thinks. *'Jim, you've gathered all these people together, procured supplies, the ship, everything,*

"God," he prays out loud, "bless Jim mightily. He went to all that trouble."

He gives in, his eyes shut, and falls asleep.

As Susan exits the bathroom, she sees that Mark is out cold.

"Wish I could do that." She mumbles to herself. "Wish I could join him, but we've got to go to dinner."

Susan softly squeezes his upper arm and whispers: "Mark, wake up. We've got to get going; they'll be waiting for us."

He opened his eyes big and stretched out his arms. "Oh yeah. Was that a dream?

"No, Dream, and you know it too. "Now get up and ready.

"It won't take me long. Got any ideas on what I should wear? I wonder how Bruce and Wendy are doing. How about the kids? Have you heard from them?'

"Mark, get in the shower. They'll be Ok."

Thomas, George, and their wives arrived early to the shore, waiting for Mom, Dad, Melody, Bruce, Wendy, and Janet to come down to the dock to take the boat out to the cruise liner.

Janet appears all spruced up, lipstick, fresh makeup, and her hair done up beautifully, looking like she had never left her job at the university. "Wow, where do you think you're going? You look fantastic," says Susan.

Bruce says, "OK, we're all here. You guys look great."

"This is unbelievable," Wendy remarks. "I'm excited. Imagine, we're going to get a meal served to us, maybe with cloth napkins, water glasses with ice cubes, and sitting around a table in comfy chairs with waiters re-filling our glasses as I snap my fingers."

Ruth, Anabele, and Janet simultaneously say: "Ice cubes?

Bruce says, "it would have been nice if we had treated ourselves to something like this once in a while.

"Well," Mark says, "yes, it would have. We started with the chicken roast. Now, let's go enjoy a good meal. Jim said that Bob is one of the best chefs and we sure will enjoy his cooking. Yes, even if it's hot and spicy. His muffins are fantastic, he said."

They all get in the safety boats and head out to the liner.

Arriving, they see that Jim is waiting for them. "Come on, you guys, we've got the tables set, the band is playing, and we're going to eat one of Bob's finest. I think he's got filets for you guys. What took you so long?"

"Hey." Mark replies: "It seems that I took a nap, and we're the guests, and remember, it's proper for guests to arrive late. But then again, you guys are guests of mine in my harbor, on my island, and things run on my time here, and don't forget it . . . you old washed-up Navy captain."

"You just won't let me forget. Welcome to MY ship, Mark. Now, let's have a good time. Wow, Janet, you clean up very nicely. Oh, you all look like you're ready to dance. Welcome and come aboard."

Entering the passenger dining room, they see it is just about full. The people are standing in small groups around the perimeter, around the tables, some sitting, some standing, and they notice about twenty small children playing together in the back. A band consisting only of a piano, trumpet, saxophone, guitar, and trombone plays softly, adding to the atmosphere.

Bruce remarks, "I feel like we're in a political fundraiser."

Jim asks, "When did you ever go to one of those?"

"The one and only one I ever went to, I think it was in 1997, at the Waldorf in Washington, when I was still playing golf, the PGA encouraged a bunch of us to be guests at a Bill Clinton dinner."

Jim says, "Come on, I'll show you your tables up front."

Mark asks if they'd be expected to give any off the cuff remarks tonight.

"No, not tonight, Mark. Some of our people wanted to hear some more from you, but I put a stop to that and instead, if . . . you don't mind, that is . . . I'd like you all to stay around after dinner and greet everyone, get to know some of the folks who've sacrificed it all to be part of history in the making, on this island, away from the civilized world. In other words, stand in a greeting line and shake hands. We will hear a few remarks from one of the pastors on board, though.

"So here we are, have a seat, and let me get these people settled down, and we can get going. I'll see you later."

Jim gets on the stage, and the band stops playing, breaking the festive mood. The people start quietly moving to their tables as Jim grabs the mike and announces, "Ok folks, let's take our seats and have a good time. The waiters will be attending the tables very soon." He gives them all a few moments to get seated and then speaks into the mike again. "Ladies and gentlemen and honored guests, let me introduce a very good friend of mine and the pastor of that mega-church in Atlanta known as Peachtree: the reverend Patrick Mooneyham.

Pastor Mooneyham enters from behind the curtains carrying a Bible in his right hand.

"Stand with me, please."

"Father God, this is an honor, a historic event in the Pacific you initiated. Your spirit has been present in everyone here today, leading and guiding them to follow your gentle signs over the past months. They have given up all to be here. These people represent all walks of life, and you have blessed their talents and abilities. We ask that you continue to bless each of us as we build a new community under your blessings and principles. Respectfully, we pray that the principles of this community under your guidance. Yes, Father, we do believe you instituted it all, and, ahh, we ask that you be a special blessing to Mark, Bruce, and their families; strengthen them, encourage them, and enlighten them daily as they will now become our guides in building this community. Let everyone agree, with the same willingness, to do whatever it takes to make it happen, to create that shining light on a hill for the entire world to see. Bless Jim, Father, for he has sacrificed so much to gather us together and bring us here today. May this food we are about to receive be a blessing to us all. Amen"

"Enjoy your meal."

Jim walks down to the main floor and walks to Mark's table. Bruce stands to his feet as Jim approaches, reaching out to shake his hand. "Thank You, Jim. Thanks again. Umm, where will pastor Mooneyham be seated, I'd like to chat with him for a minute."

Jim looks up and around. "Ah, there he is," pointing to the rear on the left.

"Thanks, Ok, I see him." Bruce makes his way through the tables, and at each table he passes, someone gets up to shake his hand and say a few words. Bruce stops and takes the time to greet each person, reaching across and circling each table as he slowly makes his way to where the pastor is sitting. "Pastor Mooneyham, I'm Bruce Wilcox."

"Yes, Bruce, I listened to you this afternoon, which was inspiring."

"I'd just like to thank you for your wonderful prayer personally," Bruce tells the pastor. "I needed it. I think we all did. I'd like to get together with you soon. You are staying around, are you not?"

"Yes, Bruce, I came to work just like everyone and hope to be here till my end. Yes, I'd be delighted to talk with you Bruce. We'll make a point of it at your convenience." Bruce then excuses himself and slowly heads back to the table.

The waiters, volunteers imitating experienced servers, make their way to serve everyone. Bob Tuit, the chef, and a helper bring the food to their table first, as another waiter fills the glasses with ice water. "Look at that: ice cubes," Anabele says, before anyone else has a chance.

Periodically, someone would interrupt their conversation, kneel next to Mark or Bruce, and say a few words.

Finishing up the meal, Susan announces that she and the ladies would like to visit the lady's room of this luxury liner. "After all, what we've become used to here has been a porta john, sometimes just behind some rocks, so excuse us as we go see what a real restroom looks like again."

Jim and Mike come over to the table and sit. "Well, how was the meal? Are you rested some? Where did the girls go?"

Bruce tells them they had to see what a real lady's room looks like.

Mark leans over toward Jim, "We've got to plan what we're going to do tomorrow, and after that, so can we chat afterward? We've got to figure out a way to get your ship to the dock and mine out of there and well . . . I don't know what you brought."

"Mike can put together an inventory list for you pronto. I had your list of supplies you initially brought, so I added more to it and additional equipment."

"The meal was great, Jim, and I'd like to thank Bob for all his work," interrupts Bruce.

Jim, pointing toward the left side door, tells Bruce: "Bob will probably be in the kitchen cleaning up."

Looking back toward Mark, Jim tells him, "Tomorrow is tomorrow, and we'll take it one step at a time, so Mark, try not to make this as only your thing. You've got all of us to pinch in, and we each have ideas about what we'd like to do first. Personally, I'd like to get some of that firewood unloaded for tomorrow night."

The ladies return, and Mike gets up to pull it out for Janet. "Thank You, Mike. Who are you here with?" Janet asks.

"I've come with Jim, and so many of the others here are my buddies. They're all my friends. Well, I need to go and get an inventory list up for you guys. See you all later." While Mike was walking toward the rear of the auditorium, Janet's eyes followed him step by step. Mike looks back toward Janet before leaving the room.

As they proceed toward the front stage, a considerable thunder is heard. Flashes of lightning are seen through the small windows on both sides of the ship.

"Here we go, another thunderstorm," says Mark. "Jim, these storms have been getting quite common lately. Fall is approaching. They come up suddenly. After it's over, the sky clears, and it's beautiful. We've been noticing that more streams and rivers are forming, depressions are becoming lakes, and more and more vegetation is emerging."

Jim gets the microphone and announces to the crowd: "OK folks, it's just a thunderstorm. Now, if you'd like to shake hands with these ten brave people, then form a line over here, as they would like to briefly meet every one of you. But please make it brief. We've got some long, hard, tough days ahead of us, and we all could use a good night's sleep before we get to work building this new community."

The line forms, and the greetings begin with each person reaching out to shake hands and say a few words. The process lasted almost two hours while the band was playing softly throughout.

The first one in line introduces himself as Jeremie Bancrof and his wife, Mary.

"Jeremie and Mary, it's nice to meet you, and welcome to this island. What kind of work did you do in the States?" Mark asks.

"Mark, I owned a small business as my wife did too. Mary ran a beauty salon, and I had a three-man carpenter shop building cabinets and staircases for the nice homes in the Phoenix area. The housing bubble bust, and then new home construction stopped, and I had to let those guys go. I couldn't afford to keep them as it was hard to get any work. We had a little saved up, so we hope to start afresh here. As this island grows, I'll be ready. It will grow, won't it, Mr. Tebonson?"

Responding, Mark somewhat satisfies the young man's question. "Well, not the island, but us, our community, Jeremie, but how soon? We'll just have to wait until then. It's good to have you on board, Jeremie and Mary. You'll probably be busy as our ladies may want their hair done soon."

Next in line was a couple introducing themselves as Ron and Diane Comestar from New Haven, Conn. Ron tells Mark he retired as a Middle school principal two years ago. "I'm just fifty-seven, Mark. They indicated that I was of the old school, resisting the new progressive ways of teaching, ah, to lower standards. The school is mixed race, and the administrators insisted that lowering standards was necessary to bring the students up to grade level. Of course, they didn't say it that way, but that's what it was. Stupidity. So when we heard about Jim's proposal, Diane and I quickly jumped aboard. I see quite a few kids on this ship, and hopefully, we can start a school system soon using our methods, even teaching the classics, Latin and Greek too. I'm ready. Diane is a teacher also."

"Thank You. We'll need to start some kind of a school soon." Mark replies. "Would you get with the rest of the teachers on board and get something organized?"

Next in line introduces himself as Ralph Banister from Oklahoma, informing Mark, Bruce, George, and Thomas, "I retired from a city job as a golf course greens keeper.

Bruce tells Ralph that perhaps we can build a course someday.

On and on it goes, one after another, each one briefly explaining why they left the States to live on a new island a thousand miles from anywhere.

The five guys playing in the band were the last ones to come over and greet the bunch. Shaking Mark's hand, "I'm Doctor Homer Hardcover, and this is Doctor Demitrius Abstra. My wife Penny, and this is Jennifer. We worked together at Georgetown University Hospital. We're here to entertain, to work shovels, tie knots, whatever, and to put on band-aids when needed."

"Thank You so much," Mark says. "And hopefully, we'll just need your shovel work, doctors. But why would you give up such a meaningful profession to come out here to no man's land?"

"Because you're here, Mark." Homer continues: "When we heard about your escape move, we started talking. Over the past decade, we've been getting more disenchanted with the medical system, the mystifyingly stymieing regulations, the paperwork, the endless documentation, always wondering when or if a group of lawyers will knock on our door, taking us to court because a patient thought we ought to be magicians pulling a gene out of a hat healing all their ailments with one pill."

"So now, doctors and nurses must submit to it all, bow down to the bureaucrats, or find another line of work."

"Doctors, Thank you. It is insane. Responsibility has given way to satisfying the flesh. Susan and I talked of getting a nice retirement home in the Caribbean somewhere on the beach and just sit back, rest, and enjoying golf, tennis, cards, taking boat rides, snorkeling, and such. But then, this island formed, and here we are. A tent as our home. Doctors, it's great to have you here. Thank you again. And if there's anything I can do for you, please let me know."

Another man had been sitting aside waiting for an opening with Mark and Bruce, so when the doctors left, he stood and approached them. "Mark, Bruce, I'm Norman Sweetwater, and Bruce, I think you might remember me."

Taking a concentrated look at Norman, Bruce says, "Well, yes, I do. You were the construction guy on that new course design I was involved in. That was four or five years ago, right?"

"Well, four years and three months, to be exact." Norman responds.

"Anyway, when I heard of your move out here, I started looking for ways to join you guys. Then I heard about Jim taking applications, and well . . . hear I am."

Mark asks him, "Norman, why would you sacrifice it all to come out here?"

"I'm a heavy equipment operator, Mark. If someone wants to remove or add a foot of sand or remove rocks from their land, I can do it, and I could slope it twelve, or three degrees. Or if they want to add just two inches of soil, I can do that. I submitted a bid on that new golf course Bruce designed, and if I remember correctly, all the permits were granted. It was approved by every local entity that could possibly be affected. The neighbors approved. The city approved. I was ready to put the metal to the ground when the EPA showed up, shutting the entire project down claiming it would disturb the newly identified wetlands. Gads

Mark, it was farmland for fifty years. Just because the land changed hands, the EPA felt the need to inspect it. Condemn it they did. And I lost thousands in the deal. That was it for me, and here I am."

Bruce adds, "Norman, you got it. That's exactly what happened."

"I'm sorry, Norman," Mark says. "But those stories are getting more and more frequent. But it's good to have you here. Do you have your family here, too?"

"Yes, Mark. My wife and two boys, ages ten and eight. My wife has been fantastic in supporting me. Getting the boys to come was not a problem, as she was home-schooling them."

Thank You Norman, we could use your services soon, I'm sure." Mark tells him.

"He's good, Mark. What he can do with a backhoe is amazing."

Mark turns his head toward the line, noticing that Melody is sitting down with a lady holding her hands while seeming to be listening intently to this thirty-ish-looking girl. Susan and Wendy are shaking hands with others, and at the front of the line is Ruth, Anabele, and Janet, surrounding others, shaking their heads in glee and loud laughter.

"Gentlemen, I see you've been patiently waiting your turn, so what has brought you guys out here?"

"I'm Patrick Mooneyham, and this is Father Steven Lumarcher."

"Yes," says Mark. "Thank you for that prayer over the meal earlier, and thank you for coming, but why?"

Reverend Mooneyham starts by saying, "The two of us went to Bible school together, so we're old friends from way back, and we have continued our friendship even though we went separate ways after graduating. I'll let Steve tell you his story first."

Father Steve Lumarcher says, "It's great to meet you guys, and I'm thrilled to be here, to be part of this from the beginning. Patrick and I have worked together on several community-wide charities over the years, and we still see eye to eye on the spiritual needs of people; we just take different paths to meet those needs. I left the protestant way, realizing that rituals are essential tools, and I desired that. Forgive me for criticizing my brethren, but I saw protestant churches seemingly heading toward looseness, a kind of relaxed, following our God's words when it's convenient. There did not seem to be an orderliness to follow. I saw the need for that. People need it.

"Even before attending school, I've always been upset about how the Protestants have split into hundreds of different denominations, each of them fighting over scriptural interpretations, each claiming they have the only way. Our understandings are finite, too. I began to see that a ritual of doing something the same way all the time is important. It's unifying. It eliminates the bickering. So, I went Catholic, entered a seminary, and became a priest. We agree on the main points of scripture. Jesus is the King of Kings. He died so that we may live, and we degenerate humans need His grace, mercy, and forgiveness."

"Thank you, Father. It'll be a blessing to have you here." Mark tells him. "Now, reverend Mooneyham, it's your turn."

"Mark and Bruce, I'm the one who is honored to be here." Patrick says. "I've been blessed to pastor a church in Atlanta, which has grown tremendously.

"But why leave that?" Mark asks.

"Well, It was because of the looseness and bickering within the Church body, accepting loud boisterous music. To me, that's not worship. It's upside down. Back in the early days, there was a sense of shame connected with breaking laws, but now shame is shunned as offensive, and demeaning.

"The church was silent during the awful years of segregation. Pastors did not speak up, leaving the civil riots to escalate. And now America is sliding toward anarchy on one hand, where the individual is king; or Statism, a type of tyranny, socialism or communism on the other hand, looking to the government as lord."

"While pastoring, I demanded that the church be respected as a place of worship when entered. All the greetings must be held in the vestibule or outside, and when entering the worship center, they would be quiet and respectful and find a seat quickly without even a whisper or hint of a wave of hello to anyone. They were there to worship rather than to socialize. The members came to respect that. They felt the spirituality of it. It worked well, and the church grew.

"It was sad to leave, but I felt the calling to be a part of this new community. I hope I can, that Steve and I can. Having heard so much of you two, I believe we're of the same mind. So, here we are."

Mark responds, "Thank you for coming, we are of the same mind, and it has been our desire from the beginning to establish a colony based on those principles. I, too, got disenchanted with the church when they put loud music first, creating a rock concert atmosphere."

Bruce tells them, "Thank you for your brief summation. I'm looking forward to more of our meetings together."

The thunderstorm continued in the area as the heavy rain pelts the ship. The ship is protected in the harbor from the larger waves created by the storm's winds. The relative harbor calmness keeps the ship from rocking much.

Jim calls the band together again. "Could we possibly have some dance music from you guys? The storm keeps us inside, so we've nothing to do but dance. So everyone, let's party tonight as the work starts in the morning. The freedom bar is open to responsible drinking."

The band starts playing softly, setting the tone for the evening. Slowly, couples approach the front, where tables are moved to create an open area.

Ruth and Anabele grab George and Thomas, entering the dance floor among the others. Susan and Mark move together to join in. Jim approached Janet, and before Jim could say anything,

Janet was on her feet, grabbing his hands and heading toward the dance area.

"Jim. This is a real treat for us, a good break from our daily work. Could I copy Andy Rooney and say: You've made my day."

As they're dancing, Jim asks, "Janet, in your opinion, what is next? How can we help? I know I suddenly surprised you guys, and if Mark wasn't so composed, he might have kicked my butt, but we must work this out. We can. These people came to help, and like me, don't want to sit around and wait but to get busy. I think we've got to hit the road running tomorrow morning. Where do we start?"

"From my standpoint, and this is mine, it's not Mark or Bruce speaking here. You caught us unaware, and I think Mark may still be upset about it. We all may be, as we were enjoying the peace. No conflicts. We were all on the same page. No one else to be concerned about, just the ten of us, and we know each other like we know ourselves. But we also knew it was inevitable that other folks from somewhere would eventually want to make this island home.

"I'm glad it was you who became the inevitable." Janet comforts Jim. "First thing though, I think, is to get this liner anchored to our dock so that whatever equipment and supplies you've got onboard can be unloaded and put to use as quickly as possible. The people will then have an easier time getting back to their quarters. Our boat will have to be moved away so that yours can take its place. That process may take up the entire day tomorrow. Beyond that is beyond that."

"I agree. Could you and Mike spearhead the details?"

"Hey, Jim." Janet quickly replies, "Mark is in charge around here, and I'm not doing anything without his knowledge and approval, Ok? You must talk to Mark about this first. You must get together with both Mark and Bruce. Ask them the same questions you asked me, and see what they say, and if that's the way they want to go, I'd be delighted to work with all. Things like where we put the equipment, the supplies, who's going to use them. What are we going to work on first, roads, buildings, homes, a meeting hall, or a church? The sewer systems, water are all important parts of a community, but what do we do first? Where will these people put their tents? Talk with them, Jim. Work it out."

Thinking the evening is still young, Jim is ready to discuss tomorrow's activities with Mark and Bruce. He leaves Janet to find them. "Hey Mark, Bruce, don't you think we ought to get together on what to do tomorrow?"

Bruce looks at Mark with that tired, not now, ready-to-call-it-a-night look. Mark looks at Jim: "You know, buddy, our schedule has been very different than what you're used to. Mostly, we climb into bed at nightfall and get up at daybreak, with no alarm clocks. I don't wear a watch anymore, Jim. You surprised our peace, and now, a good night's sleep is needed, and with this storm, I'm going to stay on the ship tonight and wake up when I wake up."

"But it's pouring rain out there."

"So?" returns Mark. "Jim, please, we're worn out . . . in a good way, and what we're going to do tomorrow can wait until the morning. Ok? Please inform everyone that we'll see them tomorrow. You're a blessing, but it's still a shock I've got to overcome. We'll see you tomorrow. Night Jim"

As they gather together for the ride in the small boat back to the dock and their ship's quarters, another lightning bolt strikes nearby, startling them all.

"Oh hell," George bursts out. "Ruth, let's at least stay here until this storm passes. How about it?"

"Yeah," Anabele yells.

"Amen to that," says Janet, as they all turn around and head back into the auditorium.

Susan says, "Is there a possibility that Jim has extra berths we could use tonight? We ought to take advantage of these comforts."

Jim sees them coming back through the door. "Well, that storm is packing in some rain. Hey, you guys could use our extra cabins aboard tonight. Are you ready for a dry night . . . to enjoy these comforts while they're available? Mike can show you where to go."

Mark leans over to get Jim's attention. "Since we're staying for the night, perhaps . . . ah . . . we could get together for a few moments talking about what tomorrow holds for us . . . if it quits raining, that is. OK?   The ladies can . . . well, Susan, Wendy, Janet, all of you can do whatever for an hour or so while we figure out what happens next."

"Ok! Amen to that." The ladies agree and thank Jim again.

Mike was behind Jim and heard the news. "Follow me, ladies, and I'll show you your rooms." Mike starts walking down a long hallway leading the ladies and periodically looking back to get a glimpse of Janet.

In the captain's room, Mark and Bruce, along with George and Thomas, get seated, and Jim starts, "The way I see it Mark, is that first thing tomorrow, we should get your ship away from the pier so that I can maneuver this liner up to the dock so we can start unloading some of our equipment, tools and supplies. Also, it would be easier for our guests to get off the ship and view some of the landscape; the children could possibly go swimming. They could do some sightseeing. What do you think, Mark? Is the pier strong enough for tractors, backhoes, and forklifts?"

"Well, we got our tractors on it, so it should be fine. And I think you must have been reading my mind."

"Mark," Jim asks; "How did you guys ever get that pier built?"

Mark says, "That was a job. I brought along some seaplane-type pontoons and some buoys that we could use as floats for the dock. We started on shore digging by hand down for our initial supports, soon finding out we couldn't get deep enough, so we built a raft-type boat out of pontoons that would support the tractor getting it ashore, and we slowly worked our way out, attaching the two by eights to the pontoons as we went. It took about three weeks to get it out far enough so the boat could pull alongside. It wasn't easy, but we figured it out as we proceeded."

"It looks good," Jim responds.

"We'll proceed with that plan tomorrow," Jim announces.

Bruce, sensing that Jim perhaps is making plans for them, pipes in and informs Jim that what happens and what we do on this Island is Mark's baby, not mine, yours, or anyone else."

"Bruce, let's not start the, er, who's on first bit, OK?" Mark pitches in. "We'll adjust as always, and now we're in this together as a team, and we've got to remember this is a team effort. Everyone has a thought on what should be done, and we should be willing to listen to anyone willing to speak up. It may take a bit longer, but that's ok."

"So, tomorrow, we'll untie our ship and motor it out so this liner can get anchored to the dock. We'll have to get our personal items we keep in our rooms of the ship transferred over here if Jim will allow us to stay the nights, if we choose not to sleep in our tents."

"Of course," agrees Jim.

Mark continues, "Mike has provided me with an inventory list, and I've circled a few items that should be unloaded first. Can we go over that list now, Jim?"

"Sure thing. Fire away."

"Dirt; we can use building up the soil for our garden right away. Tractors: we will use for everything. The backhoe we'll use for smoothing out the road(s). Concrete used to start laying the foundations of our buildings. And, of course, the people would need whatever personal items to set up their tents if they so desire. That'll probably take care of the first few days, perhaps even a week. Oops. The pier is strong enough for about four thousand pounds at a time, which Freould be max. We'll have to work around anything heavier than that and find another way. And, I'd like to get some firewood off too, as I'm ready for a campfire . . . tomorrow night. Ok, everyone?"

"One other thing, Mark," Jim says. "Do you have any thoughts of what contribution theses folks can make and how they can be kept busy tomorrow, as we'll not need them all unloading this stuff. Some, yes, and Mike is the best to handle those details.

How about the rest of them? They'll be anxious to get started on something."

"Hmm," ponders Mark. "Like I said before, they could walk around and get a sense of everything."

George speaks up. "Thomas and I would be glad to take them on tours of the place. I saw on that list, you've got several four-wheeler jeeps on board, so if we can get them unloaded, we can use those to show people around. You got a couple of trailers too.   Also, we'll probably need some more fuel, and I'd like to have the smoker unloaded, and then some beef and franks for dinner before the campfire. Yeah, beef and franks."

"Got that, Jim?" Mark says.

Bruce enters the conversation: "As the people see the area, we'll let them pick a site for their home. Perhaps we could have a lottery-type thing to eliminate the arguing.   Hells bells, we haven't begun to map out the area yet. I guess that's going to have to wait. I'm getting ahead of myself."

"In the meantime," Mark says. "If anyone wants to pitch a tent to stay in, we can point them all to the best-suited area. We'll have a tent city to begin our little town. They can always be moved. But, don't let anyone get the idea that later on, we'll share and share alike regardless of the input. William Bradford had that stupid idea for the Plymouth Colony, which proved long ago that communism does not work. Never has, never will. It still raises its ugly head now and then under different names, always making it sound like the proverbial answer that cures all ills. Governments of the world have tried it under many different names. Who was it that said 'doing the same stupid thing again but expecting different results is insanity?'"

Mark questions, "Is there anything else for tonight? I'm bushed."

They all shake their heads, either agreeing that what has been said is enough or that they are worn out and ready to give in to a deep slumber between fresh sheets.

"Good, let's get some sleep. Tomorrow will be busy, if the storm passes."

While the guys were hashing over the chores for tomorrow, the girls, having seen their rooms, gathered at a table at the bar, ordering their favorite drinks. "Well, gals," Anabele says, "this has been a great blessing. Just to get out of jeans, a dirty old T-shirt, and boots and to be served a real professionally prepared meal hovered over by servers, with cloth napkins. We needed it,"

Melody says, "Yeah, tonight was fantastic, a nice break, but tomorrow and beyond will be different than what we've become used to."

"Imagine what we'll be able to get done now," Wendy offers.

Susan, looking at Janet, asks. "Janet, how's Mike?" Pausing, she continues, "I saw that look on your face whenever Mike was near, and you even turned and followed him out as he left the auditorium. Humm? What's going on Janet? Are you getting a thing for Mike already, eh?"

Embarrassed, Janet replies, "Oh, nothing. There is nothing going on between Mike and I, so stop it? I just met the guy."

Melody says, "He's a hunk. He got my attention. I'd die right now to have someone looking like him coming home to dinner. Perhaps there wouldn't even be a dinner. I'd serve him something else."

"Janet, do you want us to help you get in Mike's way somehow?" Wendy asks

Emphatically, Janet insists, "No, now just stay out of it, OK. Don't you dare try anything? Not a thing, Nothing, Nada. Comprende?"

"I didn't notice him looking in my direction like he looked at you." Returns Melody. "Yep, Janet, I think he's got an eye for you already. You lucky gal."

"Don't you say anything! Don't you do anything! Keep out of it!" Janet warns the others. "I'm going to turn in."

Chapter 20

"*There are far, far better things ahead than any we left behind*" is a favorite quote from C. S. Lewis," Mark tells the auditorium packed with anxious people sitting down to breakfast on the liner. "Today is a new chapter in our life . . . your life now too. The plans for this new island have yet to be completed, not even started yet, as we have to make those plans together. When we came here, we had simple ideas of supporting ourselves to the best of our ability, without outside influence or outside help. It was just the ten of us, and now look around. It's now three-hundred-fifteen pilgrims to this Island.

"Yes, this changes any simple plans we had. We will have numerous meetings, some soon enough and some later after you all get acclimated to the climate and each other. The road ahead will be tedious. Physically, it will be demanding. Mentally, it will be challenging. Socially, it will be what will be.

"But, it can be done, and it will be done, and if anybody can do it, we . . . that's all of us, can and will develop a new town, a new whatever. I did not say community, this time." Mark continues. Remove the letters t and y and insert s and m, and what do you see: communism. I don't like to use that word anymore when we're talking about creating a new town, city, area, group, neighborhood or, how about this, a new village?"

The crowd erupts in applause and shouts of "village, village."

"We do not have numerous regulators watching us before, during, or after we start building. We don't have any codes to follow. We will design it to suit our needs. We're in this together, and when we. ay together, we'll enjoy building this village together.

"Jim has brought along an extensive list of supplies, tools, and equipment for us to put to work, making the job easier . . . lots easier than the limited equipment we started the process with. This morning, we will start by moving these ships so that this ship will be tied to the dock, and then we'll start unloading the equipment and supplies. Your tents and camping supplies.

"I'm sure Mike is organizing this as quickly as I want to eat this fantastic breakfast, and then we'll get to work. Hopefully, we will have a giant campfire on the beach this evening, sing songs, and enjoy the beauty of the area. Last night's storms have gone on; the rains have stopped, so we've got clear, beautiful skies to begin this adventure. Thank you all, and God bless us all and this land of newness."

"Father Lumarcher, Would you bless this meal and our beginnings?" Jim asks.

He does.

During breakfast, Susan asks Mark: "Well, what can the girls and I do this morning as you guys move the ships around?"

"Ah, it'd be great if you could gather our personal items out of our ship onto the dock, so you could move those things into our rooms here, so then we wouldn't have to take the pontoon out when we wanted to spend the night inside. We'll enjoy the cabins here."

"Consider it done."

George asks his dad what he wants them to do today. "Get with Mike." Mark quickly returns. "Bruce and I will be meeting on shore with Jim this morning, taking him up the hill to see what we've started, to see for himself the landscape so he can get his thoughts together on placing tents for the passengers. Perhaps he may have other thoughts. Everything's changed. So, we have to change with it, and need additional plans on where and what to do with all these people. I'd like to see a grouping of tents in a circle around a central open area, say ten to twenty. Twenty to fifty people per group would mean six to fifteen areas. We've got a bunch of rocks to move, to build paths or roads to connect these areas. Sitting here talking about it doesn't seem possible, but with everyone helping somehow, we'll make it happen."

Thomas says: "That sounds like Indian tribes."

"Yep, it sure does," George adds. "If it worked for them, it ought to work for us."

"But, they built them that way for protection from enemies of other tribes," Thomas adds.

"Well," Mark says, "Would we rather have rectangular areas, like the States, or circular. How about triangles? I have always admired the circular idea as all tents pointed to one spot in the middle. Say for a campfire.

Bruce perks up. "Now, why do you think the UN is spying on us, flying those drones overhead taking pictures, what we're doing, our progress, determining how to take over the island for their plans of moving indigenous peoples here? Mark my words; we will have enemies wanting this land."

"Scary thoughts," says Mark, adding, "But just as the early settlers of America originally thought they'd be left alone by the British, and they could develop the land to their liking, we have been thinking the same way. No natives are here, so our only enemy will come from outside. Sometime in the future, we may have to defend this land. Hopefully, those in power across these seas are thinking like those geologist experts, saying this island will not be ready for human habitation for hundreds if not thousands of years, and they'll leave us to die alone or give up. That's what we're counting on."

"Well, however, the tents are set up now and can easily be moved. So, shall we get to work?" Marks announces as he carefully folds the napkin and pushes the chair away from the table.

Mike is below in the cargo hold, directing the forklift operator to move pallets of supplies and equipment around. Many of the people are hanging on the railing looking towards shore, at the beach, the harbor, and the mountains in the background, staring at the numerous limestone pillars reaching up skyward and what looks like a barren land of rocks, and that's all, no trees growing on the gentle slopes right in front of them, no shrubs, and no grass can be seen. A few birds flying over are the only sign of life.

One of the passengers spurts out: "It's just rocks, nothing but rocks, big rocks and small rocks, it's . . . just rocks."

"What did you expect?" another passenger replies.

"You're looking in the wrong area. Over there, I see shrubs and vegetation appearing." Another says, pointing in that direction.

"Guys, let's get our ship ready to be moved," Mark announces as the original ten climb down to a boat and then row to their ship, tied to the dock. Upon arriving, the ladies head inside to their respective cabins as Jim is seen approaching shore on one of his rescue boats.

"Mark, are you ready to give me a tour? How long before your stuff is packed and on the pier? We have that much time for a quick look up and over this hill. I didn't get to see much of it yesterday."

George and Thomas go aboard their ship to help the ladies move the boxes, the clothes, and suitcases as Jim, Mark, and Bruce get in the Jeep to motor up the hill.

"Interesting place up here," says Jim. "Mark, what are your ideas on how to set up the tents? Wow, those are some tents you guys have there. You must have had them specially made."

"Yes, I did, and they have worked well for us."

Mark explains his thoughts of circling the tents and briefly points out where.

"Thinking ahead," says Mark, "I would like to see the buildings starting over there. Down there in the valley is our plantation. That's where Mike can start unloading the dirt. What else is on your mind, Jim?"

"I've already had people ask me about work assignments, whether we'll eat onboard every day, will they be bound to this area, or if they could move to another, and when they could start building their home, if there's a sewer, electricity, schools for the kids, if the water is safe for drinking, and if wi-fi is available out here. They're anxious to get going."

"I suspected as such," answers Mark. "That out of this many people, there will be problems with some who just might have hoped this would be a vacation paradise. That we would have the island supplied with everything in place and ready to move in. What did you tell them Jim?"

"Just what I told them when they signed up. No, to all of the above, until we, that's you, pointing my finger at their chest, and I make it happen. That's what I told them before we left. Mark, I got over twenty-five hundred applications from all over the country. I spent hours and hours, night and day for weeks, picking out those with the best potential. They were required to contribute $25,000 to the cause, and to bring their own supplies, food, and personal necessities to last them a year. I obtained additional supplies for the ships store. We sent them further information about the hardships, the lean times, the work, the adverse conditions, the unproven climate, and the dedication they must show. Then we asked for another application if they were still serious about jumping aboard this ship. So, I was surprised when I was asked those questions this morning. I thought they fully understood the nature of this adventure from the beginning."

"We'll continue to have meetings with everyone. Now, let's get the ships moved around." Mark says.

After the ships are relocated, the cargo door of the cruise ship is lowered to the dock. Janet suggested that she could help Mike by directing each load to follow Mark, Bruce, George, or Thomas on the pier, allowing Mike to work inside the cargo bay directing the workers and drivers. Depending on the contents of the load, George and Thomas led the way, driving in front of the four-wheelers pulling trailers loaded with pallets of goods up the slope and down into the valley, or left or right on top of the hill, and left or right on the beach. The ladies supervised the groups of ten or more helpers stationed in each location to unload the trailers as they arrived while others were putting up canvas shelters, opening some of the crates and boxes of tools and supplies, and storing them under the canvas. Families erected their tents.

Many of the young families with children were already having a fun time on the rock-strewn beach, having been instructed before to beware of the volcanic ash possibly still under some of the rocks and that sharks have been seen. Don't go out beyond fifteen feet.   The beach is not yet like sand. They were told not to kick up the rocks and be careful as the ash could cause skin irritations, breathing problems and to keep the children away from what may look like dark sand, but they are piles of ash. Fortunately, none of the children had problems, although one of the fathers thought it would be a good idea to move some rocks into a dam-like formation, digging into the beach and creating a mini pond in front of the sand castle he built. Well, he disturbed the ash underneath, which rose into the air as he was bending over. The young man suffered from breathing problems and had to be taken inside the ship to be looked at by the doctors. He'll recover, but he won't do that again, and neither will others as they heard about it. It was just one of those unforeseen accidents, as Mark, Bruce, George, and Thomas had played volleyball on the beach without any problems. Even Janet had surmised that if there was any ash mixed in with the sand and pebbles, it was in minute amounts. Digging down in the sand is not what they expected anyone to do.

The young man's wife was quite upset.

Janet said she would get her ash detector out again and thoroughly survey the entire beach area for signs of other pockets. She had previously used the detector on the beach, but a quick search satisfied her that the beach area was clear and safe enough for the ten of them.

Later in the day, when Mike had finished directing traffic in and out of the cargo bay, he walked down the pier toward shore, where Janet was conversing with a few workers.

"Good days work, eh?" Mike calls out to Janet.

She responds: "You did it."

And Mike's reply was, "We did it. All seemed to go well, and you did a great job of directing traffic." Pausing a bit, Mike asks, "I didn't get to meet your husband, Janet. Where's he been?"

"Oh," returns Janet. "I'm here by myself as my husband was killed in that Iraqi conflict fifteen years ago."

"I'm sorry," sympathizes Mike. "How long was he over there, and what happened?

Sorry if this is a sensitive subject for you, I'm sorry I asked. My wife was killed in a horrible car crash by a drunk driver six years ago, so I know the suffering such a tragedy causes. Sorry, I brought it up."

Janet responds to Mike: "It's OK, Mike, I'm over it. However, every once in a while, when I'm in a certain situation, the thoughts of him killed like that hits me, and I have a meltdown. He was a marine trained in IED exploration, and one day he missed one. It exploded and blew him to pieces."

"Well." Mike says, "he didn't suffer any."

"Yeah, I know. And later, the details of that calmed me. Think about it. One moment you're doing what you do, and the next moment you're up there with Jesus. No bang was heard. No crying out in pain. No suffering. As fast as the blinking of our eye."

"Oh, that's beautiful," Mike says. "Just like you." He then tells Janet that he must get back on board the ship to get with his men as the mechanics are preparing the backhoe for tomorrow.

"Mark informed me earlier that Norman was ready to work the backhoe smoothing the roads up and down the hill." He tells Janet on his way back to the cargo door. "See you later."

The process of moving the supplies took six hours to get the first day's goods in place. It was a productive day's work without incidents other than the foolish one. One of the workers inside the cargo hold got sick. Doctor Demitrius said it was the stuffy heat inside. Another man smashed his arm between the door opening and the jeep, requiring immediate medical attention.

Breaking from the day's work and sitting on the beach in lawn chairs, Jim, Mark, and Bruce review what was done. "Mark, we had a good day today, a good start, don't you think so?" Jim asks.

"It was," Mark replies. "Except for that young man who neglected to follow safety instructions on the beach. The man that hurt his arm, well, things like that will happen, but for someone to go against our instructions is unacceptable. Still, I never thought it would be as easy as it seems today. Everyone involved did a fantastic job. And Mike, what a blessing he is. Where did you find him?"

Jim tells them that he met Mike several years ago when he was planning to expand his warehouse. "It wasn't an easy job, as the only way to add additional footage was to build along the sandy hillside. All the contractors I talked with said they couldn't do it without any guarantee. Then Mike came by, looked at it, and said, 'Sure, not much of a problem. My crew can do it for you.' They did too. We've been friends ever since."

"We've got to have more meetings with everyone about safety," Bruce interjects.

"Let's go eat guys. Bob is fixing another one of his favorites." Jim interjects.

After dinner, Mark and Bruce quickly head back to the beach area to start the campfire. "I wish everyone could get around this fire and enjoy it," Mark tells Bruce as they notice the girls approaching the area, followed by George and Thomas.

"Susan, what's going on inside the ship? Is anyone coming down to join us? Jim? Mike? The preachers? Doctors? Anyone?"

"It doesn't look like it," Wendy answers. "On our way out, we noticed Jim was busy instructing the crowd on various do's and don'ts, safety first. As we were leaving, we could hear Jim shouting at them: 'People,' he was saying, 'this is not a picnic, we're not here for fun, we're here to build and work together, creating a new village for us.'

"We could hear him directing his wrath at the young families playing in the surf today. That's all we heard."

"So, it might be just us enjoying the campfire tonight," Susan adds. "I doubt if anyone will be joining us."

"That'll work for me," said George.

"Janet, you spent most of the day working near Mike. How did that go?" asks Melody.

"Don't start on that," says Janet while putting a couple of marshmallows on a rod.

Bruce asks Mark if he thought the backhoe would be ready tomorrow to work on smoothing out the trails up the hill, on the plateau, and down to the valley.

"Jim told me that Mike was working on it as it had to be disassembled to get it on the ship. It will need to be taken off in pieces and re-assembled on land. I don't understand why, but that's the story."

"Ok, let's just enjoy the fire," says Mark, withdrawing his rod of marshmallows from the fire.

George says, "A few days ago, would any of us have thought that we'd be sitting at a campfire tonight after strangers moved a bunch of supplies over the hill, as even more strangers assembled a huge tent to put the stuff under? Is this a dream? What happened?"

Wendy adds, "We were enjoying ourselves. We experienced a feeling of peace like no other, but then, at times, we missed the microwaves, the washer, and dryer. And now, look at that liner:

full of firewood, watermelons, steaks and shampoo . . . and ice cubes."

Thomas adds: "Yep, that ship has over three hundred people, supposedly with the same mindset as ours: to live free from favoritism, corruption, and compulsion imposed upon the nation by people hundreds and even thousands of miles away. Mark, how are we going to organize them? What kind of system do we need? I mean, even a community, oops, a village of three hundred, needs a governing body of some kind, right?"

"Thomas, as I lay down to sleep at night, the same thoughts come breezing through my head now and then. I wrestle with some ideas for awhile, and then I wake up. What are your thoughts Thomas?"

"From my reading of history, every society built some sort of protective mechanism. The Indians put their teepees in circles, wagon trains formed a circle, and look at that giant wall of China and all those huge Roman fortresses. They were all built to protect themselves from enemies. There have always been societies desiring to expand their territory by taking over the areas of others through aggression. How can we protect ourselves against the Russians, the US government, or the UN, if they want this land?" Thomas finishes.

Mark says, "We can't. We'd be done in just one day. We only hope they continue to think this island is unsuitable for habitation. The US and Russians could still desire to lay claim to the Island for future purposes, except that the UN would try to stop any aggressive moves by either country. All major powers have now agreed to submit any aggressive designs to the UN for approval and have provided the UN with limited oversight authority over all military operations. I don't foresee any aggressive moves by either of them shortly. The UN has a kind of soft governing advisory for all countries."

"But, it's still a possibility we can't ignore," Bruce adds.

"How can we protect ourselves then?" asks Thomas.

"You guys know about my radar and satellite scrambling device that will hack away at all incoming signals," Mark replies.

"It's like putting a tent over us so no one from above can see what's happening under the cover of the canvas. Our cell phones would also be useless. Once installed, the cameras on those drones will no longer be able see anything for a ten-mile radius of the tower. The area will look like the surrounding landscape. But I don't own the rights anymore."

George interrupts, asking, "Dad, I never heard about that invention. What happened to it?"

"When I applied for the patent, the CIA got involved and demanded all rights away from me. NASA was already working on it. They insisted that it could be used as an act of terrorism dismantling government communications. It was useless to us on that farm of ours. I once used it to disarm the radar tracking of the highway patrol. I was forced into selling them the rights. But when they came to get it: the prototype, the design, the papers, it was the FBI and the CIA who came knocking on the door with swat teams surrounding the house as if I intended to fight them off. The FBI thought they got everything. But I had one unit underground on the ranch, and it is now on our ship."

"Why?" George asks again. "How come we never heard about it?'

"Well, it was illegal, and I was just tinkering around suspecting that the EMPs we've heard about would be used by enemies dismantling our entire power grid.

"It would be illegal for me to use it. I don't know why I kept it, but at the time, it felt like the right thing to do for our protection. If we put it up, we might be giving the US or the UN the right to invade. We'd be creating an enemy, and we certainly don't want to create one, but if someone does that to us, then I'll protect ourselves. Then let them sue me."

As Mark reaches for more wood to put on the fire, he asks, "I don't foresee anyone infringing on us any time soon. Any other thoughts on what we can do to get this town built?"

Thomas then says, "While we're talking about organizing this group of people, I feel that we need some sort of policing body to judge local disputes. We should appoint a sheriff-type figure with the authority to restrain any acts of aggression, and possible physical disagreements. We can't ignore our baser instincts, the Cain and Able possibilities. I would nominate Mike as our first sheriff. He's got that presence about him, and anyone would take a second thought before coming against him. I know I would."

Mark adds, "Morally, we need a simple code keeping us all civil-minded. C.K. Chesterton had a quote that had an yearly effect on me: '*Men do not differ much about what things they call evil, they differ enormously about what evils they will call excusable.*'"

Mark then looks at Bruce, asking, "You haven't said anything yet. What thoughts do you have on organizing this little community of ours?

Bruce says, "I think Thomas is right. We will need some policing method that everyone understands and accepts, giving the sheriff the right to enforce certain codes of behavior we all agree upon. That stealing is wrong, physical abuse is wrong, bearing false witness against another is wrong, lying is wrong. I think that most people here are of the Christian faith, so if the morals of our faith, the Ten Commandments, can be integrated into our governing, we'll have a basis for harmony.

"I believe the simpler we keep it, the easier it is understood. How can anyone misunderstand the Declaration of Independence that the fathers of America agreed upon? 'That all men are created equal.' How can anyone misunderstand that? 'That they are endowed by their creator with certain unalienable rights, the right to life, liberty and the pursuit of happiness.' Isn't that clear enough? It means that our basic rights are not given to us by a governing body but from God and thus cannot be removed, restricted, or changed by any body of mere men. Life is somewhat like the game of golf; there are hazards to avoid, and we all must play by the same rules. Sports have rules to play by, and referees who see and call violations."

Bruce adds, "Here we are today on this Island desiring to have the same freedoms America was founded upon, freedoms that the government has slowly and methodically restricted. We the people let it happen by our apathy, our absentness from the process. There's a phrase in that Declaration that explains how the US federal government got so powerful, as did the British. It says: *'all experience hath shewn, that mankind are more disposed to suffer, while evils are sufferable, than to right themselves by abolishing the forms to which they are accustomed.'* Yes, we strive for security. We embrace what we come to know. Even though the familiar may be harmful, it's still familiar. The unknown scares the heebie-jeebies out of most people, so we accept the known even though we know that we might be harmed. We feel better. We feel safer. That's how crooked incumbents get re-elected time after time again. We know them. We're familiar with the name. The person with the unfamiliar name is an unknown, and we shy away from the unknown. Who wants to walk down an unfamiliar dark alley? Who knows what the unknown person might do?"

"Now I went on a rant of mine," says Bruce. "But seriously, we need a simple document that enumerates the citizens' rights and the government's responsibilities and a policing force to enforce it. If we don't, we'll eventually have anarchy or tyranny. And everyone on the ship must agree, too."

Mark says, "We're just getting started. Heck, we haven't started anything at all. We're fumbling. I feel these people expected everything to be in order." He pauses, yawns, and softly says, "I don't know about you, but I'm heading for the tent. I want to sleep outside tonight. Susan?"

Susan stands and responds to Mark, "I'm for it."

"Last to leave can put out the fire, not that there is anything that would catch a spark and start a forest fire around here," Mark tells the rest of them. "Good night, all."

On the way to their tent, Mark asks Susan. "How do you feel about all of this? And what's this with Janet and Mike? I've been hearing things about the two of them already. He just got here, and is something going on with those two already?"

"Yes, it seems like it," says Susan. "Mike is very attractive, he catches a girl's eye right away, and even Melody said she'd serve him something besides dinner."

"Melody said that?"

"Yep. Why did you bring that up, Mark?"

"Oh, I guess it goes back to that father thing in me. I could have hung that creep in front of his house. Imagine his mother saying that Melody started the whole thing, she initiated the act, and her little boy was innocent. I could have shot that defense attorney when he brought that up. And our taxes paid for part of his services. It made me so mad, and I was ready for war."

Susan responds, "Yes, you had to be calmed down. Those were awful times for us all. Now, Melody has been free of that and can possibly find a decent gentleman. She's a good-looking girl, and so is Janet."

"Yes, they are." Mark returns. "Neither one of them is someone a man would dismiss at first sight. They both would get a long second look."

Susan changes the subject inside the tent: "Overall, today went well, Mark. But, after one day, I can see that this bunch will need more control, direction, and direct supervision."

"Hey, we didn't ask for this. We did not expect Jim to show up with three hundred strangers suddenly. I'm still not over it."

"Mark, get over it. It's here. We've got to get everyone involved in something every day for a while. Some of the ladies helping us unload the crates under the tent complained about no restrooms on this plateau. One of them complained that no coffee was brought to them as they were working. I couldn't believe my ears when I heard that one. I turned around and let those gals know I was upset. No coffee service, of all things. The gal who said it apologized and said it was meant as a joke. Perhaps I over reacted. I apologized for my rebuttal, and they all returned to work and seemed to enjoy it. Later on, I apologized to her privately. I think we'll get along okay, but it irritated me when I first heard the remark. Then a little later, I stopped, looked at the other gals, and asked, where's my coffee? And, we all started to laugh."

"I know this surprise has disrupted our peace. It's not been pleasant for any of us. I'm still upset that Jim would bring so many out here all at once."

"You said that already, and I can see it in your eyes."

Changing the subject, Mark asks, "Now, tell me more about the Janet and Mike thing."

"Wendy was the first to pick up something. We have been noticing the way the two of them have been eyeing each other. When Mike enters a room, Janet keeps staring. There's a different glow in Janet's eyes when he's around. This afternoon, I noticed the two of them on the dock chatting away for quite a while. Both of them were paying close attention to each other. Janet says nothing is going on, that they're just getting acquainted. But she did volunteer to be on the dock today close to where Mike was working. That's all I know, Mark."

"Hmm! Well, perhaps there's a romance started already."

"Let's hit the sack. Mark. It's been a trying day and so different from what we've been used to. Our peace has been disturbed, but we must make the best of it. We've adjusted to so much in our lives; we can adjust to this too, right?"

"Yep, I am more tired tonight than I've been. Hopefully, the next few days will go a bit better."

They embrace, kiss, and then grab for their pillows.

Chapter 21

Two weeks have passed, during which most of the newcomers set up their tents on the plateau, somewhat organized, partially scattered. They're getting slightly accustomed to the barren environment. Norman has been busy with the backhoe and tractors clearing the paths connecting the tented circles with the beach. Another area was smoothed down the valley to the farming area and the lake. They collected the rocks for the construction of the homes. They unloaded the lumber and moved it to the plateau. They started building houses and the central hall, which will used as a school and church.

But it's all been done quickly without an organized plan.

Intermittent storms had come in, stopping work for a few days, and the next day, the heavy rains and lightning turned into a gentle shower. George and Thomas supervise the plumbers assembling the pipes to transport freshwater from the lake to the community. The fuel tanks were moved onto platforms near the shore. Work on the infrastructure projects proceeded slowly as the volcanic rocks were still formidable obstructions.

Mark and Bruce gave Jim and Mike a seaplane ride around the island, looking closely at the northern side of the volcanic mountains. For the first time, Mark saw a few whales breaking through the surf along with swarms of seals and dolphins. More vegetation appeared to be sprouting on the northern than on the southern side. They could see some depressions filling with water, and more birds were flying near the beaches. No further volcanic activity could be seen anywhere. Jim commented that the island was even more impressive than he had believed before.

Mark and Bruce pull Mike and Jim aside on the dock one afternoon, informing and questioning when Jim starts, "Guys, we need someone to direct the men, the workers, organize them, if you will, into the daily projects. Sort of keep a record of what's being done, where, and by whom, what equipment is used."

"Like a foreman on a construction site," answers Mike. "Yes, we do. I've been thinking the same thing, and I know just the guy who can do it. Bill Jacobsen. He was the guy who had a part in ramroding the dismantling of the rubble of the Twin Towers. He quit after completing half the job when the controversy of saving that Mosque arose."

"Sounds like a good match. Find him. Brief him and get his thinking," Says Mark. "It's time to organize this bunch, get them more involved, help us with supervisory roles. Would you know of any women who could do the same? Janet and Susan are beside themselves."

Mark adds, "So far, it's been just off-the-cuff leadership. Men coming to me or Bruce asking what they could do., and I'm getting tired of it. We've been disorganized. I don't know, it was like . . . ah . . . I expected people desiring freedom from regulations and oversight would find their place in building a village independently. They would self-regulate and willingly volunteer, but it's breaking down. I've been short-tempered by all this. One parent asked me where he could put up his tents for his family right after directing ten others, and I told him . . . "hey, find a spot."

"I heard about that," Jim responds.

"What were we talking about?" Asks Bruce.

"Getting someone to take over . . . someone to be a foreman . . . someone to assign and direct the work." Mark says.

Mike adds, "I could do the job, but I'd be better at the hands-on particulars . . . directing the equipment operators . . . the guys bringing the supplies to the plumbers, the electricians, the builders working on the infrastructure projects. I know where the supplies are on the ship. Bill can organize the individual assignments."

"Do it, Mike. Bruce and I and the girls can't do it all. We need to get this bunch organized. It's not a one-man operation anymore. Do what you can, Mike. Get something going. I'm tired. We were so peaceful before all of you arrived. I'm tired."

Jim speaks up, directing his remarks straight at Mark. "Mark, we need to sit down and organize a governing body, and I know just the guy to do it: Bob Simpson. He's a lawyer and historian knowledgeable in America's beginnings."

"I think we should get together and seriously plan out the governing body of this place. Every group of people needs someone to lead." Jim emphasizes again.

"Do you think Bob would be willing?" Mark asks.

Jim leans over and looks right into Mark's eyes. "Mark, you're not hearing me. We should get started on the political part of this. A city council or something. A leader to set the tone. This group is looking to you for leadership."

"Jim, I don't want any part of any political organization, not even out here . . . on this island that I saw first . . . if it wasn't for me organizing our landing . . . Oh hell, Jim, We were enjoying this island atmosphere, and then you showed up with three hundred strangers." And with that, Mark gets up and quickly leaves the three of them standing next to Jim's liner.

Mike, Jim, and Bruce look at each other and then watch Mark quickly walk away toward shore.

Almost in a whisper, Bruce turns, standing with his back toward shore to face Jim and Mike, saying, "I'm going too. Mark is right on that point. We were thoroughly enjoying our peace, and suddenly we are feeling the pressure of responsibility" as he leaves to catch up with Mark.

"Mark," Bruce shouts.

Mark continues to walk toward shore as if he did not hear, but Bruce quickly catches up to him on shore. "Mark, slow down, will you? We've got to settle this."

"I don't feel like settling anything." Mark quickly answers without breaking stride. "Dag gone it, Bruce, since they showed up, it's been a nightmare. Everybody wants something . . . and want it now. Everybody seems to expect me . . . ah . . . to pull a magician out of the hat and poof . . . everything's in place." Mark quickens his pace up the path.

"I know, Mark. I've been in the middle of it all, too. We all have. Wendy is worn out, and I know Susan is too. It just seems that George and Thomas have flowed together with the newcomers, as has Melody. I've been feeling the same as you have, Mark, but, yeah . . . but, as much as I'd like to have our little peaceful atmosphere back, we can't. It's not going to happen quickly. They're here. They came for the same reasons we left, and now we must adjust . . . for our own sake. For everyone."

"Mark, stop!"

No response as Mark quickened his pace as if he had a skate board.

"Stop and talk to me, Mark."

Again, Bruce shouts, "Did you hear me?"

"Yeah, I heard you." Mark stops, turns, and looks at Bruce. "You said stop. Okay, I stopped."

"Jim is here, Mark. He's not leaving. He came to help, and you've been friends since you got out of diapers. Now, get over it."

Taking a deep breath, Mark stretches his arms outward, slowly dropping his hands to his side, reaching into his pockets, and looks Bruce square on, takes another deep breath, sighs, and then slowly mutters: "Yes, I know. But."

"There are no butts about it. Come on. They're not going, so get over your anger at Jim. We're now in this together with Jim."

"Ah, Bruce. You're the cool-headed one. It's easy for you."

"This will blow over, and we'll start to see this new village fall together."

"But every so often, this anger at Jim for surprising us rises again. I lose my patience when these people want solutions right now, and they're all coming to me, and you too."

"It's been two weeks, and yes, it has disturbed our little world here, but we've got to go on . . . get over our . . . frustrations."

Mark takes a deep breath, thinking, *Jim did think he'd be contributing to this new venture and moving it forward quickly.* "Ah … goodness sake, Yeah. I've got to apologize to Jim. Make this right so we can move forward and hopefully use these times for the best. Forgive me, Bruce?"

"Yeah, I must also."

They turn back toward the pier and start the trek to the dock toward Mike and Jim, standing near the ship's cargo door.

Mark approaches Jim, "I'm sorry, Jim, I lost it. Forgive me. I did not intend to nor wanted to offend you. It's been hard on me and the rest of us to suddenly shift gears and be responsible for a bunch of strangers. As I told you before, I was getting rather tired of being considered the mayor, the chief of police, the governor, the CEO of the sewer company, and the guy responsible for bringing electricity to everyone."

"Mark, it's Ok. I understand and would probably feel the same if our positions were reversed. As far as being the only one here able to organize and lead this bunch, you're confusing leadership with administration and management," Jim tells Mark. "As you saw on that first day we arrived when these people greeted you standing in adoration, they admire you for sacrificing so much, for spending so much time, money, and energy, planning the exodus to this island. They naturally are looking to you for leadership. And you too, Bruce. I know all ten of you were not ready for this. I'm sorry for the unexpected surprise. I'm the one who should have been asking you to forgive me. Ok?"

Mark reaches out to shake Jim's hand, saying, "Ok, Jim, give me five, and let's butt our heads together and get back on the road. Sorry, Mike, you had to witness this."

"Me too, Jim," Bruce speaks, reaching for Jim's handshake and Mike's.

"Eh," Mike tells them. "Been there, done it."

"As for leadership, Mark," Jim says, "I see you as the one who's been through the most with the feds, who understands what a free society could look like, and is best at guiding us all in setting up this new township. But, leadership is not the same as administration. Those jobs should be assumed by the rest of us, leaving you to instill in us all the same vision you have, and we'll take it from there. I think Bill would be willing to take on some responsibilities, and Bob is ready to put together a document creating a town council."

Mark says, "We need another meeting with these guys . . . and the group again."

Bill agreed to handle the foreman aspect when approached by Mark and Jim. Right away, he hit the ground running by calling all the men together, getting input from them on their interests, abilities, and preferences, and then assigning them particular tasks.

Bob was very much interested and began discussing the details with others.

However, in spite of the attempts to install more organizational techniques, the work still slowed down. The four-wheelers had their roads. The garden area was slowly progressing and expanding with seeds for a late harvest already planted, not knowing if the winter months would allow another harvest. If the weather was pleasant, they'd have a second crop. If not, they tried anyway and wouldn't be upset because they hadn't tried. The guys created a small medical clinic.

Then again, the grumbling started to interrupt the progress.

Discussions continued on how to govern the community. More and more people started asking questions. How long before we can get a real home? Can their tent be moved down along the small lake just over the next hill? The porta johns are stinking. When are we going to get real toilets? How about electricity? When? How? When can we get a solar maximizer? How are we going to heat our tents or homes during the cold winter that is soon approaching? Will there be meters? Will we be limited in the amount of electricity we can use? Women wanted to know if they could take trips to the mainland to go shopping. Men wondered when they would be able to view the college and NFL football games. Kids wanted their video games. Will an airport be built? Does anyone know what's happening on American Idol? When more roads are built, can we bring our cars out here? Motorcycles? Boats? Water skiing? When will these trees grow taller? Can we use the pontoon boat to go fishing? Is the beach area safe enough to play badminton? Can we have a garden? How do we keep our food refrigerated? Pharmacies? Hospitals? Schools? Parks? Ball fields and games? Shopping? A McDonalds? Bowling alleys? Barber shops?

On the next trip back to get supplies, can I go and grab my ski-doo. I had a farm. Could I bring milk cows, turkeys, and chickens out here? How do we wash our clothes when the ship leaves to get more supplies? My parents are missing me, can they come join us? Dad is in a wheelchair. Shouldn't we have sidewalks? Garbage, where do we put it? On what days? Will recycling be mandatory? Will all light bulbs have to be fluorescent? Street Lights? Parking meters? Can guns be carried? Does 911 work out here? What about taxes? Dogs and cats? If some of us wanted to move to another part of the island, could we? Are the Russians coming?

The room was about half full when they arrived for breakfast in the ship's dining hall the next Saturday morning. Mark, Susan, George, Ruth, Thomas, Anabele, and Melody were eagerly ready for more of Bob's omelets, pancakes with fresh orange juice, and a full-flavored cup of coffee.

Slowly, the room starts to fill up, but there was no Bruce, Wendy, or Janet yet. The rest were already absorbed in their servings when Jim approached the table. "Good morning everyone. Hope you had a good night's sleep. Mark, we've got to talk this morning."

"Sure, Jim." "Have you seen Mike this morning?"

"No, I haven't," Jim replies.

Mark continues. "I just wanted to thank him for his work yesterday. He's been a real blessing. And Bill, too. When he took over the individual assignments, we started to get more done. When do you want to get together, Jim?"

"Just as soon as we can, Mark," Jim replies. "And if you see Bruce, bring him along too. I'll be in the captain's room."

About forty-five minutes later, Mark and Bruce enter the captain's room, seeing Jim reading a loose-leaf pamphlet.

"Morning again, Jim. What's up?" Mark greets Jim.

"Well, you guys have heard it all these past weeks, as I have. But now, I've got six families who want to return to the mainland. They're tired. They feel like they were misinformed and misled, and it's not like they thought it would be. They want out."

"What? Already?" Mark irritably questions, then quickly answers, "That's easy, Jim, let them go. Ship them out of here quick."

"But when?" Jim asks.

"Well, I guess it would mean a special thousand-mile one-way trip just to satisfy a few who are unhappy unless we can plan that when we need to restock our supplies. How are the supplies holding up, Jim?"

Jim answers, "We've got about another three months of fuel to keep the equipment running. The lumber is all onshore, some of it used. We could last through the winter, but the biggest problem seems to be that too many people are getting antsy. They wish it could all be together yesterday. Their questions are not getting answered. Some even felt like they'd been used. Some have been lounging away on deck while others are working and contributing, and the ones working are jealous of those who are loafing. The priest and pastor are seeing more people for absolution and counseling. We're breaking down. The bar is getting much more attention in the evenings than at first. A few had to be taken back to their rooms, too drunk to walk on their own."

"Hmm," Ponders Mark. "I knew there was some dissatisfaction but never thought it was as bad as you make it out to be."

Jim suggests, "We got together with Bill and Bob, but we need to get everyone together again like we did the first few days, have a dinner, and then you get them energized again with one of your speeches. Perhaps we could get Pastor Mooneyham to sermonize them. Bruce, do you have any thoughts about all this?"

Responding, Bruce says, "Well, I think you are right, Jim. It's beginning to break apart, and we must get unified again. The work has been tedious, the hours have been long, and yes, it's not among everyone. Not that it's our responsibility to make sure that everyone contributes the same amount as everyone else. But perhaps a system of rewards based on the contribution is in order. But how do we set that up, as we haven't even envisioned the need for a monetary system yet? It's just the old American dollar, and we're not transferring funds based on work performed. To do that, we'll have to set up a banking system here, our own, with a way of adding to and subtracting from accounts depending on how much each one adds to the community and then how much each takes away for personal use."

"Gads Bruce, that sounds like punching in and out on a time card," Mark responds. "We came here to embrace freedom, so let's not start regulating things that much. Ok, this is Saturday, so let's make this work for us tomorrow morning with pastor Mooneyham and Father Lumarcher providing the spiritual lift as usual, and then I'll try my best to inspire us all back to a unifying mission."

"Ok, by me, we've got to do something," Jim responds.

Mark adds, "I'll work on my speech. And Bruce, I'd like to hand that mike over to you for some inspiration from you, OK? I agree that we should appoint Mike as our sheriff, and we'll inform the people that he is the new sheriff."

"Shouldn't we institute some means of voting and any other official job?" asks Bruce.

"Yeah, you're right," Mark replies. "We will, but I think it's still early in our formation to start voting. First, I'll tell them we need a sheriff and a judge and why. As it is now, it'll be a part-time, volunteer-type job exercising his authority only when needed to control our baser human tendencies. I'll get with Mike first."

"We have been working and living without any money exchange for months. We invested our fortunes in this venture, and each person on board invested what they had for their supplies and the mutual equipment. We were not concerned with the wealth we hide away in banks but desired our freedom from the rules taxing our wealth and telling us how we should use it. When I desire to give away parts of my wealth, I do not want this government we set up to keep the biggest part of it, deciding who would get the rest based on the loudest cries for help. Big governments give our wealth to someone who either squandered their wealth or did not work to gain any, in addition to those who, due to no fault of their own, need the help. We're not yet at the point of needing a bank. We'll open a can of worms if we start organizing that."

"Hey", Mark continues. "All of a sudden, we've expanded to a small crowd, everyone desiring to do their own thing. They've left a very structured, organized society, and now they're living in a very unstructured society, and there's no escape."

"Heck, we've got to get the water system working, the sewers built, the common areas defined first, or we'll have anarchy. Our common areas must be planned as soon as possible."

Jim gets back into the discussion, saying, "Leaders and administrators tend to meddle because something may not be working for the benefit of everyone. Soon enough, someone will open a store to sell their homemade goods, restaurants will be serving tacos and burgers, and a mechanic will set up a business repairing 4-wheelers, a plumber will organize the installation of the water lines into these homes we're building, and electricians will get into the act for wiring these homes. Mike and Bill will probably offer contractor services for our homes and businesses. People with teaching skills will drill the children on their ABCs and two-times-two's, and on and on. It'll expand on its own. Someone will open a barber shop for men, and another will cater to women.

"We can't plan all that. That should be left alone and let it happen naturally from the bottom up. Slowly, these people will start the process on their own. Some of those businesses will succeed, some will fail. If we got involved from the beginning, we'd be partially responsible, and they'd look to us to help the ones that failed."

Mark says, "There's no way that the three of us, or twenty of us, could possibly set up a community-wide system that will meet the needs or desires of everyone on an equal and fair basis and do it in a month. We'd screw it up somewhere, and then we'd have to make corrections on top of what we messed with, adding to the mess of trying to enforce the rules we made up."

Hmmm? Mark adds, "That sounds like the federal government involvement in everything. Can't let that happen. No way. At this stage, the people will determine the process.

"But we do need some organization, some structure, some policing method, some kind of system to hold us together," Jim interjects.

Bruce adds, "Yes, we do. But what? I've never read anywhere about how three hundred people came together and built a town on a brand new island., and did it all in one month."

"No, I haven't either."

Mark continues as Jim and Bruce quietly sit and listen to Mark, "As far as I know, it took the pilgrims months, and they had to reorganize to get those who did little while the rest got after it.

Like here, we've had those sitting around on the deck all day, not contributing to the work outside. We've got to stop that somehow. In my speech, I'll address that, somehow encouraging their participation. I'll level with the people and tell them our predicament, that this is all new, and we've got to have patience, knowing the vision of a new colony takes time to construct."

"Governments continually consider additional laws and regulations to improve the failed ones. The new laws are added on top of the existing laws already in place. Lawyers make sure the rules of fairness, equality, diversity, and equity are not violated. The advancement for minorities rules are not harmed, the equal opportunity act is not violated, nor the act against racial inequality, the act of equal pay for equal work, the act for the advancement of the transgendered, along with the rules forbidding union insults, Islamic insults, minority insults, gay insults, handicapped insults, red hair insults, blonde female jokes, among hundreds of other regulations that could be affected, that none of them were violated in any way. That's one of the reasons why we're here."

"But we need some sort of unit to oversee the common areas." Jim adds, "Sure, I know that governments grow bigger and bigger and eventually get out of control, but we're only talking about three hundred people here, not three hundred million."

Mark continues as if he did not hear Jim. "We were tired of it. We desired to escape those legalities and insanity. The laws should be simple and few. If all men are created equal, why are the laws unequally applied? Now, let's get to work on this, Jim. I'll inform the pastors." Mark concludes as he starts to leave the room.

"Oops," Turning back to the table, Mark realizes he did not allow Bruce to say what's on his mind. "Sorry Bruce, I got too involved in what I was thinking. What will you say?" as Mark sits down, ready to listen to Bruce.

"Well, it's the old story plaguing human history since Eve took a bite of the forbidden fruit. People being people. They're not perfect. We're not perfect workers, nor even perfect renegades.

We're certainly not perfect leaders either. Ten of us getting together is easier than three hundred coming together as a cohesive unit, and we've been blindsided when these strangers show up with nothing to do, no office to go to, and no schedule to keep, expecting us to have everything planned out for them. It's going to take time. Back home in the States, we had our schedules. We became used to doing things a certain way. Even our free time had some organization. We learned how to plan our day around the must-do things to keep the cash flowing for our support. Then, for us, all of a sudden, the entire system is gone."

"Yes", Mark interrupts. "Yes, but they willingly gave those things up when they came here."

Jim says: "Yeah, but we need something like a town governing body to hold this bunch together. A city council of some sort. Something they agree to and have a part in creating. Just knowing that there is a governing body, I think, would relieve some anxiety. Knowing there is a place where they could take their grievances would add to their feelings of community. A judge of all, like biblical times."

Again, Mark goes on another rant, not paying attention to Jim. "Even so, after awhile, these things become ingrained. They are even thought of as rights, just as those NY protestors said they had a right to a job, had a right to a home, a right to a college education, and at someone else's expense. Those are not rights. But, over time, we became used to them. We reach into the refrigerator, grabbing a package to put in the microwave. We do not have to physically turn over the dirt several times, rake it, and then slowly and methodically plant seeds, then make sure it gets enough water, but not too much, and then wait months before enjoying the fresh taste. No, it's easier to start the car, comfortably drive a few blocks, listening to music while out of the nasty weather, drive to the huge indoor market, buy what we want and even more than what we came for, and drive back home, put the package in a microwave and sit down three minutes later to eat in front of a sixty-inch screen to get entertained. To leave all of that for the shovel is hard. Why did we? Yet, here we are, and in this ship, three hundred others thought this would be easy, that instantaneously they'd be satisfied forever. It's no wonder we are having problems. The easy acquisition of anything was left behind, and now it's a physical grind getting up and having to stand in line to use the potty. These discomforts that we now experience every day will be our way of life for some time. But, the ten of us adjusted and we were enjoying the changes when you showed up."

"You don't have to keep bringing that up Mark."

"No matter what we do, the easy life does not look like it'll be coming here any time soon. We miss it. We'd like to have both. But we can't. We also know that to have that easy life requires trade-offs. Our forefathers traded their previous life for the unknown in a new territory. They were willing to sacrifice their lives and their fortunes to be free of the tyranny and persecution that existed in England at the time. But back then, technology was not yet, and daily life in the homeland was not that much different from the new physical life in America. Our changes are dramatic. We've left the microwaves. The battle between the two is hard to keep personal and quenched, so it erupts, and we get short-tempered and antsy, not knowing how to deal with it. I'm surprised we haven't had more fights, but it's just been people questioning whether they did the right thing by joining our forces. Our humanity is being exposed."

Bruce adds, "We've got to convince them again that freedom is worthwhile and tyranny is evil. It takes continual vigilance to gain and to keep freedom. We don't want to be slaves or subjects under the ever-watchful thumb of another. We came here possibly hoping that over time, the result would be a revolution tearing apart the current system that's on top of another system, layers upon layers of bureaucratically instituted rules; a system we allowed to develop over decades by our apathy. Tyranny destroys the will of the individual. It makes subjects out of them. We've got to re-convince them that what we're doing is worthwhile, that trading off the easy life for freedom is the only way we can escape the life of being watched over, regulated by someone who thinks they know what we need . . . for our good, they tell us. We must show them the difference between freedom and tyranny, selfish anarchy and cohesiveness, between microwaves and Coleman stoves. They need reminding. That is what I'll try to tell them. Mark."

"Well, OK. Now, what are we going to do today?" Mark says, "I need to continue working on the solar power and installing the rest. I only brought along ten units, and that's not enough for everybody. Bruce, what do you plan on doing today?"

"Mike, Janet, and I are working on a sewer system. George and Thomas are laying pipes for a water line. We've got lots of help."

"Are you making any progress?" Mark asks, "Let me know if you need something. Oh, and something else was asked of me. I almost forgot. A lady wanted to know if she could get a dog or cat the next time in town."

Sunday morning comes, seeing most everyone in the dining hall in good moods as last night Mark invited everyone to enjoy a huge campfire up on the plateau. He planned a campfire that would be big enough for all. Beforehand, Mark had asked the musicians if they'd play and direct some songs. They were delighted. During the evening, Mark got up and thanked everyone for their sacrificial work over the past weeks. He assured them that positive steps were being made. Mark likes to use the analogy that building a town from scratch is like assembling a puzzle. You've got a picture in mind, but the pieces don't exactly fit together where you first thought they would, so they've got to be moved to another location, piece by piece.

Before sitting in the camp chair to relax and enjoy the atmosphere, he again thanked them for coming across the sea to an island the experts said could not be habitable for humans for a thousand years. "We're proving the experts wrong, and nothing inspires me more than proving that the governments' self-appointed experts are wrong."

Over the past several weeks, breakfast on the liner has been just a once-a-week affair on Saturdays, leaving Sunday mornings free for the people to come on board for worship services by Pastor Mooneyham for the Protestants and a Catholic service led by Father Lumarcher. Some stayed in their tents, some took walks, and some just hung out among themselves, but this Sunday morning, most everyone was up early enough to enjoy breakfast, having been informed last night of the meeting this morning.

Susan remarks that breakfast this morning was exceptional. She excused herself to go to the ladies' room. Melody, Wendy, and Janet get up to join Susan, leaving Mark, Bruce, George, Thomas, Ruth, and Anabele at the table.

"It doesn't take long to appreciate a well-planned and prepared breakfast, does it?" Ruth remarks. "There are times when I like to be waited on," she continues, "and that's becoming most of the time."

Anabele adds, "Yes, I know those feelings."

Mark, directing his remarks to the ladies, says, "Am I hearing you correctly, or am I reading between the lines here? It almost sounds like you're ready to give up and go back to the States when you said 'becoming most of the time.' Do you want to go back?"

George adds, "Mark, what the ladies are saying is that yes, it is appreciative to be waited on, but that does not mean they'd give up their love for freedom."

"George, I want to hear it from the ladies." Looking at Ruth, Mark says, "Go on Ruth."

"Mark, don't you ever wish you could lean back in a nice comfortable lounging chair getting into a twilight zone watching a ball game? Sure you do. You are as human as the rest of us, and there are times that I would like to, . . . well, you know, sit back and, yes, enjoy the easy life, enjoy those machines we had that did make it easier for us. Pushing a button to activate the chair to massage my back while I relax in its comfort is easier than climbing on a table and having George rub my back. Out here, it's not easy. It's continually hard. Washing clothes is a burden as we scrub the shirts with a rock against another rock, forcing the dirt out. At the same time, I'm thinking about the washing machine I left behind. Technology has removed the tediousness and given us the easy. Thomas Edison made it easier for us to read a book at night. Henry Ford made it easier to mass-produce cars. The Wright brothers made getting from New York to San Francisco easier."

Ruth expounds more about her wish to bring the easy out to the island. "So, please don't get up there and rant and rave about any of us voicing our wish for the easy life. If these activities make us happy, then that's guaranteed in that Declaration of Independence you so often quote. Yes, Mark, we willingly gave in to the concept that has slowly crept into modern society, a concept that is called by all sorts of names: socialism, Marxism, Communism, despotism, and tyranny, and the politically correct term: progressive liberalism. Basically, it comes down to my freedom to make decisions about my life. But I'm here to stay; I desire that freedom more than the washing machine. But, Mark, if I complain about rock washing, then just turn your other cheek. That's all I have to say, Mark."

"Very well put, Ruth, and thank you."

"Anabele, do you want to add anything?"

"Yes, I do," she replies. "I agree with Ruth on all those points. Do you think we'll ever get to that point on this island? Will we ever again be able to relax on that lounger and doze off watching "Sleepless in Seattle?" Will Thomas ever be able to play ball with our son in a fenced-in backyard while I plant flowers against a picket fence and around the redwood deck, proudly watching the two of them? Will our son have a college here on the island to go to? I've been just recently pondering all that. Those things became part of the American pursuit of happiness thing long ago. I've asked myself a dozen times if I am pursuing my happiness here, or am I pursuing Mark's dream?"

Mark interrupts, "Did I interpret what you said correctly? Are you expecting? Are you two going to have a son?"

Anabele bursts into a joyful "Yes, and Yes, I am, and we are."

Mark exhales, saying, "I'm going to have a grandson. Ya Ha!" Ruth is sitting there as her tears of joy overcome her, her hands wiping away the tears rolling down her cheeks. Mark gets up and joyfully hugs Anabele while reaching out to Thomas to shake his hand. "Congratulations, you two, this is fantastic. You've made my day. Does Susan know? Have you been able to let your parents know back home?"

"No. Thomas and I just found out about it the other day when Doctor Abstra examined me in the clinic."

"How does he know it's a boy?" Mark asks.

"He doesn't, but we both want a boy first, so that's what we're hoping . . . . and expecting."

Ruth reaches across the table, grabbing Anabele's hands, "Oh, I'm so happy for you. This is fantastic, but there you go, beating me again."

"This is wonderful. Can I announce it this morning?" Mark asks.

"Anabele and Thomas look at each other and say, "Of course, and Yes," simultaneously.

"Good, Thanks, but ah . . . do you want to tell the ladies first when they get back?"

"Let's go tell the ladies now," Ruth announces, getting up from the table, pulling the chair out for Anabele, and reaching down for her hand to help her up.

"Ruth, I don't need your help."

Thomas says to Mark after they leave, "She's been suspecting this for a few weeks now. But it won't change anything we're doing here, Mark. The medical clinic is finished and furnished; the doctors can now do their stuff. We've just got to get more generators up and running. Possibly build a dam."

Anabele and Ruth caught the other ladies coming out of the restroom.

"Would you all join us inside for a minute," says Ruth. "Anabele has something she wants to share with you." They all enter the restroom anxiously, looking at Anabele, waiting for her to say something.

Anabele bursts out, "I'm pregnant." They look at each other and start jumping up and down in excitement and joy, their arms going together around Anabele and Ruth as they continue jumping up and down, shouting out: "She's pregnant. She's going to have a baby." "I'm going to be a grandmother."

"Oh, this is fantastic." Then, the usual questions. "When did you find out? How? Do you know what it is? How far along are you? What does Thomas say? Does he know? Does Mark know?

Ten minutes passed, and other women entered the waiting room after hearing the announcement. "We're going to have a baby, the first on the island." A woman says, exiting the restroom and entering the hall. The word spreads like a tsunami throughout the packed dining hall.

Seeing the crowd and realizing that the word is already spreading, Mark gets up on the stage to make the announcement. "Ladies and gentlemen, let me have your attention for a minute. I wish to make an official announcement."

The crowd partially quiets down as their attention is still toward the rear as the six ladies enter the hall escorting Anabele. "Ladies and Gentlemen, I'm going to be a grandfather. Anabele is with child." Everyone in the hall applauds as Anabele is escorted through the tables to join Thomas.

"I'm embarrassed," Anabele says to Thomas as she reaches the table. "It's just a baby. Why all the fuss? Now, everyone will look at me as if I'm an invalid needing help all the time."

"That's just the initial excitement, honey," says Thomas as he reaches out to help her sit down.

"See, there you go, helping as if I can't do a thing for myself anymore," Anabele bursts out at Thomas. The rest of them quietly take a deep breath.

As he gets up from the table, Mark tells them, "Before we have the services this morning, I need to get with our preachers for a few moments."

Mark finds the Reverend Mooneyham and Father Lumarcher behind the stage. "Gentlemen, could I have your attention for a minute? Did you hear the announcement I made just a few minutes ago?"

"Yes, we did." Answers Father Lumarcher, "And we're excited for you. Congratulations to you, your son, and Anabele." After a short pause, Father Lumarcher asks, "There is something else on your mind, Mark, isn't there?"

"Well, yes. There is, but I don't care to bother you with it." Mark sheepishly says.

Bending over to get closer to Mark, Rev. Mooneyham says. "Yes, you do. You did not come in here to tell us about your future grandson. There is something else bothering you. Spit it out."

Mark starts telling the spiritual leaders that he was going to stomp down hard on everyone this morning about their moaning and groaning, the complaining about missing the conveniences they all left behind: the simple things like washing machines and microwaves, the ability to go shopping in a mall, watching ball games on TV. Lounging in an easy chair stuffed in cushioning fabric. "But, when I heard Anabele announce she was expecting, all of that stuff seemed out of order." Mark opens up to his sense of confusion. "What do I say now?"

Father Lumarcher answers: "Mark, what do you think you should say?"

Mark replies, "Perhaps it's me, and I'm causing the grumbling. I've been pushing all my ideas on everyone, so perhaps it's time I let go, let go of thinking of myself as the ultimate leader of this, thinking that I'm in charge of everything all the time, and if I don't direct the traffic the cohesiveness will fall apart. It seems as if it's falling apart under my direction. And now all that has changed. I'm trying, but not very well."

"Mark, you are not a community organizer. You're an inventor and businessman. You've never wanted to get involved in the political realm." Pastor Mooneyham says, "Kings, Rulers, and tyrants have yearned to organize the human spirit throughout, but it has always failed and always will. This is not your SimCity. Mark, it's harder to step aside. We advise you to step back and let the market work."

"I kind of thought you'd say something like that," Mark replies. "I've been forcing my dream on everyone, haven't I? Anabele suggested I was."

"Mark, you're primarily a businessman with great curiosity, but these people are not your employees. They feel they have the right to come and go as they please. Those three young men who took off to walk around the island were following their desires. Gads, Mark, you felt relieved of the pressure of following rules when you arrived here, and now you want them to follow your rules. That's what community organizers do: set up rules for the community. You desired that everyone appreciate the peace you found here and tried to get them to lean back, rest, and find that peace as you did. They can't, Mark. It's their own path they must find. My advice is for you to shake it off. Think instead of the rules our creator set up for mankind and follow those. Simple rules like love one another, be honest, do not covet, honor your parents, and do not replace the creator with another god."

"Be candid with the people this morning, Mark. Let them know what you were thinking, and then assure them you're just like them. . . an individual desiring to live free or die. Is freedom worth the struggle? Will the island be cooperative?"

Finishing his advice to Mark, pastor Mooneyham says, "You asked for our advice, and there it is . . . take it or leave it."

"Thank you, and pray for me when I'm up there acting like I like it," Mark says on his way out. *Now I've got to find Mike,* Entering the dining hall, he sees Janet sitting at the table along with the others. "Janet, do you know where I could find Mike?" He asks.

"Ah. . . well, I haven't seen him this *morning.* I suppose he could still be in his room, as it was early, and we were up late." Mark heads out and down to Mike's quarters. Finding it, he knocks on the door. Shortly, Mike opens the door, still in his pj's.

"Can I come in? I would like to talk with you before the meetings today." Mark informs him.

"Sure, Mark, come in and make yourself comfortable while I get dressed," disappearing into the bathroom.

"What's up?" Mike shouts out to Mark from behind the closed door.

"Take your time, Mike, and we'll talk." Less than a minute passes, and Mike sits opposite Mark.

"Ok, what's up?"

"Mike, I'm sure you are aware of the grumbling going on and know about the few instances of rowdiness, misbehavior, and fights there've been, and some families want to go back to the states. Jim, Bruce, and I have been discussing how we can control some of that. The idea was floated that we need to appoint a sheriff, a judge to handle those things, a sheriff that the people will respect. And I think that if everyone knew that someone had that authority, it would be a deterrent to such behavior. Mike, we would like you to be that sheriff. For now, it would be on a needed basis, a voluntary position, with our full cooperation. This community is building fast, faster than I ever imagined, and recently there have been instances indicating the need for authority by someone to oversee, what shall I call it? . . . ah, provide a safety net, a protective layer, a shield protecting ourselves from any aggressive actions against anyone else. Would you consider it?"

Mike does not appear to be surprised. "Sure, Mark. I'll do it. Rumors have been flying, so your question is not a surprise to me. I thought you would have approached me several days ago. Do you have a badge I would wear? I'm into badges," he says with a big grin.

"There's one other thing, Mike. You know that in the States, sheriffs are elected and not appointed. We haven't set up an election process, not even a single government document or anything of that nature yet, so this will be our first process of governing this community. We don't even have a name yet. I don't own this place, so I have no legal right to run it. We had some simple ideas when we first came here, and then you and Jim showed up changing everything, so I'm learning to sit back and let it happen, which is not easy. I do have some ideas, as almost everyone does. How to get those ideas out and to choose is still a mystery. We're just three hundred people who came here to escape government regulations and endless rules. I've been somewhat bewildered on how to set up a governing body that is fair and open, one that regards the free exchange between people as supreme."

"Mark, I've been pondering the same questions on my own, and Janet has let a few cats out of the bag as to what you have all talked about. I don't have any astounding ideas either, Mark. But how about this? You've planned to have meetings with us this morning. At some time, let me get in front of the people, and I'll bring up the subject of naming this community, ask for suggestions, and then vote. If they'd like to vote on it, I'll say a few words about needing a sheriff or a judge sometime in the future. When? How? We'll let democracy begin."

"That would be terrific," Mark says, "Now, can I get personal? I'm curious. How are you and Janet doing? I'm hearing some good news about you two. Usually, the bad news gets to me first, but I do not often hear the good news. I guess it's like the mainstream media in the States, where the bad news gets all the attention on the broadcasts. Bad news sells. Controversy sells. If the media does not have any bad news coming their way, they go out of their way to create some. Cameramen and on-site reporters have become a big pain in the butt, pushing their way into closets to get a ten-second sound bite from a victim of anything. It's sickening. By tuning in, we help support those perverted methods of keeping us informed. Too much of the current news is none of my business, but those self-anointed experts say we have the right to know. And then those victims call friends and neighbors to watch the news, as they'll be on TV, live, and in living color."

"How did I get off on that? How are you and Janet doing?"

"We're doing just fine, Mark," Mike responds. We enjoy each other's company, and that's all I'll say about it. Ok? But please, no reporters, no camera guys watching us."

"Sure, Mike, and forgive me for asking. But Janet is a special lady to Susan and me. We feel about her as we do our kids." Mark tells Mike. "You two are adults, and I'm confident you will do the right thing. Just take it easy. . . one step at a time."

"Sometimes, Mark, your control freak comes out. You have to be in charge, in control of every little detail, don't you? I'm not your employee, Mark." Mike snips back to Mark.

"I guess I do, Mike. It's just me. I learned that by building my businesses. I like to relax, sit back, and watch other people. Still, when I see someone heading into unknown territory, perhaps a disaster, it's hard for me to watch without doing or saying anything, especially when I've been there before. Sorry. I shouldn't have said anything."

"Of course, Mark."

"Good, and thanks again for your many contributions to this place and for your suggestions just now. I can always count on you. I will call upon you sometime this morning to express your thoughts. Ok?"

"Ok," Mike gets up and starts to open the door for Mark, saying, "Now I need to get ready. See you later, boss," emphatically amplifying 'boss.'

When Mark entered the hall, Pastor Mooneyham was at center stage, leading the group in hymns with the band playing in the background. Making his way toward his seat, Mark notices that there's a good majority turnout of people this morning, even though most of them had been sleeping in their tents on the plateau. The people are singing out: "Standing on the promises . . ."

The hymn ends, and pastor Patrick starts, "Well folks, here we are together on this luxury liner parked on a dock leading to a barren rock-filled no man's land. Are we standing on those promises we just sang about? 'When the howling storms of doubt and fear assail, By the living Word of God I shall prevail.'

"We shall prevail. Imagine Noah as he assembled his family, spending years building a boat bigger than a football field in a deserted land. No rain had fallen for years, and he was building a boat, of all things. His neighbors thought he had gone off his rocker, watching him and his lonely family diligently putting together a boat that could never be moved to the ocean, a ship so big that every person in the village in the surrounding area could get on board. Then, the word was out that it was for animals.

"If PETA had been there, they would have stopped it. They would've ridiculed him. They would have called him names. They might have insisted that he stop, and as people do now, some would have gone to the authorities and filed a lawsuit claiming the ship is destroying their view of the desert and should be moved to another location. 'They can build if they want to, but somewhere else, and not in my backyard. I've got a right to my unobstructed view of the desert, don't I?"

"Jump forward a few thousand years to the streets of New York. A crowd pitched their tents in the streets and parkland, so many of them that the store owners had to close up and go home as shoppers were intimidated by the rowdy bunch. The stores closed, and their windows got smashed while the police were held back, protecting this group and their right to assemble. Someone in that group used a police car for a urinal. Some were having sex outside their tents. Those living in Utah, Oklahoma, Maine, and around the world saw all of this on the television sets while reporters and cameramen filmed the ruckus. The police forces were standing in a ready position but just watching, instructed by their superiors not to interfere.

"Now go with me to a smallish town in Colorado where a group of people had gathered in front of the city hall holding up signs saying 'protect our children,' another one saying 'babies have rights too.' The police demanded these people to go home, as they could not assemble on public property without a permit. In another town, the signs read, 'Put the Ten Commandments back in schools. ' They were told to go home. In another town, the signs read 'Obama must go,' and the media labeled these people as racist."

"You've heard about them all through that magical invention called television and the internet. We witness it as it happens. To some, these events were disturbing. We went about our daily life, not directly being disturbed. It did not matter to us as the mall was still open, and a game was on another channel. Just turn the channel if you don't want to watch that stuff. Click on a button, and another channel is a commercial for Viagra. Click it again, and two people are making out. Click it again, and the news shows the results of a tornado hitting a town in Missouri. Click it again, and you see a commercial for Diet Coke. Click it again, and someone will show you how to paint a room. Click again, and the president is making a speech. Another station has five women talking. Another has five men talking. Then you remember all the recordings in that tiny box under the TV and sit back to watch Clint Eastwood for two hours.

"What's for dinner? Where are the kids? I'm going to take Jimmy to soccer practice this evening, and Judy must go to dance lessons, so there's a dinner in the refrig you can warm up. Ok?"

"It's the modern life folks. It's been called progress. Modern technology enabled this progress. It's made our life physically much easier, but then we become dependent on that technology. What will we do if that technology was just suddenly disabled? Someone somewhere may be able to do that with an EMP device."

"Now here we are on this rocky land without any of that. It's so peaceful, we've gotten bored and, yes, bored. Partially, we came here to escape all of that gibberish. Partially we came here because we were fed up with the police just standing there doing nothing. Police are protecting terrorists rather than us, doing nothing to protect our borders while allowing people to side-step our own immigration rules. And heaven forbid that girls might sell lemonade that the FDA has not approved. In another town, swat teams broke down the front door, invading an innocent man's home, having received the wrong address from the chief. In another town, the owners of a piece of property desired to build the home of their dreams. The local permits had been granted, but then the feds came and shut it down, declaring the land to fall under the new rules of wetness.

"Partially, we came here because the government has grown to an uncontrollable monstrosity that even the government does not know what the government is doing, as one agency overlaps the authority of another."

"We're here because of one man who had a dream, a vision. Willingly, we left the progressive life to follow that dream. No one forced us to give up the convenience of it all to pursue a different life, a life so different it's been hard to adjust to the hardships, but also so peaceful without the six o'clock news, and now it does get boring. We think the work day must immediately stop at five pm and we must have Saturdays off. "

"When the rains came, and that ship began to float, Having to feed all those animals was getting stuffy down below. It must have stunk. Noah did not know about television, the internet, and had no idea what a microwave or washing machine was. He didn't think about when his cell phone would work again, or when he could watch football, baseball, or soccer again. No refrigerators keeping the food fresh for those forty days. He did not look back, thinking about ball games or when the misses could get to the mall, but still, he must have wondered about some things in his past.

"Yes, my friends, Noah's life and ours have changed dramatically. I believe we've been called out from among the rest to have our lives changed dramatically, pursuing a new life without interference from powerful people on the public payroll who set down the rules for us to follow. We need to wash our hands of the old and start anew."

"Thank you, and God bless you all. And now, I am pleased to bring Mark out here again."

Mark walks onto center stage and says, "Wow, pastor Mooneyham. That was inspiring. Thank you. I never thought of Noah like that before. It reminds me of an article someone in our times had written about the early settlers and their wagon trains heading into the plains of Colorado. The author wondered if the EPA had cleared the path, if the Fish and Wildlife Service had inspected the route for endangered species, if the Department for Public Safety had inspected the wagons for seat belts, and if the Department of Health and Human Services had insisted on a nurse being aboard every wagon, if Homeland Security had inspected all the wagons for possible terrorists and if there were any illegal weapons on board."

"Folks, if our current government had been around when the folks threw that tea party in Boston, the party would have been stopped for polluting the waters."

"Ladies and gentlemen, I don't have much to say this morning. Abraham Lincoln once said: '*As I would not be a slave, so I would not be a master.*' I did not realize at first that this project had to change when Jim showed up with you; it was no longer just my family and me. Three hundred strangers here for the same reasons we came here. My family came here to escape from the bureaucracy of big government, a government that has lasted beyond its years. The United States is no longer acting as a Republic but as your master."

Mark takes a deep breath. "I also, do not intend to act as your master. I'm an inventor of sorts, and for a while, I thought I could invent a town where everyone would be happy and contented for the rest of their lives. Utopians have been trying that for centuries. What a foolish thought. I'm sorry. I shouldn't have.

"We've completed six homes so far, with eight more soon to be finished. The first homes went to a few young families with children. Although these homes are not what you'd find in a good neighborhood in the States, for now, they're adequate. Perhaps we now need a lottery system for choosing who gets the next, as it will take time before you all have a home. Perhaps another system would work. A central hall and a medical clinic is finished. We're on our way, but it's getting to the point where perhaps a city council should oversee the rest."

"Folks, I'm just an inventor farmer and a very lucky businessman. So, let's open this up to your suggestions somehow. Let's open the process. Your ideas are needed. I'm going to concentrate on expanding our power grid. So, that's all I want to bore you with this morning. Now, I'm going to turn this discussion over to Mike Galloway. Mike, come on up here, please."

Mark leaves the stage, and Mike jumps up and says, "For a moment there, I thought he was going to appoint a sheriff to control me. Most of you know a bit about me and my moans and groans about not having electricity, not having a sewer system, and no running water. How come? Let's get with it. After all, how much time does it take to build a neighborhood, something we can call a town, a village. Habitat for Humanity can build a home in about a week. We don't even have a name. What are we going to call this place anyway? Ah . . . yeah . . . thinking about that, let's name this. Any ideas? Write them down, and we'll vote."

"I vote for Mike as sheriff." Someone from the audience bursts out. Another one shouts, "we need a city council first." Another, "I vote for Mike." And another one standing up says, "We should elect a town council first and let them appoint a sheriff." Then another replies, "sheriffs are elected positions in our town." A woman stands and begins, "People, I think Mark has done a fantastic job here so far, and I don't want to see him out of the process. He should be the first mayor of this town. Let's name it Village Mark, or Marks town."

"Why do we need a city council? It'll just get bigger and bigger, and soon enough, we'll have to pay taxes to pay their salaries," another one shouts out.

This continued for another ten minutes until Mike finally grabs the microphone and says, "People, people, let's have order in the house. Order, please."

"Mike for sheriff." A man in front shouts out.

"Order, please."

Another shouts out, "No taxes."

Slowly, the room grows quiet.

"Ok," Mike exclaims, "we've started the process. So, if someone would post some paper in the back, you could write down your suggestions as a name for this place, and then we'll get together and vote on it. The same goes for the town council, the mayor, and the sheriff. We'll get together to decide what responsibilities the city council will be given and what authority the sheriff will have. Write them all down, folks. Let's see what develops. Let's meet again on the plateau on Wednesday evening."

"Now, what else is on the agenda for this morning?" Mike asks, looking in the direction of Mark and Jim. Both of them shake their heads, indicating that's it, shut it down. "OK folks, I think that's it for this morning, and thank you for being here."

Mike returns to his seat, and the band starts playing as the people leave.

"Thanks, Mike, that was good," Mark tells him.

Janet reaches out to Mike, patting him on the shoulder. "You did good. Will I have to call you Mr. Sheriff? Are you going to write me a ticket for speeding and not wearing my seat belt on the Jeep?"

Shortly, Jim approaches the table, pulls out a chair, and tells Mike and Mark, "I liked it, the speeches and especially the sermon of pastor Mooneyham. It fit. Ah . . . Remember the families I told you about who desired to go back home, well, they still do, and some others heard about it and have joined them in a desire to return to the States. So right now, there are fifty-two quitters."

Mark replies, "Are they still disgruntled about missing their toys?"

"No, that's not all of it," replies Jim. "More than half of them are older, missing their families and their grandkids, and they also want to be able to get in their RV and travel the States, enjoying the latter years of life. They say the fight for freedom is not theirs but the younger generation. They want to enjoy life, feeling their early struggles have allowed them to relax and enjoy, putting the hardships aside. They feel they have that right."

Mark; "There we go with that concept of rights. But, yes, they do have that right."

Bruce adds, "Yeah, I can understand their desire to sit back and let someone else."

Susan then adds, "I sympathize with them. I would miss our grandkids too, but thank God our children are here. I still miss seeing my parents now and then. There are still weaker moments when I wish we had taken the Caribbean route. This is not easy. But neither was farming. But here, the peace is transforming."

"Life has never been easy." Janet adds her two cents; "It wasn't easy for me to finish my university courses while having to support myself, and it wasn't fair that I was reprimanded over and over for telling my students that democracy is dead in America, that the ruling class of bureaucrats and lobbyists run this country, with the media echoing, the entertainment industry pushing, and academia censoring. And it hasn't been easy to bear the loss of my husband."

"Freedom is not easy. Slavery is not easy either," Mark says, "Don't they realize that driving an RV is getting harder and harder to do, the availability of fuel, the endless regulations governing campground use, and putting up with and protecting oneself from the rowdies entering those campgrounds looking for an easy retired couple to harass and rob. Even reading a newspaper is depressing."

"Jim, what do we do?" Mark asks. "Mike, do you have any ideas?"

Mike says, "Let them go, as even a meeting with them will not change their minds. What was previously said did not change a thing."

"Yes, I agree," Jim concludes with Mike. "Let's find a way to get them back to the States as soon as possible so this infection will not spread."

"Do you fear that it will spread?" Bruce asks.

"No, not really," Jim answers. "I feel the rest are as hardcore as we are."

"But then why did you warn us that it might," Bruce questions.

"Well, it just might because of the uncertainty that most of us have had, that this island will never be a land of plenty. We have wondered if it will become a land with abundant trees, forests with roaming wild animals, and without a threat of the UN invading our paradise." Jim responds. "That's the main difference between us and the early settlers of America. They came to a land ready for a harvest, whereas we came to an Island of rocks. When the trees grow, and the animals somehow get here, that threat of being invaded will increase and will always be unsettling. There's no way that we'd be able to fight against an aerial attack. We all know that."

"They know it too." Mark adds, "Well, you're right about that. There's nothing in the near future we can do to settle those fears. So, Jim, let's work on returning these people to the States. We need to re-stock our supplies anyway, so make it happen quickly. Ok? Does everybody agree?"

"Yes" and "yes" all around the table.

"And," Mark tells Jim. "Let's get with everyone who is staying and get orders for those large tents for those who'd like one for six hundred dollars. They'll need to write a check to the company. Those camping tents are only good for short stays. We all know it will take us many more months to build homes for everyone. We'll need more solar panels, too. They can be shipped to Anchorage."

Chapter 22

Another month has passed, and the unknown winter season is just around the corner, the evenings cooling down closer and closer to freezing. The discontents returned to the States, and Jim returned with the supplies replenished along with seventy-two new tents. What started as ten suddenly increased to three hundred fifteen and is now down to two hundred sixty-three people in this village named Freedom.

During Jim's absence, Mark had four more generators up and running, expanding the electrical grid. There have been a few blackouts and a few days when the storms were heavy, disabling the system. Still, the invention of Mark will suffice until a more powerful permanent power system is implemented.

George, Thomas, and Norman have completed the water lines delivering fresh water from the lake. The water lines are adequately designed for their present needs, relying on gravity to move the water down the slope to the community. As long as the rains keep coming, the lake will always have plenty of water as rivers flow from the mountains down to the lake, the valley, and eventually the ocean. More and more vegetation is emerging, and some trees are almost three feet tall. Grasses and weeds sprout in well-watered areas. The beaches have become sandier as the sandstone slowly break down. Several men erected a twenty-foot high cross on the beach right beneath the plateau's cliff. They wanted anyone entering the harbor to know where they stand. One hundred ninety people are still living in their small camp tents.

A few have hung up signs offering their services. "Hair cuts." "Home Made Muffins." "Wash Your Duds." "Cell Phone Repairs." "Scrubbing." The garden plot is beginning to expand in the area, presently at six acres, so next spring, they ought to be able to grow their food, expecting that the soil brought from the states mixed with the desalting chemicals over the ocean floor dirt, together with the sun and rains working their magic making the soil rich in nutrients. Janet has planted hundreds of tree and shrub seeds, deciduous and evergreen, in one and five-gallon pots.

Upon his return to the Island, Jim informed them that thousands of people all over the country seemed interested in moving to this isolated island. Hundreds of thousands have mentioned the island on their Facebook pages. The Media has been dismissing it all as just another phase of discontent, interviewing a few of them, portraying them as uninformed radical right-winger nobodys.

"It's disgusting how the media will showcase the ones who can barely speak a sentence without slang," Jim says. "Then, they summarize that all the discontents are uneducated. But Mark, a movement is growing where thousands are looking for ways to join us."

"I'm not surprised," says Mark. "This island is big enough for thousands of people, and I would not be surprised that someday we will start to see others settling in various areas and possibly wanting to join our town. We'll handle that as it comes."

Mark, Susan, Mike, Jim, and Janet sit together on lawn chairs around the campfire before anyone else shows up for the weekly song fest and storytelling.

"Jim, you've been gathering our supplies for over a month, enough for us to last through the winter, a winter of which we're not sure what the weather will bring our way. We thank you for that and are thrilled to see you back. Jim, we all decided that keeping the name simple is best, so we officially adopted Freedom.

Mark explains, "To get you up to date on some of what has happened, first about the name. We had many suggestions, but our historian, Tom Simpson, opined that the French philosopher from the 1700s, Baron de Montesquieu, best illustrated our views and position on this island. Tom noted that the founding fathers were very impressed with his writings, especially 'The Spirit of the Laws.' In it, he said: *"Countries are well cultivated, not as they are fertile, but as they are free."* This Island is certainly not fertile, but we are free. The quote was to the point and short enough to be inscribed below the name on the sign. It expresses our political stance. It will be put on our stationary, letterheads, and such when we get to that point. We all seemed to like it when Tom made his suggestion.

Montesquieu said during the Enlightenment period three hundred years ago, *"constant experience shows us that every man invested with power is apt to abuse it ... it is necessary from the very nature of things that power should be a check to power."*

Tom also introduced the Mayflower Compact, which the pilgrims signed, binding them all under a common purpose. Tom suggested we form our Freedom Compact by reading quotes from the Declaration of Independence and the Mayflower Compact in part.

'We hold these truths to be self-evident, that all humans are created equal, that they are endowed by their Creator with certain unalienable Rights, that among these are Life, Liberty and the pursuit of Happiness. That to secure these rights, Governments are instituted among Men, deriving their just powers from the consent of the governed.

We, the undersigned, have undertaken, for the Glory of God and advancement of the Christian Faith, a voyage to plant the first colony on this Island we herby name Freedom.

We solemnly and mutually in the presence of God and one another, Covenant and Combine ourselves together into a Civil Body Politic, for our better ordering and preservation and furtherance of the ends aforesaid; and by virtue hereof to enact, constitute and frame such just and equal Laws, Ordinances, Acts, Constitutions and Offices, from time to time, as shall be thought most meet and convenient for the general good of this colony, unto which we promise all due submission and obedience.

So Help Us God, we mutually pledge to each other our Lives, our fortunes and our sacred Honor.'

"Agreement was unanimous." Mark continues. "He purposely left out of the document that part that gave honor to the king and country, as we no longer honor the government of the United States. All of the adults signed it. So, now, it's your turn, Jim. You can be the last."

Mark adds, "It feels like we're together, Jim. We're a community of like-minded. A town council of seven was settled. Mike is the sheriff, and Tom Simpson is the first mayor. The town council has had meetings soliciting ideas from the entire group, debating and deciding.   So far, this is what they've come up with. They've surveyed the land and have decided how the town would be arranged into neighborhoods if you wish to call it that. George has used his architectural skills to design the layout. They've located two hundred sites for homes in half-acre lots, two-acre, and ten-acre lots, which will be auctioned through a lottery system. It's pick a number out of the hat where number one gets first choice. The half acre lots will be $200, the two-acre lots at $800, and the ten-acre ones at $4,000, with the proceeds going to the town for the continual construction and care of the infrastructure projects, streets, sewers, electrical grids, and such.

It's all been laid out and marked with posts and rope. Each plot is numbered. Certain areas are reserved as town future projects, fire stations, commercial areas, schools, parks, and churches. At first, they wanted one of those town squares as a park, a town hall, or a church in the center with stores and shops around it. But instead of a square, they decided on a circular pattern, with the church in the center.

"They've done a marvelous job," Mark tells him. "There's been minimal bickering, just lively open debates. Those plans were presented to the group and approved, and a copy of the town layout has been posted in our meeting hall."

"The people also voted that the first order of business was to introduce into our governing document, first and foremost, that no public official could ever be elected more than twice and that all laws passed would apply equally to all citizens and all elected officials. There would be no career lawmakers on this island, and they would not enjoy special retirement plans, compensation plans, or special privileges. Neither would we make laws favoring one group over another. Lobbyists are forbidden. When the time comes to install a tax system to support our public infrastructure and safety, it would apply equally to all; there would be no exemptions or deductions for this and that, and businesses would not be taxed. We all agreed that taxes should be placed on consumption rather than production. Knowing that taxes tend to become behavior modifiers, we've guarded against leaders using taxes to do that. Production should be encouraged, and we should all conserve consumption. Thus, they agreed that a sales tax on the consumption of goods is fair."

"So far, that's it, Jim. We've started the process. This will be a system guaranteed to be from the citizens, for them, recognizing that all humans are created by the creator God, endowing each with inalienable rights to their life, their liberty, and their pursuit of fulfilling personal dreams and ambitions, respecting that all others have the same and equal rights, respecting the personal rights of property owners and that governments are created to protect those freedoms, provide for the public infrastructure, and to ensure a civil togetherness. Those rights cannot be removed or changed by any agency."

We've transmitted our declaration of statehood to the UN and the US, declaring ourselves to be an independent homestead on this particular island named Freedom by the residents. All of the adults signed it, and it is so. We are independent. We have denounced our previous citizenship in the United States, desiring to retain our visas for the next ten years. We have yet to receive an acknowledgment. That's it, Jim."

"Now, let's enjoy the camaraderie a campfire extends."

Hope you enjoyed it.

Friedrich Hayek: *"The freedom that will be used by only one man in a million may be more important to society and more beneficial to the majority than any freedom that we all use."*

About the Author.

Arnold Kropp

The author of this novel is an unknown average American like millions, a quiet, unheralded voice from the heartland of America. Arnold Kropp was born and raised in Chicago, Illinois, the home of the Cubs, the Bears, and some fantastic museums. He went on to college after high school but could not find a subject, a major that captured him, so he enlisted in the Army and served in Germany during the years the Berlin Wall was built. He stood there in front of the barricades of the Brandenburg Gate; stood alongside the barbed wire fences gazing into the guarded open areas, looked at the bricked closed windows of homes, and watched diplomats and businessmen cross over at Check Point Charlie.

Those walls in Germany were needed by a political ideology of fascism, of communism, to protect the ideology itself, not for the protection of individuals.

Seeing what effects Soviet communism had on the people of East Germany left an impression. Arnold would return to America, the land of the free and home to the brave, free to pursue his dreams. Now, 60 years later, elements of political ideologies other than a pure democratic republic are being welcomed and are unfolding here in America.

The idea for this book came about when he and his son were sitting on the deck, discussing the political disaster that America has undergone since 9/11/2001, and the idea of the storyline for this novel evolved. A new island develops, capturing the interest of some citizens who desire to leave their comfortable life behind to establish a new colony on their own terms.

www.ingramcontent.com/pod-product-compliance
Lightning Source LLC
Chambersburg PA
CBHW060903140726
47996CB00001B/96